Stalking White Crows

How Evidence and Altered Consciousness Bring Us Better Living and Better Dying

Stalking White Crows

How Evidence and Altered
Consciousness Bring Us Better Living
and Better Dying

Jack Crittenden

BOOKS

Winchester, UK
Washington, USA

JOHN HUNT PUBLISHING

First published by iff Books, 2019
iff Books is an imprint of John Hunt Publishing Ltd., No. 3 East Street, Alresford,
Hampshire SO24 9EE, UK
office@jhpbooks.com
www.johnhuntpublishing.com
www.iff-books.com

For distributor details and how to order please visit the 'Ordering' section on our website.

Design: Stuart Davies

UK: Printed and bound by CPI Group (UK) Ltd, Croydon, CR0 4YY
US: Printed and bound by Thomson-Shore, 7300 West Joy Road, Dexter, MI 48130

We operate a distinctive and ethical publishing philosophy in
all areas of our business, from our global network of authors to
production and worldwide distribution.

Contents

There are vast realms of consciousness still undreamed of, vast ranges of experience, like the humming of unseen harps, we know nothing of, within us.

D.H. Lawrence "Terra Incognita"

To All My Students
Here is a lesson that I never taught but should have:

Life is an open ocean;
Dive out of your boat.

Foreword

By Ken Wilber

Stalking White Crows is a smorgasbord of delightful reflections on some of the least discussed yet utterly most important topics in today's world. Take a list of the topics that are not discussed in polite company, and you have the table of contents of this book.

And when I say, "least discussed," what I mean is, the way that Crittenden discusses these topics involves some of the least heard versions of these ideas—which is a real problem because, I believe, he's basically right in what he says, and it is a deep shame that our cultural wisdom does not reflect more of these profound perspectives.

Take religion and science, for example. That's a fairly hot topic, no doubt. The problem is, most of the suggested solutions to how these two crucial endeavors are related to each other are truly off the mark. They almost always involve trying to show the major limitations (or even total illusions) of the rejected approach; or they attempt an actual integration by trying to prove that the leading-edge sciences of today (usually something like quantum mechanics) show us the very same "ultimate reality" that you can find in the world's great mystics—namely, a completely interwoven, unified, interrelated world, a "oneness" that is the true nature of reality itself. The only problem with that approach is that it spectacularly doesn't work in any pragmatic terms. If modern quantum mechanics, for example, showed us the same world that you see when you have a mystical satori in Zen (an enlightenment or awakening experience), then professional physicists, who fully understand quantum mechanics, would be having *satoris* left and right—and, alas, virtually none of them do. Whatever it is they are doing, they are not getting in touch with the same reality that the Zen student is.

So what is the typical Zen student doing? Well, Crittenden points out, let's first ask what the typical scientist is doing, and then see if we can find any similarities. Science, he maintains (and here he adopts a view similar to mine in *Eye to Eye*), basically has three fundamental strands: an injunction, an illumination, and a verification. The first step, an injunction, simply means that most forms of conventional knowledge have a requirement for some sort of preliminary activity—it's of the form, "If you want to know this, do this...." So, if you want to know if it's raining outside, go to the window and look. If you want to know if a cell has a nucleus, get a microscope, learn to take cell sections, stain those sections, put them in the microscope, and then look. This strand is the part of the scientific enterprise that Thomas Kuhn focused on—and he concluded that all science is based on a particular paradigm. "Paradigm" does not mean "theory" but "practice" or "injunction," which Kuhn at first called a "paradigm" but then, upset with how that concept was being horribly misused (in a way that implied science was nothing but a relativistic construction that created facts and didn't discover them), he started calling instead an "exemplar," which shows its basic nature as an injunction (a series of exemplary actions taken as fundamental to any particular knowledge). So that's strand one.

Strand two is, if you complete the injunction correctly, then you will have an experience, an illumination, or what's more typically called "data" (which William James explained basically meant "experience"). Those who complete the same injunction correctly will have the same type of resultant experience, illumination, or data. And notice that this strand does not say what type of experience that must be—it could in fact be a sensory experience (or a datum produced by an extension of the senses, such as a telescope); or it could be a mental experience—such as doing mathematics or performing a logical deduction (this is an interior experience); or it could be a spiritual experience (also an interior experience). This is the strand of scientific knowledge emphasized by the empiricists; it is, in any event, what makes all science evidence-based.

Strand three is the verification strand — either a confirmation or a rejection of the data. If you complete the first two strands and keep getting the same data, then you have somebody else complete the first two strands and see if they get the same results. If so, then that data becomes widely accepted, and it can enter a stream of hypothetical deductions meant to explain the existence of the data itself. The capacity to reject the data is the core of Karl Popper's notion of falsifiability. (Hence, this approach integrates the Kuhnian, empiricist, and Popperian theories of scientific knowledge.)

But look what else it does. It divides religion right down the middle, into those religions that themselves follow these three strands of good knowledge versus those that don't. We mentioned Zen, for example. Zen has been producing satori experiences in students for almost two millennia, and it does so precisely because it follows all three strands of true scientific knowledge. Strand one for Zen is meditation — if you want to know if you have Buddhanature (that is, if you are one with the Ground of All Being), then you must do this: sit in a comfortable position, count your breath from 1 to 10, then repeat, and do that until you can repeat the process 50 times without mistakes. Then take up a koan practice, meditating on the meaning of the koan until you think you understand it (a koan such as, "Show me your Original Face, the Face you had before your parents were born"). These can't be solved by logic or any conventional mental means, and it will therefore force you to engage types of consciousness that are radically different from your normal state.

Which, if you stay at it, will lead to strand two, and you will eventually have some sort of profound illumination called in Zen a *"kensho"* or a *"satori."* This is a direct and immediate experience, which is a first-person experience or direct datum, and which announces itself as being a truly ultimate reality, a Ground of Being, a sense of being totally one with both an ultimate Reality and the entire manifest universe (an "ultimate unity consciousness"). This carries a staggering degree of certainty (no matter what one's educational background or training; doctors and lawyers as well as actors and waiters all report the same overwhelming certainty).

Still, to see if you have truly completed the injunction correctly, you must check your satori understanding—check your data—with both the teacher and the community of practitioners. This is strand three, the verification strand. In grueling tests of authenticity, your illumination is checked against the background of the entire community of knowledge. In this "scientific" fashion, Zen has been passed down for centuries. (And it enters that class of meditative practices around the world that have all reported experiences of an "ultimate unity consciousness" and a perfect oneness with a Ground of All Being.)

Is that a genuine "scientific" knowledge? Well, it certainly follows the essential steps of all typical science: it clearly follows all three strands. We might object and say, "Yes, but it's not exterior sensory data, it's only interior, so there's no way to really check it." But that is to simultaneously say the same thing about mathematics and logic. Nobody has ever seen the square root of a negative one running around out there in the sensory world. And surely Zen is not just a "private" knowledge, because it can clearly be trained (and has been for centuries), and a trained knowledge is a public knowledge.

What this does do, however, is separate spiritual systems into those that are a type of "interior science," like Zen and other meditative and contemplative practices around the world (which notoriously report very similar experiences or data, as all real science does), versus those that are based primarily on "mythic-literal" stories, like the Old Testament. Zen differs from, say, the science of physics because Zen focuses, not on sensory experience but on spiritual experience (satori); and it differs from the science of mathematics or logic because it focuses, not on mental experiences but, again, on spiritual experiences. But as for being dependable, repeatable, authentic knowledge—a real "science"—it's very hard to see how Zen does not meet the necessary requirements.

Jack Crittenden certainly thinks so. And if we do this—if we recognize that the type of knowledge that injunctions like Zen give us are true and genuine knowledge—then this would involve a stunning revolution in how we think about science and religion in the first place. It wouldn't matter if the vast majority of the world's religious believers were following a mythic-literal religion that is no more valid than a fairy tale, all we need is one example of what turns out to be a real religious knowledge in order to open the whole field up. And this is where Jack gets the title of this book. Using a metaphor first employed by William James, if I am trying to prove that crows are not all black, I don't have to prove that all of them aren't, I only have to find one white crow to prove it. And religions like Zen—which apparently do indeed involve a type of interior scientific knowledge of a spiritual reality—involve a fair number of white crows which prove the point quite conclusively.

In this book, Jack is in search of a series of white crows that convincingly prove a point often taken to be wrong. That's what makes this book so truly enjoyable, as well as educational (and educational as fun, not dreary). He looks at topics such as the capacity of consciousness to survive death (with evidence involving Near-Death Experiences and reincarnation). He points out that the various meditative traditions around the world point to a spiritual reality that is experience-based, and thus, following the three strands of all good scientific knowledge, give us a spiritual knowledge that is real and genuine, and not merely a mythic fairy tale (Zeus, Apollo, Aphrodite, Jehovah). And when it comes to those mythic fairy tales themselves, they have actually evolved, so you can read the Bible itself through a developmental lens. He looks at the existentialists, and suggests that an evidence-based. spirituality gives a much better way to interpret what they were saying. He moves to recent discoveries, and shows what psychedelics can tell us about death and consciousness (especially when used with people having terminal illnesses).

When it comes to discussing the idea of whether consciousness can exist independently of the material body, Jack examines items like reincarnation, and draws on the brilliant researcher the late Ian Stevenson, who, in books with such unassuming titles as *20 Cases Suggestive of Reincarnation*, gave absolutely stunning empirical (sensory-based evidence) cases that are virtually impossible to explain without some sort of reincarnation. (You'll see what I mean when you read that section.) But this is typical of the types of evidence that Jack uses throughout this book: very, very hard to disagree with; white crows everywhere.

Jack is particularly hard on scientists that use their version of science to ham-handedly deny all sorts of realities for which there are actually many white crows. And this includes scientists who deny sensory-based evidence for "far-out" realities—such as paranormal events (the evidence for some of which is absolutely overwhelming)—as well as scientists who don't acknowledge that science itself can definitely cover higher experiences (including mental experiences and spiritual experiences), in addition to the standard sensory experiences (which, if true, would mean that mathematics and logic were not scientific).

Jack ends—in "Robots Won't Be Hoarders"—with a discussion of what our near future would look like if knowledge of these white crows were more common. This brings us back to the point that I started with: this is a book about some of the least discussed topics that there are—in the sense of perspectives that are the least realized to be true. We don't think science and religion can fit together; we don't think consciousness exists independently of the material body; we see religion as nothing but a series of fairy tales; we're not aware of the deep openings that psychedelics can give people (especially in areas such as terminal illnesses); we have no official room for things like reincarnation. Do robots really dream of electric sheep—and are they ever hoarders?

This is a wonderful, exciting, truly illuminating book—and it will awaken you to a host of ideas for which you mostly have already decided just can't be true. Until they are. Which is what this book will likely do with every item it covers for you. So sit back, relax, and prepare to have your mind and your accepted world blown—and descended upon by a murder of white crows where you thought there were none.

Acknowledgements

I have friends, avid readers, who always turn first to any book's Acknowledgements pages. Their hope is that here, especially with academic writers, will be found the most transparent, if not to say bare-naked, prose. Guards are down, and the authors pour out interesting, even unique, ways of saying "thanks," while simultaneously permitting themselves to be funny when being vulnerable, grateful, and kind.

Alas, this is not such a page. For example, my children are grown; my dues are paid. So I could write this book without the guilt of too many nights away from my family or neglecting my parental duties or, further afield, postponing grading papers for another evening revising yet again another chapter. Thus I need not apologize to or necessarily acknowledge them. Oh, my sons exist, for which I am grateful beyond words. But they have little bearing on this book, though Todd, our middle son, was the impetus when he was 10 years old for the first chapter. Invited, he never read it. He acknowledges a modicum of regret for not having done so, and I here acknowledge that it matters not a whit to me; I love him nonetheless.

Four people deserve acknowledgement. First, and most important, is my wife and best friend, Pat, who edited the manuscript with her penetrating eyes and deft touch. She is the best editor I know, something I realized over 40 years ago, when we shared on a blind date our love for the Oxford comma, which quickly burgeoned into a love for each other. We've now had a lifetime together to argue about splitting infinitives and the like.

Another person to acknowledge is my good and great friend Ken Wilber. As always, Ken read the entire manuscript and spent hours with me on the phone talking about points large and small. He graciously agreed to write the Foreword to this book, with nary a complaint. It is not the first and surely will not be the last favor that he has done for me. He has remained in good humor over the 45 years that I have given him a stream of IOUs.

The third person to acknowledge is my former student and now friend Rory Varrato. As is customary with Rory, he read the entire manuscript with great haste, as I surely demanded. It was not a page-turner, but Rory put his shoulder into it and met whatever arbitrary deadline I had imposed on him. Since he was not a student of mine at the time of his reading, I can only conclude that he read it all as a courtesy to me. He provided ample feedback, which I appreciate about him to no end.

Finally, I owe both acknowledgement and gratitude to Dr. Julie Beischel, the Director of the Windbridge Research Center. Julie and I became friends after I convinced (cajoled?) her to serve twice as a guest speaker in my college seminar on life-after-death. Since then, I've joined her Board of Directors and have tried my best to serve as her archival spelunker and fulfill her requests to retrieve articles from ASU's Hayden Library. In the summer of 2018 Julie received an e-mail from Bernardo Kastrup, the publisher of Iff Books, telling her that he was in search of new manuscripts. During a meditation session, Julie had what she calls a "yogapiphany" and realized that Bernardo might really like the manuscript that turned into this book. She brought us together, and the result of that effort is, indeed, this book. I might have found Iff Books on my own, having some familiarity with Bernardo's own work. But who could, or would want to, overlook the magic in this serendipity. The universe was talking!

Meanwhile, along the same lines of acknowledgement, let me thank Bernardo and the staff at Iff Books and John Hunt Publishing. Their work was rapid, thorough, transparent, and encouraging all along the way.

Over the years that I wrote this book, many friends and several family members (sons included) asked to see manuscript chapters related to some interest of theirs. I sent off the requisite manuscript pages. I can say without exception that not one of them ever commented on those chapters or, as far as I know, read much of them. They might have read enough, however, to know that they could not or did not want to continue. Hearing the reasons for that might have helped make the manuscript better. Was their silence and possible neglect a better outcome than their harsh comments? Possibly, because to date the relationships continue unabated. I acknowledge fully that their skipping over these chapters could reveal keen insight on their part. Yet I must also acknowledge my own largess, if not magnanimity, in letting them slide with no recriminations or whining on my end...until now. When the book becomes a best seller, I'll even let each of them pretend that he or she was the singular exception, the one white crow, to read the chapters in manuscript form.

Introduction

This book is about making up our minds and about the makeup of our minds. Making up our minds, as I argue, involves using evidence—that is, reason and fact-based propositions, beliefs, ideas, and claims—in arriving at our conclusions about how best to live. The makeup of our minds involves recognizing consciousness. The makeup that interests me and that appears in the book is altered and elevated states of consciousness.

Both of these views are under attack. Currently we live in a climate where feelings trump reason and evidence, where lies are treated as "alternative facts." At the same time, it seems that our culture does not want us to treat altered and even higher states of consciousness seriously, especially, for example, altering consciousness through psychedelic drugs, even in clinical settings.

Focusing both on evidence and on such states of consciousness can reorient our attitudes, as I argue in the book, about life after death, about the basis of morality and the essence of spirituality, about the meaning of happiness, about the path of dying, and about the proper role of work in our lives and how education connects to that role. These are significant existential facets of our lives, and I discuss them all. Another writer might well have chosen different topics central to how we live, but for me these are the topics most salient and worthy of exploration. Experiences of and the evidence on altered and higher states of consciousness can lead us therefore to better lives and, what is more overlooked, to better deaths.

As far as we can tell, we are the only species that knows we are going to die. Knowing this, why then do we seem so ill prepared for death? One reason is that our physicians are too often unwilling, or unable, to talk straightforwardly to patients and families when a patient is dying. Too often, doctors think that a patient dying is their failure. Another reason is that our principal knowledge-gatherers—scientists—are too often unwilling, or unable, to look at the evidence for life after death. Failure to talk openly and to look at the evidence means that dying remains a taboo subject, and living in the face of death is thereby made more difficult. At the very least, missed in our experiences of and around dying is the chance to awaken to the value and purpose of the life we lived. Philosophy, Plato wrote, is preparation for death. We should take him at his word and ponder what he meant—wonder, that is, how death figures into aspects of how we live.

In this book I do just that. I look at evidence about consciousness that could help us both live better and die better. In doing so, I uncover some white crows; that is, exceptions that probe our rules, norms, and mores. I'll have more to say about white crows later in this introduction.

My focus in the book is best captured by a series of "what if" questions:

- What if morality were based on reasons and evidence and not on God and sacred texts? Is it scientific evidence that establishes our morality?
- What if Jesus had never lived? Would Christianity have any value? What if our spiritual pursuits, and the Bible itself, were not matters of history and faith, but were matters of evidence?
- What if happiness lies not in what we think, how we feel, and what we long for, but in living in the present and in the dying of the self itself?
- What if we could overcome our fear of death by taking a single small pill?
- What if robots eliminate all of our jobs? Where will those who identify with their work find meaning and worth and dignity when jobs are dying or dead? What kind of

educational system do we need to meet this predicted eventuality?

These "what if" questions led me to address and explore possible answers that involve altering, and perhaps elevating, consciousness, because consciousness is perhaps the ultimate perplexity: It uncovers what makes us distinctively human. To explore states of consciousness I focus on evidence, on finding evidence, exploring its basis and implications, and following the evidence when we establish our perspectives and beliefs. We use evidence, or should, whenever we investigate propositions and opinions, our own and those of others.[1] The evidence of interest to me, and that serves as the basis of this book, is that which surrounds, informs, and provides insight into a straightforward but knotty question: Where does consciousness come from? That leads to a second question: Does personal consciousness disappear when we die? From there I take a turn into ways to deepen and/or expand consciousness.

To those who think that the physical world—the world that we maneuver in and can explore through our five senses and their extensions—is all that there is, consciousness is the product of the brain. Thus, when the brain dies, our consciousness dies with it. But is that so? I went in search of evidence to help me understand whether consciousness is independent of or produced by the brain. Through writing this book, I also grew evermore interested in the evidence we use as it relates to states of consciousness in which and through which we form, maintain, and change our views on morality, religion, happiness, and, of course, death.

Something is wrong with our understanding of morality, religion, happiness, well-being, work, and death. In each case the misunderstanding can be rectified, as I argue, by following the evidence about altered and higher states of consciousness. By doing so, we can indeed live better and die better, though this involves looking at the misunderstandings in new ways, ways that can uncover exceptions or white crows.

To be honest, this book is not wound tightly around a single central thesis. It is instead, as its title conveys, the pursuit of white crows: reorienting evidence on consciousness that relates to topics of existential significance to us human beings. Thus the chapters of the book are woven loosely together by looking at evidence on or related to altering, raising, and reexamining states of consciousness.

Since this book is about consciousness, I feel obligated to say something at the outset about what consciousness is. I'd prefer not to, since like "truth," "beauty," "goodness," or an adept cat burglar, apprehending consciousness is difficult. Most often consciousness is thought of and defined as awareness or attention. As a general concept, the idea of awareness or attention seems informative but not fully adequate. More to the point, and more to my liking, consciousness is the subjective experience that we all have of our internal life—for instance, pain, instincts, desires, emotions, thoughts—and of the world. We are aware of, attentive to, or conscious of...something. We are always conscious of some object or feeling, some thought or sensation.

We report to others what we experience by describing these subjective states. Sometimes that reporting is not verbal but nonverbal, as we can communicate anxiety, elation, sadness, puzzlement, and the like through body language and facial expressions. Nonverbal communication is the kind of report that we receive from animals, whom we assume are conscious. We don't know much about their subjective experiences, other than that they have them. We know that something is going on inside when Barney the Beagle is asleep and yet his legs are moving as if he is running. We assume that he is dreaming, given his movement and rapid breathing, and dreaming is a subjective experience that can be scientifically detected through, for example, EEG machines.

We cannot measure the subjective experience of another, other than to hear his or her report. Absent such a report, we cannot know another's subjective experience directly except by some extraordinary means such as mind reading or telepathy, about which I shall have more to say going forward. So, consciousness seems to be something that we assume on the basis of the techniques that we currently use to gauge subjective experience.

The kind of consciousness that interests me in this book is the kind that we humans describe as self-reflective and self-referential consciousness; that is, states of internal awareness that we can attend to and reflect on, including our own thinking. Of course, when we are conscious, as I wrote earlier, we are always conscious or aware of something; we cannot be aware, however, of consciousness itself. Or can we? Can we be aware of pure consciousness; that is, of consciousness without an object of attention? I doubt that many scientists think that we can; philosophers might be able to imagine mental constructs that include the idea of pure consciousness; but mystics often discuss that possibility as a lived reality. But if consciousness is, as I said, our subjective experience, our first-person experience, then how can we be conscious of something that we don't experience? How can we experience consciousness itself, which would be without anything to experience? Those who have experienced this declare that it can happen. I'm among them. This is a significant white crow. I'll have more to say about this later and throughout the text.

I am not suggesting here that we are always conscious or aware of what we do and why we do it. We know that much of our daily lives is taken up with behaviors and functions that are subconscious or at least subconsciously driven. But that fact makes consciousness itself all the more mysterious, since we can then ask, "If much of our life is subconsciously driven, what purpose does consciousness itself serve?" Well, somehow those subconscious drives arise into consciousness to some degree if we are to act on those drives.

My concern in this text, however, is not whether we humans could do without consciousness. The point is, we *are* conscious; we *have* consciousness. One of my concerns in this text is where consciousness comes from. I consider that question in the first chapter. The upshot of that chapter is this: If, as many scientists and even philosophers argue, consciousness is the product of the brain, then what are we to make of numerous cases within the world of psychic phenomena that undercut that perspective? Once that perspective is undercut, then we are free, I think, to explore other manifestations of consciousness that don't rest on brain chemistry or neural pathways—though surely there are physiological correlates to altered states of consciousness. Released from a physical or materialist grounding, such states of consciousness can be described and referred to as real. That is, they are not illusions or hallucinations. Indeed, in some instances, as you, dear reader, will see, some of these states of consciousness may well reveal depths or heights of reality that render our own material world a mere shadow of that deep or heightened reality. This, then, is another concern explored in the text: Where can consciousness take us?

What Readers Will Find in the Text

Chapter 1 addresses the initial "what if" question: What if our memories, thoughts, and whole personality lived on after we died? What if there is life after death? As I shall discuss in the text, science is now showing us that this might well be true; most scientists, however, deny it. Why do they?

It turns out that scientists are human. We tend to think of them as persons driven by experiments and data who remain neutral and objective until the evidence is in. Then they make up their minds. But that isn't always the case. With some (and as I'll discuss in the first chapter, "some" here equals "most"), when the evidence runs against their deeply held beliefs, especially about the scope and nature of scientific inquiry itself, then they close their minds, look away, and flee from the ghosts. The ghosts are possibilities that they don't want to look at.

One ghost is the possibility that we live on after our brains die. There is ample evidence today, scientific evidence, that consciousness survives bodily death. It is that evidence and other evidence-driven adventures that constitute the heart of this book.

I am by training and perhaps temperament a political theorist. But as a long-time meditator, I also have an abiding interest in states of consciousness. A few years ago, I began thinking about the materialist/physicalist proposition that consciousness is a product of the brain, so that when we die and our brains stop functioning, then our consciousness—and all it entails: for example, memories, plans, thoughts, personality—dies too. How might we put this proposition to the test? I thought that one way might be to examine recent (and not-so-recent) experiments in paranormal phenomena that show some remarkable results in demonstrating the ongoing existence of personal consciousness after death. I even went so far in my explorations to offer twice a semester-long seminar on life-after-death. This, you can imagine, was unusual in a political science program and was greeted, when colleagues paid attention, with raised eyebrows.

These explorations led me to the scientific work on medium readings of the dead, on near-death experiences, and on reincarnation. Thus, the first chapter ("Stalking the White Crow" and the origin of the book's title) is on medium readings, with a special focus on the ongoing work by Dr. Julie Beischel at the Windbridge Institute. Here I challenge scientists to examine her research protocols, because Beischel uses rigorous research conditions in her work.

Beischel's work is really a continuation of serious scientific inquiry into parapsychology that began at the end of the nineteenth century and continued into the twentieth. In 1896, in his presidential address to the American Society for Psychical Research, William James declared the evidence from medium Leonora Piper to be so stunningly revealing and consistent that she was a "white crow" that destroyed the proposition that all crows are black.

In short, Leonora Piper was the exception that destroyed the rule. James understood the role of exceptions. Today we often follow the cliché that "the exception proves the rule." Logically, of course, that is nonsense. The cliché derives from the sensible proposition that exceptions *probe* the rule, which we can see in the phrase's Latin origins: *exceptio probat regulam*. When an exception probes sufficiently and discloses anomalies, then the rule must be changed. The presence of a white crow is not an exception that thereby proves the rule that crows are black.

"Prove" in this context refers to the sense of the word as in "proving ground"—a place to test something. For James the tests of Mrs. Piper that she was receiving information from the dead produced evidence that was so overwhelming that he thought that our scientific understanding of consciousness and the afterlife had to be fundamentally rethought. Her work demonstrated beyond doubt that all crows are not black. As you shall see, Mrs. Piper was hardly alone. Today, research scientists are uncovering a murder, or a bunch, of white crows.

Scientists who dismiss out-of-hand such paranormal studies are abandoning the very open-minded attitude—the probing—that led them into science in the first place... or should have. Chapter 2 is also a dispassionate examination of two other paranormal phenomena: near-death experiences and reincarnation. Both chapters focus on the veridical or independently verifiable evidence that comes out of many of these studies. The evidence from these two other paranormal phenomena reveal their own white crows.

In Chapter 3 I move on to ask whether the evidence from the

paranormal undercuts our theistic Abrahamic religious views. Most particularly, I ask whether we can have morality without God. This is an important question, especially in an era when feelings today compete with or even supersede facts. According to a Pew poll conducted in May, 2014, 53 percent of Americans think that one must believe in God to be a moral person.[2]

This is a dangerous perspective, because acts sanctioned by interpreters of God's word can otherwise show all the hallmarks of immoral acts. Religious sanction cannot be anything but the beginning of the search for establishing a moral code.

Nor is religious experience itself sufficient. Without further investigation into the claims engendered by the experience, that experience can be little but confirmation bias and the applause from a self-congratulatory group. We must demand more, and in this chapter I discuss the form that that "more" ought to take: investigations using reason and evidence. Such investigations can provide a white crow against claims of moral relativism.

Chapter 3 is a companion-piece to Chapter 4, which is on the topic of "divine knowing." My view is that religious or spiritual experience needs to be verified and can be verified following precisely the same steps, as Ken Wilber argued, that establishes epistemological validity in both science and morality. Thus, insights into or revelations from altered, and maybe higher, states of consciousness must be and can be epistemologically verified through proper testing, again using reasons and evidence. This testing also provides a white crow against the view that spirituality is only or can only be feelings and metaphysical musings.

Arguably, the insights gained from meditation or contemplation, given their metaphysical or paranormal content, can reflect a higher level of consciousness. Those insights undercut our theistic traditions by providing practitioners with direct experiences or even direct apprehension of the supernatural. Such experiences permit and encourage us to jettison the absurd historical events depicted in the scriptures of the three Abrahamic religions. A reliance on history causes nothing but trouble, or should, for practitioners of those religions. Without that reliance practitioners can concentrate on direct transcendental or spiritual experiences through altered and higher states of consciousness. To this end, I offer in Chapter 5 a transition away from historical paralysis and toward liberation by reading the Bible as a history of moral development. This reading interprets the Old and New Testaments as expositions on the three stages of morality as discussed by psychologist Lawrence Kohlberg (among others) and shows their progression to the teachings of Jesus.

Having argued in Chapter 5 that transcendental or Christic consciousness is a level of development—psychological and spiritual development—that all of us can undertake and that many of us can attain, I then discuss, in Chapter 6, three spiritual teachers today—Eckhart Tolle, Gangaji, and Bernadette Roberts—who are exploring and explaining this state of consciousness and in some cases offering practices to help us attain it. I discuss these three teachers in the context of Existentialism. We often think of Existentialists as writers and philosophers focused on freedom of choice, of course, but also on certain by-products of unbridled freedom—fear, dread, nihilism, alienation, meaninglessness, and, best of all, absurdity. In this sense, "happy Existentialists"—the title of the chapter— may seem oxymoronic. But Albert Camus introduces us through Sisyphus to the idea of happiness in the face of an absurd world, and Nietzsche, a progenitor of Existentialism, clearly sees a way to a joyous, even a happy, life. I focus heavily on a couple of Nietzsche's philosophical concepts that underscore ideas related to the psychological states explored today by teachers of non-dual awareness or elevated consciousness and to their views of happiness.

In Chapter 7 we arrive where we started: the topic of death. We don't die well in America. Though most of us wish to die at home surrounded by our loved ones, most of us will die in a hospital, connected to machines that we don't want and surrounded by people dedicated—and their work is dedication—to keeping us alive. I find it impossible to imagine how dying in a hospital could lessen the fear, anxiety, depression, and discomfort that many experience as they face and tumble down into death. Yet even at home or in a hospice, making persons physically and emotionally comfortable might well not be sufficient to ease them into a peaceful death.

Based on recent research, I think that giving them psychedelic drugs in a controlled setting could help immensely in providing that ease. The chapter is a fictional account, though based on research, of two persons immersed in the dying process and how the use of psychedelics might play a significant part in relieving fear and anxiety for those facing death. If there is one condition that almost all Americans face, in addition to all of us being terminal, it is that we fear death. Overcoming that fear can be instrumental in helping us live better, more fulfilling, more flourishing lives. Altering states of consciousness through the use of psychedelic drugs, administered in accordance with strict scientific protocols, is showing us how that can be done. Again, a white crow appears: Psychedelic drugs are not to be feared, but are useful, often necessary, elements in treating anxiety, depression, phobias, addiction, and even PTSD.

I taught political theory at Arizona State University for nearly 30 years. In our introductory theory class on Political Ideologies, I asked students to wrestle with one of the profound questions of human existence: What is human nature? Every founder or every exemplar of a political ideology has a view of human nature—what a person is and can become. So this is no idle question within the study of politics.

In the course I presented the views of human nature that lie beneath political ideologies, but I didn't dwell on those views.

That was not the purpose of the course. But it should be the purpose of *some* course and some course that has connections to politics—how we can live together and flourish as individuals and societies. Indeed, I think that the question about human nature is merely one variant of a deeper question—what is the nature of life itself? Concomitant with that is the question of whether there is life, the continuation of personal consciousness, after death.

No political theory course, let alone any political science course, asks such questions. They are relegated to different disciplines. I think that this is a mistake, because until we find, derive, develop, or steal some views on these deeper questions, I fear that politics will be nothing but the parade of different faces in positions of power all practicing some variant of the political ideologies that we already have. That is, nothing fundamental will change politically until we have sorted out and come to terms philosophically, psychologically, and metaphysically with these other questions. Fundamental and structural political change is just what we need today. As I discuss in the final chapter, Chapter 8, the industrial world is on the cusp of widespread and, for many, catastrophic change in the availability and the meaning of work. Our jobs are dying out. In the face of this kind of death, what are people who define themselves by their work to do? If work can no longer be the source of personal and social identity, dignity, and respect, then what are people to do to find and live out a flourishing life? With the advent of robots, Artificial Intelligence, and other technological innovations, work will no longer be the source. This new era of the machines will be, then, a test of the flexibility of our human natures. What appears at the outset as a disaster may actually be a white crow: an era of increased leisure time and thus an opportunity to increase and intensify our adventures in consciousness, as we explore the further reaches of human nature.

This book, therefore, might be a prelude to the kinds of

adventures in consciousness that people will explore and the kind of attitudes toward inquiry that they might well adopt as we move into a full "robo-economy."

These and other adventures in consciousness can begin with identifying the exceptions or white crows:

- Materialism is a powerful framework for understanding the world, except in light of what science itself can tell us about the survival of personal consciousness after bodily death.

- Values and morality are relative to different cultures, except when we see evidence for ways to universalize moral codes.

- Science is divorced from spirituality, except when we see how science can investigate the paranormal and how valid knowledge in both realms shares the same epistemological process.

- The Old Testament, the New Testament, and the Koran are steeped in history and rely upon historical figures and events, except when new frameworks for interpreting those texts provide coherent and consistent readings independent of alleged historical grounding that violates what we know of how the world works.

- A life without a sense of self or ego is a life of "nothingness," of nonexistence, except where that emptiness means fullness and can be lived as such.

- Psychedelics are harmful and thus dangerous drugs that must be eliminated from research protocols, except where those drugs are shown in clinical studies to have salutary and lasting effects on those who take them.

- Finally, with predictions of our jobs dying off, never to be replaced, life for those who identify with and find dignity in their work will be left to flounder, except where new social, political, and educational developments can use the dearth and death of work as an opportunity to turn leisure time into productive ways to expand and elevate consciousness.

Regardless of how the future looks—for example, full of robots or full of jobs—the topics discussed throughout the book are germane, I think, to our future human flourishing: How different might our lives be if we based our notions of spirituality, morality, happiness, and life-after-death on reasons and evidence and not on feelings, emotions, and beliefs? The world—our societies and cultures and the planet itself—is changing at a dizzying pace. But disorientation can transform into reorientation with adequate preparation. Your reading this book is such preparation, if you remain on the lookout for, and even hunt for, white crows.

Chapter 1

Stalking the White Crow: When Exceptions Become the Rule

Science advances one funeral at a time.
Max Planck

Blind certainty: a close-mindedness that amounts to an imprisonment so total that the prisoner doesn't even know he's locked up.
David Foster Wallace, Commencement Address, Kenyon College

How might a talented Cambridge- and Harvard-trained biochemist and botanist veer away from a promising career in biochemistry and into the shadowy and questionable world of parapsychology? In the case of Dr. Rupert Sheldrake, just such a biochemist and botanist, it happened by following the evidence.

Once, years ago, while a fellow at Clare College, Cambridge, he and some graduate biochemists, relaxing in the tearoom, laughingly dismissed as rubbish ideas about telepathy in particular and paranormal or psychic phenomena in general. Sitting nearby, eavesdropping as it were on their conversation, was Sir Rudolph Peters. Sir Rudolph, formerly Professor of Biochemistry at Oxford, had retired from that position and at the time was working in the biochemistry lab at Cambridge. Sir Rudolph interrupted the group by saying to Sheldrake, "Have you looked at the evidence for telepathy?" Sheldrake, of course, as an ardent materialist, had not. He had already concluded that telepathy had to be rubbish. Why bother looking at the "evidence" when it could not possibly be scientific or, for that matter, evidence? Sir Rudolph then responded, "Well, I have, and I think there might be something in it."

Of course, even moments like this, when one is pressed by a senior professor or a distinguished colleague to look at the data, can fail to persuade materialists to look at something that, to their minds, cannot have any merit. But Sheldrake was intrigued by a story that Sir Rudolph then told:

An ophthalmologist friend of Sir Rudolph's, E.G. Recordon, was treating a boy who was severely disabled, nearly blind, and mentally deficient. Recordon asked the boy to read the eye chart across the room, which the boy then did flawlessly. At first, Recordon thought that the boy had simply guessed correctly, but there were too many letters for that. Then he thought that the boy might be reading the chart through his mother. So, Recordon asked the mother to leave the room, and the boy could no longer read the chart.

Recordon told Sir Rudolph about this, and the two of them created an experiment in which they separated the boy and his mother by a screen, showed the mother a series of letters and numbers, and the boy immediately revealed what they were. They then set up another experiment with the boy in one English town and the mother in another. They showed the mother cards of letters and numbers, pre-randomized. The boy would then say over the phone what the cards showed. The boy should have been right 1 out of 26 times or 3.8 percent with the letters. He was actually right almost 40 percent.

The findings were significant, as Sir Rudolph had declared. Sheldrake then asked to listen to the audiotapes of the experiment and, having done so, came away agreeing with Sir Rudolph's conclusion. Next, Recordon, Sir Rudolph, and Sheldrake enlisted magicians to listen to the tapes to ascertain whether there was any subtle cheating going on. They could not detect any. After this initial encounter in the tearoom with Sir Rudolph, Sheldrake has since gone on to make investigations into telepathy a significant part of his research.[3]

Telepathy is a form of communication with or information transmission from one person to another without the aid of any sensory mechanisms, as far as we can detect. It is, therefore, the direct link of one person's mind or consciousness with another's, with no physical interaction—no talking, no reading of body language, no nonverbal cues—between one person and another.

The nature of consciousness itself is a tough question for any scientist: What is it? Where does it come from? How does it arise? In a material universe how does the physical brain produce subjective experience? How do neurons and chemical substances create an invisible and immaterial phenomenon?

For many scientists consciousness is housed in the brain. More than housed there, for them it is created there and is, as well, destroyed there when the brain dies. Neuroscientist Daniel Bor sums up this attitude: "Of course consciousness is a physical thing."[4]

But scientists don't know this scientifically; that is, they have yet to demonstrate empirically that consciousness is a physical thing. Because scientists have yet to demonstrate this, they can't know it. They can only believe it, which many do because the belief follows logically from their view that the brain produces consciousness, which ends when the brain dies.

Could consciousness—our awareness, our memories, and even our personalities—however, be independent of the brain? Could consciousness live on after the brain has died?

If we wanted to answer those questions, where would we look? Wouldn't one area be anomalous experiences, those that seem to defy the idea that the brain produces consciousness and thus defy the idea that the brain can be the same as the mind? That would seem to be a likely and possibly fruitful place to look to test whether the material-mechanistic view of consciousness is the true view.

Anomalous experiences of consciousness are also known as paranormal phenomena and, more narrowly, psychic experiences, one of which, not surprisingly, is telepathy. As one form of paranormal phenomena, telepathy's existence would be evidence of anomalous information reception,[5] which is part and parcel of evidence of consciousness independent of the brain. Evidence of consciousness independent of the brain is itself the basis for claiming that life survives bodily (brain) death. If we get demonstrable results from telepathy experiments and if we eliminate cheating and fraud (for example, everyone involved is lying), then what explanations remain? That is a good question, and it is one that should interest mainstream scientists, because Sheldrake, for one, is getting demonstrable results.

Yet, despite the history of experiments on the paranormal and despite the current level of scientific investigations into the paranormal, Dr. Mark Leary, Professor of Psychology and Neuroscience and Director of the Social Psychology Program at Duke University, comments that "many scientists...remain disdainful" of those researchers who explore the paranormal (2011). "Disdainful" doesn't mean that they debate the methodologies used. It means that these scientists ridicule, dismiss, and denigrate the entire field and those who work in it.[6] Why are they reluctant, when this seems one promising avenue for exploring and explaining the nature of consciousness?

"Many scientists" does not comprise, of course, *every* scientist. So another question is: Why are some scientists open to evaluating the scientific investigations into the paranormal, even if their motivation is to debunk such studies, while others refuse to do so? Why Rupert Sheldrake and not, say, Stephen Hawking?[7]

Are we surprised that a highly trained scientist like Sheldrake would spend time exploring telepathy, one form of paranormal phenomena? It is difficult to ignore the tug on your sleeve when the pull is by a renowned and respected scholar like Sir Rudolph Peters, but it's less difficult when so many of your peers reinforce the preconception that these phenomena are "rubbish," to recur to Sheldrake and his colleagues' earlier conclusion or, in actuality, their earlier assumption. And it is an assumption, because they hadn't looked at and evaluated the methods, the evidence, or the results. Their objections to paranormal research are not based on studies or experiments or counter-evidence. Instead, most of the objections are subjective reactions and impressions without evidence. This strikes me as a most unscientific attitude.[8]

Scientists with such an attitude are not unlike fundamentalists. This may seem to be an overly dramatic charge, but the charge rests on what we mean by the term "fundamentalist." Malise Ruthven, author of *Fundamentalism* (2007), states that the term now bleeds into, among other ideas, doctrinairism and ideological purism.

Ruthven himself suggests that such nonreligious uses of the term aren't really analytically useful (p. 22). But we're not looking for one-to-one correspondences among the practices of antiabortionists, animal rights activists, Islamic agitators, and Six Day Creationists, or even family resemblances among them. To support our charge we are looking for foundations of perspective. In that sense, using the term fundamentalism outside of its historical religious context makes sense, because all fundamentalists show the same dogmatic adherence to beliefs or a set of beliefs and do so without evidence. It is not that they won't compromise on these beliefs. The issue is starker than even that. It is that the alternative perspectives, the "other side," are wrong, evil, or "rubbish."

But are scientists as materialists the same as believers in religious dogma? Are we really talking about beliefs and belief systems for scientists? I am not suggesting that science has no starting assumptions that themselves cannot be proven. I'm suggesting that science and the scientific method as processes move us beyond beliefs and into evidence and experimental results. Yes, the processes do, or, rather, they should. But too often they do not. When some scientists refuse to examine the evidence for the paranormal collected in a scientifically valid way, then such scientists are clinging to some beliefs that preclude them from following the very methods and inquiries that they otherwise proclaim and around which they structure their own work. They are behaving like fundamentalists.

This attitude is encapsulated in this observation by neuroscientist Sam Harris and psychologist Paul Bloom: "Philosophers and scientists remain uncertain about how consciousness emerges from the material world, but few doubt that it does."[9] This is the very problem: Few scientists doubt something for which they have, at this point, no scientific evidence or, for that matter, grounded scientific explanation. The closest they come is to say something like this: "Humans are meat machines. Therefore, we should be able to build conscious living robots if we replicate human mechanisms."

Happily, there are scientists like Sheldrake willing at least to look at new evidence. Perhaps his turnabout doesn't even surprise us guileless souls, since Sheldrake is, after all, a scientist who wants, as so ably spoken by Galileo in Bertolt Brecht's eponymous play: "not to prove that I was right but to find out *whether* I was right" (1966, p. 96; emphasis in the original). This, we might well think, is the attitude of scientists, because it is the scientific way: "What we find out today we will wipe from the blackboard tomorrow and reject it—unless it shows up again the day after tomorrow. And if we find anything that would suit us, that thing we will eye with particular distrust" (1966, p. 96). So let us be led by the evidence, not by our prejudices; let us look through the damn telescope.

There is a lot at stake in maintaining a materialist worldview. Not just careers are built on it, but so, too, are purpose, meaning, and identity. Biologist Richard Dawkins is on record as saying that the existence of the parapsychological phenomenon of telepathy would "turn the laws of physics upside down."[10] And with those laws the worldview and understanding built on and of those laws turn upside down as well.

Along similar lines, two leading skeptics,[11] both psychologists, Richard Wiseman and Chris French have declared that the evidence for telepathy is so strong that "by the standards of any other area of science, [telepathy] is proven."[12] But the evidence is downplayed or ignored. This state of affairs reinforces Dawkins's observation: If telepathy is true, then the scientific understanding of the world as portrayed in the orthodox scientific paradigm is wrong in some significant ways. That's difficult for many scientists to stomach. Still, a failure to be open to scientific studies that stretch or push the scientific worldview leaves us to think that the very existence of "scientist" as an identity and of "science" as a community rests solely on a single, hegemonic, and shared understanding that will brook no renegades. Even if the scientific method reveals anomalous data, materialist scientists cannot look at or tolerate that data, though they risk by their intolerance the generation of a new worldview that could integrate the anomalous data.

So reputations and worldviews are at stake. Yet why isn't there pressure on reputation and scientific growth from the opposite end? Why don't those scientists themselves who practice the scientific method when investigating the paranormal press their colleagues to conduct experiments on psychic phenomena? Why aren't they calling out in the media those scientists who refuse to examine the evidence of the paranormal? After all, it is the scientists investigating the paranormal who are living up to the standards—and, indeed, the reputation—of science itself. It is they who are following science's call, as Brecht says, "for valor. She [Science] trades in knowledge, which is the product of doubt" (1966, p. 123). These are the true scientific explorers. Scientists, on the other hand, who refuse to consider the experiments in, methods of, and evidence for the paranormal are, ironically, in the very same spot as the Church officials who refused to look through Galileo's telescope. Those officials claimed already to know, with no distrust or doubt whatsoever, that there was no evidence there. So today's intransigent scientists, fixated on a materialist worldview, take the blind positions that they say they oppose and thereby become the very thing that they hate.[13]

Cognitive Dissonance and TMT

There is a host of possible reasons, reputation aside, why scientists would avoid looking at the methods and results of studies of the paranormal. Freud's "cathexis" might be one: Scientists develop a strong emotional attachment, often unconscious, to an idea—say, the materialistic structure of our world. Evidence against the idea is bypassed or ignored. Another candidate might be "post-hoc rationalization," where we tend to invent reasons for accepting something that we have already accepted. A similar phenomenon is "confirmation bias." In this case, the scientist doesn't simply invent reasons to support what he already supports. Instead, the scientist listens mostly, if not only, to the reasons and evidence that give support to his positions and ignores the reasons and evidence that challenge those positions.

Another powerful motivation is "cognitive dissonance"—the discomfort that comes from holding two conflicting beliefs simultaneously. Faced with challenges to one's self-concept and worldview, a person really only has two choices—fight or flee. Fleeing seems the easier course, as one simply pulls his/her cognitive hat over the face and refuses to peek out. What is really lost by dismissing as "utter rubbish" scientific studies of the paranormal? From the perspective of one who fully accepts the materialist view of the world, very little. What is saved through the dismissal is one's identity and worldview. Fighting would require confronting the evidence, looking to see what is there.

In jeopardy by doing so is the world of meaning constructed throughout one's life, thought, and work. At risk is one's very identity.

The challenges raised by cognitive dissonance are, of course, not peculiar to scientists. They are part and parcel of every human life, for challenges arise all the time. This is how we grow or arrest, how we progress or regress. There seems no middle ground.

One clear example of "fight" within cognitive dissonance is the case of journalist, blogger, and public intellectual Andrew Sullivan. Sullivan was an unabashed champion of the US invasion of Iraq. In the days after 9/11 he moved in lockstep with the neoconservatives. But then came the release of the photographs of prisoner abuse from Abu Ghraib, and Sullivan had to confront the use of torture and the neoconservative attempts to justify it. For Sullivan this was nothing short of a total loss of all moral basis for the war.

That admission, and recognition, led Sullivan to a critique of neoconservative positions on war and foreign policy. Sullivan did not stop there. He found himself in profound disagreement with the Bush Administration's policy of off-the-books funding of the wars in Iraq and Afghanistan, which shook his fiscal-conservative sensibilities, as did the ever-rising costs of funding the Bush prescription-drug program. By the end of the Bush Administration Sullivan was recommending a full Justice Department investigation into what Sullivan viewed as the war crimes committed by Bush and Cheney.

One can find more pertinent views of dismissal and contempt in philosopher Neal Grossman's article "Who's Afraid of Life After Death?"[14] And here is an example from my own small world at Arizona State University: A philosophy professor denies categorically to one of my students that mediums can gain information from the dead. Okay, my student retorts, but what about the quintuple-blind studies on mediums coming out of the Windbridge Institute showing positive results (see below for more on Windbridge)? The philosopher's response: There aren't any good grounds for thinking that they are actually studying talking to the dead. Well, then, my student continues, what are the weaknesses of the methodology? "Don't know," he said; "I haven't looked." It's easy to conclude that there are no "good grounds" when one hasn't bothered to look at the methods.

Perhaps the most powerful motivation of all for dismissing dissonant studies emanates from our human nature. Most humans fear death. That fear, stemming from awareness of our own mortality, affects our lives and life choices. Beyond the natural survival instincts that come from just being living animals, humans strive, in numerous ways, for immortality, which can mitigate the fear. One extensive line of research examining the effects of this "immortality seeking" is Terror Management Theory (TMT). The researchers involved hypothesize, and their studies bear them out, that much of our thought and actions is based on the need to deny physical death, which is seen as the end of human existence. That is, people seek ways to dispel or offset the terror of finitude, our deepest existential dread.

One frequent strategy for avoiding this paralyzing terror is to find ways to bolster one's self-esteem, which is centered around and dependent on one's cultural worldview. Self-esteem, therefore, is sustained and even increased "by maintaining faith in the validity of one's worldview and the belief that one is living up to the standards of value that are part of it" (Dechesne et al., 2003, p. 722).[15]

We can readily see, then, the importance for some scientists to defend their materialist worldview and to enhance their self-esteem by adhering even more closely to the values and features of that worldview. There is every reason, therefore, to eschew claims and studies that could undermine that worldview and with it one's self-esteem; there is every reason, also, to embrace, if not cling to, those who help defend and maintain the worldview.

At stake here is not just reputation; at stake is one's very identity and meaning in life. Enhancing self-esteem protects the person from death fears by linking one to the "symbolic immortality" of the worldview. You might well die, but your cultural worldview—the constructed conceptions of reality and of how the world works that you share with others—and thus your work and purpose and meaning in life will continue after you.

Adherence to symbolic immortality provides a "sense that one is a valuable part of something larger, more significant, and longer lasting than one's individual existence" (Dechesne et al., 2003, p. 723). Being an ardent scientist makes you a member of a community holding a worldview that can extend into eternity. Defending that community and its concomitant worldview against such perceived threats as dissimilar values, unconventional ideas, or alternative views of reality strengthens one's symbolic immortality. It is in the best interests of a scientist, therefore, to denigrate those alternative conceptions of the world—such as data from and scientific explorations of paranormal phenomena—that undermine or diminish his own belief, even if the subject of and the evidence from the scientific explorations of those alternative conceptions could help dispel the fear of personal finitude.

William James's White Crow

It might well seem, then, a Herculean task for any scientist, in light of the obstacles, psychological and reputational, confronting him to review the findings of scientific investigations into the paranormal, let alone undertake such studies himself. At the end of the nineteenth century and into the twentieth some of the researchers who both reviewed studies and initiated their own were not simply intrepid, but were renowned. Among them were Henry Sidgwick, Professor of Moral Philosophy at Cambridge University and author of one of the seminal books in moral philosophy that exerts influence even today—*The Methods of Ethics*; Sir Oliver Lodge, physicist and central pioneer into wireless telegraphy, electricity, and spark plugs; and, of course, William James, famed psychologist and philosopher, an intellectual force at the turn of the century, and whom philosopher Clancy Martin called "as rigorous a man of science as early twentieth-century America produced" (2011, p. 14).[16]

Here is how James described the impetus to get involved in psychical research when the British and American Societies for Psychical Research organized in the 1880s:

...[H]ow great a scientific scandal it has been to leave a great mass of human experience to take its chances between vague tradition and credulity on the one hand and dogmatic denial at long range on the other, with no body of persons extant who are willing and competent to study the matter with both patience and rigour.[17]

The psychical researchers at the two Societies were certainly willing and competent to undertake their studies with both patience and rigor. As James concluded: "Science may keep saying: 'such things are simply impossible;' yet as long as the stories multiply in different lands, and so few are positively explained away, it is bad method to ignore them" (p. 7).

One of James's most consistent and remarkable sources of impressive results that could not be explained away was Mrs. Leonora Piper. Mrs. Piper, stated James, presented "phenomena so chronic and abundant" that they cannot be dismissed as "chance-coincidence" (p. 4). That leaves fraud, then, as the only other explanation, an explanation that James's confederate, Richard Hodgson, did his best to demonstrate.

Mrs. Piper was so significant for the studies of anomalous information reception—knowledge that she gained through sources other than her "ordinary waking eyes and ears and wits"—that James dubbed her his "own white crow." Commented James: "...a universal proposition can be made untrue by a particular instance. If you wish to upset the law that all crows are black, you mustn't seek to show that no crows are; it is enough if you prove one single crow to be white. My own white crow is Mrs. Piper" (p. 5). For James the evidence coming from Mrs. Piper's paranormal abilities would revolutionize the scientific understanding of consciousness.

Leonora Piper (1859-1950) was the daughter of a Boston shopkeeper. All her early life she fought against her psychic abilities (Blum, 2006, p. 98), wishing only to become a mother and a respectable housewife. This reluctance was one significant reason why she agreed to be examined for over 30 years by a range of scientists and investigators: She hoped to bring some light to herself and to the world on her "gift."

Piper came to the attention of James after his mother-in-law (Mrs. Eliza Gibbens) and his sister-in-law (Ms. Margaret Gibbens) reported to him on their own remarkable readings (Blum, pp. 98-9). James and his wife, Alice, went to Mrs. Piper for their own reading soon after the death of their son, Herman. James came away suspicious, but also curious and impressed.

Other researchers, sent by James, went for readings, and most also came away impressed with her abilities. So by 1886 the investigators of mediums from the American Society for Psychical Research had come to a conclusion similar to Richard Hodgson's in his later report: "[N]early all professional mediums are a gang of vulgar tricksters who are more or less in league with one another" (Blum, p. 117). Nearly all...but not Mrs. Piper.

For James the next logical step was to invite the best, most hardheaded investigators to examine Mrs. Piper. And so Richard Hodgson, the chief investigator for the British Society for Psychical Research and a man with a reputation as a debunker, came to Boston for the sole purpose of investigating whether Mrs. Piper was a fraud. Hodgson's goal was "to quickly reduce

Mrs. Piper to the ranks of exposed imposters" (Blum, p. 133). He couldn't and he didn't during the 15 years that Hodgson studied her.

Mrs. Piper was a trance medium. As with other trance mediums, Mrs. Piper would go into a trance at which time a "control" or the disembodied spirit of a deceased person would take over her voice and body. Here was the most obvious element of fraud. First, was this trance simply pretend? Second, was the control anything other than a fiction contrived by the medium or dredged up from the medium's subconscious?

Piper's first control claimed to be a Frenchman, Dr. Phinuit. But investigators revealed that there were no records in France of any such person, even though Phinuit/Piper was quite specific.[18] Plus, he spoke poor French.[19] James and other investigators concluded that Phinuit was probably a creation of Piper's subconscious.

The trances, on the other hand, seemed quite real. To test the trances Hodgson went to some extremes: "He'd put ammonia-soaked cloth under her nose, dumped spoonfuls (sic) of salt, perfume, and laundry detergent into her mouth, pinched her until she bruised, all without producing a flinch."[20]

When Piper traveled to England at the behest of James and other investigators to disrupt her familiar environment and routines (thinking that this might affect her abilities and, perhaps, disrupt her cheating) and to undergo additional tests by members of the British Society for Psychical Research, the investigators there—Sir Oliver Lodge and Fred Myers—also tested her trance. They "pricked her with pins, burned her arm with a match, held ammonia under her nose" (Blum, p. 164). Again, Piper showed no reaction to any of this while in her trance.

Finally, G. Stanley Hall, the American psychologist and a staunch critic of all things paranormal, asked for sittings with Piper. Hall had little interest in doing anything but debunking her (Blum, p. 303). He tested her trance by dripping camphor (a slightly toxic mixture known to sting and numb) in her mouth. "To [Hall's] surprise she did not startle awake" (Blum, p. 303). But once out of the trance Piper did remark that her mouth was numb, and the next morning her lips and tongue were covered with blisters.

At another sitting Hall tested her trance by using an esthesiometer, a device employed by slowly screwing a weight against the skin to test the sensation of pressure. Hall thought that as the pressure increased, Piper would awaken. She did not. But afterward, she feared that she had lost the full use of her hand.[21]

Clearly, Piper's trance was a real altered physiological state. Hall's attempted debunking of that had been thwarted.[22] So there was virtually no doubt that Piper's trances were real. But what about the information that her controls passed along to the various sitters? Hodgson then concentrated his efforts on that side.

Hodgson had, of course, his own readings with Piper. Initially, Hodgson did not give his name or reveal anything about himself, including his affiliations. At one early reading, Phinuit told Hodgson that he had a message for Hodgson from his cousin, Fred. Long dead at the time of the reading, Fred was the son of Hodgson's uncle. Phinuit told Hodgson that the two of them, Fred and Richard, had gone to primary school together and had played all sorts of roughhouse games, of which leapfrog was Fred's favorite. Athletic as a youth, Fred loved gymnastics, fell from a trapeze, injured his spine, and died from the injury. Phinuit through Piper told Hodgson about this precise accident, saying at the end of the description: "You were not present at his death" (Blum, p. 135).[23]

Hodgson was stunned. Perhaps it isn't difficult to guess that young boys loved to roughhouse, but to pull out a) the name of his cousin, b) Fred's favorite game, and c) a description of the very accident that killed him seemed beyond luck or guesswork.

During this reading, Phinuit went on to deliver a message from another deceased friend, a woman: "Please be sure to keep the book of poems that Hodgson had given her and that her family returned to him after her death."[24] After the reading, Hodgson returned to his apartment, where he kept that very book of poems, Tennyson's *The Princess*, to ponder what had just happened. He concluded, having eliminated guessing and luck as explanations of Piper's information, and given the level of detail, that the only reasonable explanation was that Piper was spying on him. So Hodgson hired private detectives to follow both Piper and her husband for the next month (Blum, pp. 134-6).

After the month of surveillance the detectives reported to Hodgson that they had found nothing suspicious in the couple's behavior and nothing linking them in any way to Hodgson or any other sitters (those coming to Piper for readings). "Neither Mrs. Piper nor her husband had been heard asking questions about [any] sitters. They had no mysterious meetings, made no unexpected journeys, checked out no past issues of newspapers from the library, and visited no cemeteries" — all common practices of fraudulent mediums (Blum, p. 141; Sage, pp. 35-6). Nor had the Pipers hired their own private detectives to do such work for them, not that they could have afforded to do so, for her yearly earnings from her readings was never more than 200 Pounds (Sage, p. 36).

Now obsessed with Mrs. Piper, Hodgson paid the local news seller to limit the family's information by only delivering morning newspapers and only on those days when Piper had no sittings scheduled. He began sitting in on Piper's sessions, which she approved as a condition of the scientific investigation into her abilities.[25]

During his stay in America, Hodgson met a young philosopher and writer named George Pellew, who was an inveterate doubter of psychic phenomena. At age 32, Pellew was killed in a fall from his horse.[26] Later that spring (1893) Pellew appeared as a control of Mrs. Piper. Hodgson called this control "G.P." (Blum, pp. 185-6). This "coincidence" is astonishing—someone whom Hodgson knew personally now becomes one of Mrs. Piper's controls. Taking on a persona or control whom Hodgson had known was a tremendous risk, because Piper could easily be caught in her cheating. So it is difficult to imagine that Piper would have taken on Pellew if she were faking. In short, this seems a massive blast of arrogance on Piper's part...unless G.P. really was the discarnate spirit of Pellew, or unless Piper had read and could read Hodgson telepathically. Both of those possibilities, however, still point to consciousness beyond the brain.

Pellew's arrival as Piper's control provided Hodgson with either a gold mine of fraud or an additional case of compelling evidence. Hodgson devised a test of Piper's new control, this discarnate personality. He made a list of Pellew's family and friends and then invited from this list as many of them as would agree to come to have an anonymous reading with Piper (Blum, p. 186). Over a five-year period Hodgson brought 130 different visitors for sittings with Piper. Of the 130 visitors 20 were friends or relatives of Pellew's; the rest were strangers. Hodgson insisted that the visitors could offer no clues about their possible relationship to Pellew, and none of them revealed their names.

With one exception G.P., the control, identified all 20 and greeted them correctly as friends or relatives. Nor did he misidentify any stranger as a friend or relative. The one exception, his one "miss," was an 18-year-old girl whom Pellew had met when she was 10 and had not seen thereafter (Blum, p. 217). In the intervening years the child had become "a tall young woman." So at the first sitting G.P. did not recognize her at all. But at a subsequent sitting, he did: "I did not think I ever knew you well," G.P. said, "you used to come with Mr. Rogers," which was correct.[27]

While in England, with Piper out of her familiar environment, additional tests yielded other kinds of evidence. In one test, Sir Oliver Lodge wanted to rule out telepathy as an explanation for her abilities. He figured that if he presented her with a case that he himself was unfamiliar with, then she could not be picking up clues from Lodge's mind or from Lodge himself.

Lodge had an uncle living in London to whom Lodge was not close. He wrote to this uncle, Robert, and asked him to send Lodge an object, which Lodge would return, that had belonged to Robert's twin brother, who had been dead for 20 years. Since Mrs. Piper showed some ability for psychometry—getting information on people by holding and reading some possession of theirs—Lodge wanted an object "no one in the house [had ever] seen or [knew] about" (Blum, p. 165). Robert sent Lodge a gold watch that his twin brother had worn.

Lodge arranged a sitting with Mrs. Piper on the morning that the watch arrived. When Mrs. Piper went into her trance, Lodge produced the watch and handed it to her. This is what she told him: "This belongs to one of your uncles. The owner of the watch was very fond of another uncle. The name of the other uncle is Robert. In fact, Robert is now the keeper of the watch."

When Mrs. Piper spoke next, her voice was smooth and quick: "This is my watch and Robert is my brother and I am here. Uncle Jerry, my watch" (Blum, p. 165). The name of Robert's dead twin brother was, indeed, Jerry, and, of course, the watch had belonged to him. Piper had accurately named the deceased uncle/brother as the owner of the watch. But Lodge knew that, and so Piper could have read his mind. What Lodge needed was evidence that he himself did not know.

Piper, now using Phinuit, then told Lodge about how as boys the uncles had swum in a creek when it was dangerous, and the boys came close to drowning once. Also, the boys had killed a cat in Smith's field, and Jerry owned a small rifle as a boy. Jerry, Lodge was told, also treasured a snakeskin.

Lodge knew nothing about any of these details, and so he wrote to Robert for verification. Robert verified risky swimming in the creek and that he also possessed Jerry's prized snakeskin. But Robert wasn't sure about the rest. So Robert wrote to his younger brother who "remembered all of these events: the way the creek flowed past a treacherous millrace [the fast-moving current that drives a mill wheel], the stiff action of the rifle, and even the poor cat, trapped in Smith's field" (Blum, p. 166).

Yet boys in the country swim in creeks; there seems little unusual about that and it could be an easy guess. But what of the details and the rest of what Piper told Lodge? Lodge, ever cautious, thought that Piper might have learned about the boyhood adventures from others in the town where the boys grew up. So he sent private investigators to the town to ascertain whether Piper or anyone could have discovered the details related to these anecdotes. The detectives reported back to Lodge that there was no indication that anyone had inquired about the Lodge boys at all, nor were there any records in any local newspapers of these incidents and the details (Blum, pp. 167-8).

Lodge, like William James, came to the conclusion that Mrs. Piper's gifts were genuine. After 83 personal readings with her, Lodge concluded: As to the means by which she acquires her information, "I can only say with certainty that it is by none of the ordinary methods known to Physical Science" (quoted in Tymn, p. 35).

Yet in an article for the *New York Herald* (Sunday, October 20, 1901), Mrs. Piper herself claimed not to be a "telephone to the spirit world." Instead, she said that her information came from her unconscious or from telepathy (Gardner, 2003, 258). Perhaps her information did come from telepathy, but that is no less an anomalous source and still points to consciousness being independent of the brain. How else to explain how information can pass from one mind to another without any obvious communication?

Windbridge's Murder of White Crows

It is perhaps difficult to accept the evidence from a case that was investigated, though exhaustively (The American and British Societies for Psychical Research investigated Leonora Piper for over 30 years.) over a century ago. But today, through the Windbridge Institute, we have the possibility not simply of one white crow, but, indeed, of a murder of white crows.[28]

Along with her research partner and husband, Mark Boccuzzi, Dr. Julie Beischel, a doctor of toxicology and pharmacology, co-founded the Windbridge Institute in Tucson, Arizona, to conduct scientific investigations into how mediums work. Over the course of the past several years, Beischel has certified nearly 20 mediums as research partners.[29]

She has done so through experimental readings involving a medium and a sitter. Beischel has gone to some lengths to ensure that the medium is "blinded" from the sitter (the person receiving the reading); that is, the experimental controls are such that the medium never has any contact with or knowledge of the sitter. This blinding prevents the medium from reading the sitter through body language or other subtle means of detecting clues. The experimental controls also prevent the medium from gaining knowledge of the sitter, and thereby the deceased person the sitter wishes to contact, through the Internet.

So the medium never meets the sitter. Indeed, the medium doesn't even know who the sitter is. Over 1000 people have volunteered to participate as sitters in Beischel's experiments. From this group a sitter is chosen at random by computer. The medium only knows the first name of the deceased person whom the sitter wishes to contact and does not know the sitter's name at all. This name itself does not come from the sitter or Beischel, who herself, if she knew who the sitter was, might have information about the sitter and thus might somehow convey some of that information to the medium. So Beischel herself is blind to who the sitter and the deceased are.

To ensure that the medium isn't guessing, the experiment involves providing the medium with a list of specific questions to which the medium must receive answers so that the information conveyed to the sitter cannot be general. The medium must provide a physical description of the deceased, plus the deceased's personality, hobbies, and cause of death. "It would not be possible," writes Beischel, "to accurately guess the hair color, eye color, height, weight, personality, activities, and cause of death of discarnates [deceased] named Jennifer, Barbara, Anna, Linda, James, Michael, Jessica, Margaret, Brian, Joe, Nicholas, or John," which are actual names of deceased persons named by sitters in Beischel's experiments with mediums.

To limit "rater bias," Beischel provides the sitter with two readings—one from the medium reading the actual deceased person named by the sitter and one "decoy" reading not intended for that sitter. This prevents the medium from simply giving general information. "If a medium reports very general information, all the sitters will score all the readings as accurate."

The experiments are even more complicated than I'm depicting them, involving how the decoy readings and other factors are established to prevent cheating. For simplicity's sake and to appreciate the level of blinding involved, consider this summary: The medium doesn't know who the sitter or the deceased is; she (Most mediums are women.) knows only the deceased's first name, let's say "Tony." So, from all the Tonys who have ever lived and died, the medium is to make contact with the right Tony, the sitter's Tony—or, to be true to the mediums' own experience, the right Tony contacts the medium. The experimenter is blinded both to which medium is doing the reading and to the sitter. The experimenter involved with the medium during the phone reading (another way to prevent the medium from picking up any cues) is blind to all information about the sitter and about the deceased. From this information the medium is to present a reading for the sitter that is accurate enough for the sitter to identify his/her "Tony."

To be a certified Windbridge medium, the medium must attain a certain level of accuracy in her readings. Beischel says that about one-quarter of the mediums tested did not achieve passing scores. Those 25 percent may or may not be legitimate mediums. They might simply have had bad days when giving readings during the experiments. Beischel reports in one study that "16 out of 21 (76 percent) of sitters chose their own target reading as the one they felt was intended for them...If the sitters were choosing purely by chance, we would expect 50 percent to pick the right reading. At 76 percent this data is also statistically significant."[30]

Beischel concludes that her experiments reveal that these mediums acquire information about deceased persons that could not be gathered by normal means. Thus, their method of gaining this information can only be described as "anomalous." Hence, as mentioned before, Beischel refers to the medium's method as AIR: Anomalous Information Reception.

Notice that Beischel is not claiming that mediums necessarily contact the dead. They might just as well be dipping into an immense reservoir of information, like a gigantic library-card catalogue and information shelving. This is known as the "Psychic Reservoir." But that doesn't quite match what happens in Beischel's experiment. Since the medium knows only the first name of the deceased, how could the medium diving into the reservoir come up with the right "Tony"? Equally telling, if the right Tony is contacting the medium, then how does that consciousness arise out of the reservoir? Something else, therefore, must be going on with the reservoir information. It seems to be, for the sake of parsimony, that making contact with the consciousness of the deceased—the discarnate personality— is a better explanation. Mediums themselves favor this explanation.[31]

Beischel's work provides a murder of white crows—far more populous than James's single white crow—and Beischel's research (and researched) mediums are available for anyone to book for a reading. As one example, a student of mine, Robert C., researching mediumship in my undergraduate seminar on life after death, had a personal reading by Eliza Rey, one of Beischel's certified mediums. The 40-minute reading was conducted entirely over the phone; at the reading Robert gave Eliza his first name and the first letter of his last name (as I have done here), and he answered only "yes" and "no" to her comments and to most of her queries. His story, authenticated via an affidavit signed under penalty of perjury, follows:

- Initially, Eliza told Robert that he had a dog on the "other side" and described the dog accurately.
- Eliza told Robert that he ate too much acidic food and frequently got heartburn, which Robert verified to me: "I eat nothing at ASU (Arizona State University) but corn dogs, Burger King, and Dr. Pepper; I constantly experience heartburn." Although this information has nothing to do with afterlife consciousness, it does show another side to Eliza's ability to receive anomalous information.
- She told Robert that he has a relative from the early 1900s who follows him. This relative didn't like to talk; had short, dark hair, "a military haircut almost," and was blind in one eye. Robert knew nothing about any such relative, but family members of Robert's later identified this person as Robert's great-grandfather. Later, Robert was shown a picture of him, showing him blind in one eye and with the short hair. Robert challenges anyone to try to find out anything on the Internet about his great-grandfather,[32] even if Eliza could somehow have discovered a connection between him and Robert.

- Eliza asked Robert whether there was anyone in particular whom he would like to contact. He said, "Yes, Aunt Margaret," giving Eliza nothing but her first name and the relationship. Margaret, through Eliza, greeted Robert in the unique way that she always used. She commented that she hated being called "Margaret," which was true. Eliza then described how Margaret had died in a car crash in ice and snow, and how Margaret had told her family two months before she died that she was soon going to die and they should prepare for it. Eliza then described Margaret's personality, as well as Margaret's kitchen and the window Margaret liked to look out of to see her yard at her house; Eliza said: "There was a spot in her kitchen where she would often stare out the window." Eliza also described the view. All of Eliza's statements were accurate and confirmed by Rosemary (Margaret's sister) and Ann Marie (Margaret's daughter).

- Eliza then asked Robert whether he had any specific questions for Margaret, and Robert asked Margaret about her daughter, Ann Marie. Eliza then gave personal messages to Robert for Ann Marie that made sense, Robert commented later, to both Ann Marie and Rosemary. All of these statements, Robert said, were completely accurate. For example, Margaret told Ann Marie to stop changing her hair, which, Robert said, was funny since Ann Marie dyes her hair all the time. Margaret also told Robert (through Eliza) to tell Ann Marie to stop seeing the guy that she was dating and not to become engaged to him. Margaret had been asking Ann Marie for this for five years.[33] Margaret also showed Eliza Ann Marie's dog, who died, and told Ann Marie not to get a new one. Her dog had died a few months before the reading, and Ann Marie had already made plans for a new one.

- Eliza also told Robert things that he did not at the time

of the reading understand. Margaret appeared to Eliza with her daughter. Robert found this puzzling, since her daughter is Ann Marie who is alive and quite well. But Ann Marie later confirmed to Robert that her mother had miscarried a baby girl about 12 years before.

As Robert's experience demonstrates, Julie Beischel's work with mediums at the Windbridge Institute has made the search for reliable paranormal readings far easier than was the case for William James at the end of the nineteenth century and the beginning of the twentieth. Rather than search around the Internet or around one's own community for a reliable medium, Beischel has certified hers. Another student of mine wrote up the reading that a friend of hers, Sarah, had with a certified Windbridge medium. The medium contacted Sarah's grandmother (Actually, according to the medium, her grandmother came to the medium.), whom Sarah had never met. The medium accurately conveyed the following information about Sarah's grandmother, confirmed by Sarah's mother:

1. The grandmother's name was JoAnn.
2. She died when Sarah's mother was eight years old.
3. She had six children and two miscarriages.
4. She died at a young age from metastasized cancer.
5. She went to her favorite beach house in her final days.
6. Her last words to her children were harsh and hurtful.

Sarah had the reading face-to-face with the medium. She gave the medium her first name only, and Sarah had no contact with the medium before the reading. The medium consulted no phones, computers, or documents during the reading, and she did not ask Sarah questions about her grandmother.

At this point, having looked at some "white crows" of mediumship, we can ask whether we have evidence of life after death. The mediums provided some information that they could not have gotten through normal physical means, but was the information from persons deceased? Tested mediums like Leonora Piper and Eliza Rey got the information from somewhere, though not necessarily from someone. They might be retrieving it from a psychic reservoir and not from the consciousness of someone in some form who lives on, to say nothing of a deceased person whose personality remains intact after death. So can we say at this point that we have evidence that consciousness—if only as constellations of images, statements, and symbols from the deceased—is independent of the brain and survives bodily death? It seems, based on these studies and on the evidence of and from anomalous information retrieval, that consciousness is independent of the brain, but is that also evidence of survival of bodily death? Perhaps not yet.

Two other sources or forms of paranormal phenomena, however, may provide better evidence of such consciousness and even of personality remaining after death. Both near-death experiences (NDEs) and reincarnation offer white crows of their own and also provide, as did the medium investigations, veridical evidence. I shall examine some of those phenomena and this type of evidence in the next chapter. Nevertheless, regardless of the outcome of that examination, I think that at this point scientists owe Beischel's work a serious look. Her protocols are scientifically rigorous, and her results are robust. After that look, the scientists either must explain how her studies are flawed and the evidence faulty—how, that is, all crows remain black—or must concede that the evidence from mediumship "probes the rules" of mainstream science to the extent that they must now rethink whether consciousness is produced by the brain.

Chapter 2

Out of This World and Back Again: Veridical Evidence in NDEs and Reincarnation

There may be little or much beyond the grave, but the strong are saying nothing until they see.
"The Strong Are Saying Nothing" by **Robert Frost**

It's been too hard living, but I'm afraid to die
'Cause I don't know what's up there, beyond the sky.
"A Change Is Gonna Come" by **Sam Cooke**

Anyone, scientists included, looking into the scientific investigations of the paranormal, especially life after death, wants not just evidence but compelling evidence. The most compelling, to my mind, is veridical evidence. Indeed, any evidence short of that seems suspect, if not flawed. Veridical evidence in this context refers to any perception reported by someone who has undergone a paranormal experience where information is revealed that can be independently verified or corroborated later as actually having happened in our material or physical world. For the person undergoing a near-death experience, for example, these are perceptions that could not have been available to the ordinary senses of the person, since he or she was clinically dead. In a study published in 1954 Hornell Hart identified 288 published cases of possible out-of-body experiences (OBEs), characteristic of many near-death experiences (NDEs), where the person floating outside the body perceived events that could not have been witnessed from within the body. Of those 288 cases, Hart found 99 that had veridical evidence—events that were independently verified after the person had experienced them (Hart, 1954).

Veridical Evidence and Near-Death Experiences (NDEs)

Veridical evidence, it seems to me, is what can move skeptics from doubting the existence of the paranormal to accepting it. This evidence comprises experiences that those pronounced clinically dead should not have been able to have; it includes knowledge that from within our material paradigm and physicalist worldview people cannot be said to have had. But people did have these experiences; people do have this knowledge.[34]

We have encountered examples of veridical evidence in our medium readings: among them, the escapades of Sir Oliver Lodge's uncles when they were boys, the friends and relatives of George Pellew correctly identified by the disincarnated G.P. when brought for a reading with Mrs. Piper, and the description of my student's, Robert C.'s, great-grandfather. All of these statements were later corroborated as facts. But, as I suggested earlier, NDEs seem to provide better veridical evidence of consciousness itself surviving death or near-death. Consider this example from Brown University clinical psychologist and neuroscience researcher Willoughby Britton:[35]

A woman was riding with her boyfriend on her boyfriend's motorcycle. Her boyfriend had a collector's Harley-Davidson with an Indian-Head penny embossed on the side of the bike. The two skidded on some gravel, the motorcycle went down, and the woman slid underneath the bike. Suddenly, she found herself outside her body, looking down on herself, her boyfriend, and the bike. Then she saw the penny pop off of the bike and fly across the road and roll into a bush. Weeks later she returned to the scene of the accident and found the penny in the bush. Because she was underneath the bike, this event was something that she couldn't have seen if she had not left her body and had not then been floating above the scene.

While the motorcycle accident was clearly traumatic, and while the woman might well have thought that she was going to die, she was not at any time dead or near-death. So trauma can trigger an out-of-body experience. Still, that is not a near-death experience. At the same time, it might be possible that the woman had later seen the damaged motorcycle without the penny and then, weeks later, went hunting for it. In short, without more information, we don't know that she didn't lie. So consider another example:

Dr. Lloyd Rudy, a pioneer in cardiac surgery, tells of the time that he and his team lost a patient during an operation. The patient, through an oral infection, had an infected native valve that required an emergency valve resection. Once the resection was complete, the surgical team could not get the patient off the heart-lung machine. After numerous efforts, the team concluded that they would have to pronounce him dead. The anesthesiologist turned off his machine; the bellows that breathed for the patient stopped. The patient was clinically dead and was prepared for a post-mortem exam.

The machine that recorded the patient's vital signs continued to run, with the paper spilling onto the operating-room floor. The heart-monitor machine also continued to run. Dr. Rudy, the head surgeon, and his assistant surgeon changed out of their gowns and gloves. They returned to the operating room and were standing in the doorway discussing what other measures they might have taken and what medicines they might have used to save the patient. About 20-25 minutes had passed since they declared him dead: no heartbeat, no blood pressure, no brain activity.

Suddenly, the doctors looked over and saw some electrical

activity on the monitor. Then that activity turned into a heartbeat. The doctors assumed that it was an "agonal" response with the heart continuing to beat. But soon the patient was generating a blood pressure. The doctors weren't doing anything, no intervention at all. Dr. Rudy immediately called for the team to return. They returned to the patient and helped him recover without needing to reintroduce the heart-lung machine.

The patient fully recovered, as Dr. Rudy says, "with no neurological deficit." He had been clinically dead for 20-25 minutes.[36] Yet what occurred next shifts our attention, or should, elsewhere: Dr. Rudy asked the patient what he had experienced, if anything. The patient then gave a version of a classical NDE. What astounded Dr. Rudy, however, was the patient's description of the operating room and of Rudy and his assistant surgeon, after they had declared the patient clinically dead, standing in the doorway with their arms folded, which was true.

But most amazing of all was the patient describing a string of post-it notes on the television monitor. These post-its were calls that Dr. Rudy received during surgery. A nurse jotted down the name and phone number of who had called. None of these notes appeared before the operation, and thus the patient when entering the operating room would not have seen anything posted. "He claimed that he was floating around the ceiling...He never woke up during the operation, and he was out for a day or two as he recovered in the Intensive Care Unit."[37] Dr. Roberto Amado-Cattaneo, the other cardiac surgeon in the room with Dr. Rudy, later verified all of this information to researcher Titus Rivas (Rivas et al., 2016, pp. 74-7).

Verification of the information by Drs. Rudy and Amado-Cattaneo is crucial in this episode. Both doctors are on record as verifying that the details of what the patient observed, and that they corroborated, occurred when the patient was dead. Veridical evidence is also the foundation of James's declaration that Mrs. Piper was his white crow. But NDEs and reincarnation have their own white crows. Let's begin by considering one such exemplary case—one possible white crow—from the near-death experience literature.

A debate on life-after-death included noted atheists Sam Harris and Christopher Hitchens, as well as two Rabbis: Rabbi David Wolpe and Rabbi Bradley Shavit Artson.[38] During the debate Hitchens dismissed categorically the phenomena of near-death experiences. Hitchens stated, "I've read a lot about this stuff." He went on: "the most persuasive example, and I get it [hear it] all the time, is about a woman who floated out of her body, floated out of the bed, made a tour of the outside of the hospital, noticed that there was a running shoe on one of the window sills, woke up, and reported it to a nurse whose name we've never been told, who went to look and there was the shoe." Hitchens then scoffed with heavy sarcasm: "If that doesn't prove [life after death], I don't know what does."

Hitchens was right about this case, the case of the blue sneaker. It is often, perhaps always, mentioned in the NDE literature and thus is presented as something of a white crow. Here's why:

The patient, Maria, a migrant worker, had a heart attack in 1977 while visiting friends in Seattle. Her friends took her to Harborview Medical Center, where she was admitted. While there, she had a second heart attack and had to be resuscitated. After she regained consciousness, Maria became so agitated that the nurses called in her social worker, Kimberly Clark (now Kimberly Clark Sharp). Maria told Clark that after her heart attack she had found herself floating out of her body, hovering above her body and above the medical team seeking to resuscitate her. Maria then floated out of the hospital, and she described to Clark the layout and design of the emergency entrance. Clark assumed that Maria had simply unconsciously gathered this information on her way into the medical center and was retrieving the memories.

Then Maria got to the shoe. Something on a ledge on the third floor caught her attention. She floated over to this thing, which Maria identified as a man's tennis shoe. It was dark blue, well-worn, with one lace tucked underneath the shoe's heel, and with a scuff mark where the little toe would be. Clark then says, "Thinking that it might make Maria feel better to know that someone trusted her," Clark went off on a "futile search" of the third floor ledge to find the shoe.

First, she walked the perimeter of the building to see whether she could spy anything on any third-floor ledge. She could see nothing. Next, she went on a room-by-room search of the third floor. Having inspected the rooms on the east side and the north side, she went to the west side. There, by pressing her face against the window in one of the rooms, as she had done in all the others, she saw on another ledge the tennis shoe. "I felt my heart go 'thunk.' There it was."

Clark retrieved the shoe. All of the details that Maria conveyed were accurate.

Compare this version, taken from Kimberly Clark Sharp's book (2003), with that of Hitchens. First, of course, we know the "nurse's" name. Second, notice that Hitchens offers no explanation for what occurred. He insinuates that the story is singular and thus not persuasive of life after death. Perhaps not, but it is a white crow in that it offers veridical evidence of a paranormal occurrence that shows that Maria's consciousness operated independent of her body and that her awareness outside of her body could gain information about a material object that she could not otherwise have had. Or does it?

Let's look for alternative explanations. In 1994 two students from Simon Fraser University, Hayden Ebbern (an undergraduate psychology student) and Sean Mulligan (a graduate student in biological sciences), visited Harborview in Seattle three times and had several conversations with Kimberly Clark. Despite their best efforts, Ebbern and Mulligan could not locate Maria, nor did they find anyone other than Clark who had had any contact with her. Is the implication here that Clark lied? But if Clark lied and made up this story, what possible motive would she have? Well, Clark herself is prominent within NDE circles; she is the founder and president of the Seattle International Association for Near-Death Studies, which her book jacket describes as "the oldest and largest group of its kind in the world." You can also find her on YouTube describing her own NDE from 1970. That year was seven years before Maria was admitted to Harborview. Thus Clark already had some interest in and knowledge about NDEs. Might it be to her benefit to fabricate or at least to embellish a tale such as Maria's to draw attention to herself and to the phenomena of NDEs?

Next, Maria was a cardiac patient and was surely not out of her bed traipsing about the medical center visiting different rooms, let alone different floors. At the very least the monitor leads attached to her would restrain her movements. Perhaps, on the other hand, one of Maria's friends, with time to kill, wandered about the medical center, found the room on the west side, peered out the window, saw the shoe, and reported this back to Maria. Then Maria either pretended to see the shoe or unconsciously recorded this information and thought upon revival that she had seen the shoe. But could the details of the shoe that Maria described be seen from that window? Still, if Kimberly Clark could reach the shoe to bring it in, so, too, could the friend…to retrieve it or to place it there.

The same students, Ebbern and Mulligan, planted a running shoe on a third-floor ledge to determine whether they could see the shoe from outside the hospital. They were "astonished at the ease with which they could see and identify the shoe" (1996, p. 7). Because of that ease, these authors suggest that hospital personnel might have seen the dark-blue tennis shoe and might well have commented on the "novelty and whimsicality of its location" (p. 8). Maria, who spent three days in the hospital before her second heart attack, might have overheard such comments. Or, again, as a form of cryptomnesia,[39] she might have absorbed the story unconsciously and then recalled the specifics as a visual image believing honestly that she had never heard that information before.

But could anyone from outside the hospital have seen the details that Maria reported? Ebbern and Mulligan do not say, but given that the shoe was on the third floor, it is difficult to imagine that anyone could see such details. Additionally, if the shoe were so clearly visible, why did no one remove the shoe from the ledge? Whimsicality or not, who would leave the shoe there?

Part of Hitchens's sneering dismissal of the blue-shoe incident is that it is a singular event, the only one that those within the near-death community refer to or use as providing veridical evidence. But that is not the case.[40] Consider two more. The first is taken from the immense study by cardiologist Pim van Lommel of cardiac-arrest patients in 10 Dutch hospitals; the second is the case of Pam Reynolds, another frequently cited NDE white crow.

The Denture Case

A 44-year-old man in a coma was brought into the emergency room of a Dutch hospital. He had been found unconscious in a public park, where passersby administered CPR until the emergency services arrived. When the cardiac patient arrived at the hospital, a medical team immediately began resuscitative efforts. As part of that procedure, a nurse tried to intubate the patient (that is, place a hollow tube down his throat). When he did so, he discovered that the patient had dentures. Before intubation, the nurse removed the upper set of dentures and placed it on the crash cart. The nurse reported: "Meanwhile we continue extensive resuscitation. After approximately ninety minutes, the patient has sufficient heart rhythm and blood pressure, but he's still ventilated and intubated, and he remains comatose" (van Lommel, 2010, p. 21).

After more than a week in a coma, the patient returned to consciousness. When the same nurse entered his room to deliver his medication, the patient said to him: "You know where my dentures are...You were there when they brought me into the hospital, and you took my dentures out of my mouth and put them on that cart; it had all these bottles on it, and there was a sliding drawer underneath, and you put my teeth there" (van Lommel, 2010, p. 21).

The nurse was amazed, because he reported and had verified that the patient had been in a coma when the incident with the dentures occurred. In addition, the patient described both the small room where the cardiac patient had been resuscitated and the people who were in the room. All of this, the patient claims, he saw when he floated out of his body.

The case drew the attention of Dutch-Australian anesthesiologist Gerald Woerlee. Although Woerlee never saw the follow-up interview of nurse "T.G." (The nurse used only his initials to protect his privacy.) by Ap Addink, the anesthesiologist thought that this case, like all NDEs, could be explained in materialistic terms as the observations of a conscious patient. Woerlee argued that

1. The patient was conscious because the cardiac resuscitation was successful; his hearing and sight were restored;
2. Extreme oxygen deprivation of his brain paralyzed him, rendering him unable to move or speak and thus to inform the doctors and nurses of what he was experiencing;

3. He felt his dentures being removed and heard them clank into a metal drawer, whose opening and closing made a distinct sound;

4. His eyes were opened periodically to check pupil size as a sign of oxygen deprivation, and so he could see the room and the people in it (Smit, 2008, p. 49).

5. By checking the transcript of Addink's interview with T.G., Rudolf Smit challenged Woerlee's assertions. To the assertion that the patient was conscious Smit countered with T.G.'s description of the patient when first brought into the hospital: He had no pulse; he was not breathing; he had been lying in a meadow for a long time and showed signs of "post mortem lividity"; and he was clinically dead. The hospital team began resuscitation only because the patient was so young.

6. Woerlee claimed that the patient might have been conscious and thus had his eyes open some of the time. But T.G. said that the patient had "no pupillary reflexes whatsoever, which is a clear sign that the supply of oxygen to the head had stopped. During regular checking of the pupils there was no reaction...He was unconscious in any case. Thus he was unable to see" (Smit, 2008, pp. 51-2).

T.G. reported that after 15 minutes of efforts to revitalize the patient the team was convinced that they were working on a dead man. "We all had the feeling: what for heaven's sake are we doing here? Because the man was ice cold..." (Smit, 2008, p. 51). But after much more resuscitative effort the patient did establish a heartbeat and a low blood pressure. He was then transferred to the intensive care unit where he remained in a coma.

As for the dentures, Woerlee's assertion that the patient could feel them removed and hear them placed in the metal drawer is without substance. T.G. removed the dentures at the beginning of the resuscitation procedure so that they could intubate the patient. At this point, as we've seen, the patient is clinically dead and could not have seen or heard anything.

Moreover, T.G. did not immediately place the dentures in a metal drawer and close it: "I took the dentures out and placed them on the crash cart" (Smit, 2008, p. 53). He had placed the dentures on a sliding shelf, a flat wooden plate sticking out from the cart, and left them there. T.G. left the dentures on the shelf. "[A]pparently during tidying up...those dentures got lost somehow. I [did] not see them again" (Smit, 2008, p. 54).

Obviously, there were no sounds of dentures on metal or of sliding drawers, even if the patient could have heard such sounds. Additionally, according to the patient himself, this was the first time that he had ever been admitted to a hospital, and the crash cart, as T.G. says, "is unique in the entire hospital. Nowhere else in the hospital was such a crash cart available" (Smit, 2008, p. 54).

T.G. remained at home for the next five days and did not visit the patient for a couple of days after that. In total he did not see the patient for over a week: "I was surprised to see that...he recognized me, because the last time I had seen him he was still comatose! And his eyes had not been open, except for the times when I checked his pupillary reflexes [those pupils had given no reaction whatsoever]" (Smit, 2008, p. 55).

The patient then told T.G. that he had seen from above T.G. removing his dentures and placing them on the crash cart: "There was a sliding plate upon which you put the dentures" (Smit, 2008, p. 55).[41]

From this example, if the reports of the nurse are to be believed, there is no way that the patient could have had the experiences and formed the memories that he did if his consciousness was the product of his brain. Did his consciousness float out of his body and watch the proceedings from above? Whatever the method involved, the patient could not have known what he described except by some anomalous means.

The Pam Reynolds Case

Pam Reynolds entered the Barrow Neurological Institute in August, 1991, to undergo a radical procedure called "hypothermic cardiac arrest," which seemed the only hope for dealing with her brain aneurysm. The procedure required reducing her body temperature to 60 degrees Fahrenheit and stopping her heart and breathing. At that point, the doctors would drain all of the blood from her head. To assure that she was "clinically dead" — that is, that she had no heartbeat or brain function — the doctors inserted at 7:15 a.m. earpieces that emitted 95-decibel clicking. Once her brain stopped reacting to the sound — as loud as a rock concert or a jackhammer going off in her ears — then the doctors would know that there was no brain activity at all, not even in the brainstem.

Before this procedure, doctors gave Reynolds intravenous pentothal and general anesthetics and taped her eyes shut. So with her eyes taped shut she could see nothing in the operating room; with the clickers in her ears she could hear nothing in the operating room.

At 8:40 a.m., the neurosurgeon, Dr. Spetzler, incised her scalp and removed a section of her skull with a bone saw. Meanwhile, a female cardiac surgeon made an incision in Reynolds's right groin to prepare the femoral artery and vein for the cardiopulmonary bypass. But the female doctor commented that the blood vessels were too small and so incised Reynolds's left groin instead.

At 11:05, with Reynolds's body temperature at around 73 degrees, the doctors induced cardiac arrest. By 11:25, with her body temperature at 60 degrees, with no clicks registering and thus with total brain shutdown, the doctors drained the blood from her head. With no blood in the brain there could be no brain function whatsoever. Dr. Spetzler then repaired the aneurysm.

Pam Reynolds claims that she was "awakened" by the sound of the bone saw, which, as a musician, Reynolds described as "a natural D tone." The sound, she claims, pulled her out of her body through the top of her head, where she lighted near Spetzler's shoulder. She saw with total clarity (Recall: Her eyes are taped shut.) the cranial saw, which she described as like a dentist's drill and not at all like what we might associate with a saw. Dr. Michael Sabom (1998), who wrote up this case and is himself a physician, was startled by Reynolds's description of the saw, since he himself did not know what this cranial saw looked like. More startling than this, Reynolds described someone conducting a procedure in her groin area, which surprised her since she thought that she was only having a brain operation. Reynolds says that she heard a female voice say that the vessels were too small on the right side and then a male voice telling the female to try the other side.[42]

Some of what Reynolds reported—the bone saw, the cardiopulmonary bypass, and the comments from both doctors about that bypass—certainly seems to be veridical evidence. But veridical anecdotes such as these require investigation, though it also seems to be the case that patients in the state that Reynolds was in will not be able to hallucinate accurate empirical details when they are clinically dead...unless Reynolds was not dead or unless consciousness is independent of the brain. Still, it is possible that Reynolds could have researched the bone saw, for example, before the operation. But what about the other elements? How do we account for them?

In the case of Pam Reynolds one doubter, Keith Augustine (2007), argues that her experience occurred before the cardiopulmonary bypass began. Thus clinical death had not yet occurred. Hence, her experience could be filed under "anesthesia awareness," a well-documented phenomenon.

On the other hand, how did she hear the conversation about her blood vessels? First, anesthesia awareness is most often attributed to a patient being under-anesthetized, which Reynolds was not as her brain was being monitored thoroughly and extensively throughout the entire procedure.

Next, two of those monitoring devices were the earpieces used to measure response in her brainstem. As Holden reports, Augustine does not mention them. Recall that these earpieces emitted 90-100 decibels at a rate of 11-33 clicks per second. That is as loud as "a whistling teakettle...a lawn mower or a subway tunnel when a train is going through it" (Holden et al., 2009, p. 198). Holden also reminds Augustine that these earpieces are molded to fill the ear canals completely. The idea that anyone could hear a normal conversation when this was occurring is fanciful.[43] Since the clicks began after the introduction of general anesthesia and at least an hour-and-a-half before the operation began, and if the clicks produced no reaction in the brain, then that can only mean that there was no response in the brain at all, not just in the brainstem. This means that Reynolds, by every clinical measure, was dead. As Sabom reported to Holden, Reynolds never even mentioned hearing any clicks.

Science needs to be able to explain how persons can have experiences, vivid and often life-changing experiences, when they are declared brain dead or show all of the signs of brain death. Here is Dr. Spetzler's (her doctor's) own view of what happened to Pam Reynolds: "I don't have an explanation for it...I find it inconceivable that [through] your normal senses, such as hearing, let alone the fact that she had clicking modules in each ear, [she could] hear what she heard...I don't know how it's possible for it to happen, considering the physiological state she was in" (Holden, 2009, p. 199).

Perhaps there are flaws in Reynolds's case (though I think that that is quibbling) that don't render it a white crow. Still, highly skeptical readers might have to admit at this point that it is worthwhile examining further whether consciousness is somehow independent of the brain. On the other hand, perhaps the most skeptical reader needs more. Therefore, consider, another case, quite similar in nature, which might be an even stronger candidate as a white crow: Sarah Gideon.

The Sarah Gideon Case

Dr. Allan Hamilton reported this case in his book, *The Scalpel and the Soul* (2008). Hamilton, chief of neurosurgery and chair of the Department of Surgery at the University of Arizona Medical School, had heard about a case at Barrow very much like that of Pam Reynolds. But in this case the patient's entire operation had been recorded via audiotape and video camera. To understand this case, the case of Sarah Gideon, Hamilton reviewed, in addition to the usual medical records, 300 sheets of continuous brainwave readings, as well as the audio and video tracks that were taped during the surgery.

The facts are that Sarah Gideon, 34 years old, worked for an architectural firm in Phoenix, Arizona. One day at work she suddenly began to see twinkling lights everywhere. Moments later she developed an excruciating headache and passed out. The cause of her symptoms, like those of Pam Reynolds, was a cerebral hemorrhage or a "basilar tip aneurysm." The usual result of such an incident is death. But Sarah Gideon didn't die, and so the aneurysm could be repaired.

Because the aneurysm had engulfed and surrounded two important arteries in her brain, the operation would be difficult. If the aneurysm ruptured during the operation, Gideon would die.

The doctors at Barrow decided, as with Pam Reynolds, to stop all blood flow in Gideon's body and to her brain. Then, when in a deep hypothermia with all brain activity stopped, the surgeons could dissect the aneurysm without any bleeding. The doctors estimated that there was a 50 percent chance that Gideon would die during the operation; without the operation, however, the chances were 100 percent that she would die. According to Hamilton: "the brain simply will not tolerate being deprived of its blood for more than two to four minutes. Longer than that and the brain dies. Instantly. Irrevocably." Cooling the body temperature drastically can extend the time that the brain can be without blood.

Doctors proceeded with the operation. During the 17 minutes when Gideon was "as a corpse," when the aneurysm was sealed off, the doctors and nurses chatted casually. One nurse, Rita Hightower, informed the group that she had just gotten engaged. The audio recordings picked this up. Rita wore no engagement ring in the OR; she had scrubbed in for the operation. She described her ring to her colleagues during the operation as a "one-and-a-half carat square-yellow diamond."

Rita also described how John, her fiancé, had gotten down on his knee at Morton's, a steakhouse in Phoenix, and proposed. In fact, one of the waiters didn't see him, tripped over his foot, and fell into a wine case. One of her colleagues in the OR asked, "Where is the ring from?" Rita responded: "Johnston Fellows," one of the most exclusive stores in Phoenix (2008, p. 194).

Dr. Hamilton reviewed the video and audiotapes to verify that Rita had conveyed these details when Gideon was clinically dead, with no blood flow to or activity in her brain. This is significant, because in the recovery room Gideon told the head surgeon that she had heard a conversation about a diamond ring from Johnston Fellows and about Morton's where somebody proposed.

Upon hearing this from Gideon, the head surgeon called in the anesthesiologist, who himself then questioned Gideon. Then they watched the video of the operation. When the conversation occurred, Gideon was clinically dead, with no blood flow to the brain and no EEG activity whatsoever. Her brain had no function at all. In that state, comments Hamilton, "it would be utterly impossible, from a biochemical, metabolic, and physiological point of view for this woman's brain to create a memory."

Later, after more conversation with Gideon, doctors discovered that she could describe everyone in the operating room, most of whom she had not seen before when on the table. And she could accurately describe parts of the procedure and the equipment used, but none of that happened or had been introduced until she was anesthetized.[44]

How can we explain Gideon's accurate recall while clinically dead? My first thought was "contamination." Could Gideon have overheard a conversation in the recovery room between a recovery-room nurse and a nurse who had been present during the operation? Was that notion far-fetched?

It so happens that my sister-in-law is a recovery-room nurse in Arizona, and so I asked her whether there was much, if any, interaction between recovery-room nurses and nurses coming out of the OR after surgery. Her response was unequivocal: "All the time." It turns out that a patient must be escorted from the operating room to the recovery room by a nurse from the OR and by the anesthesiologist. Thus, recovery-room nurses know well the nurses from the OR. Given the unusual details in the marriage proposal, it is possible that the OR nurse would have shared the story with the recovery-room nurse. And so Gideon might have overheard parts of the conversation.

Furthermore, I decided to ask Dr. Hamilton what he thought about this possibility, and so I sent him the following e-mail:

I had a question that I wonder whether you considered and pursued when you investigated this case. Is it possible that the recovery-room nurses could have heard about Rita's engagement (even with the details about her fiancé tripping the waiter into the wine case) and her engagement ring either from Rita herself or from other OR nurses? Could those recovery-room nurses then have been talking about the proposal, given the unusual features, while Sarah was coming out of the anesthesia? Thus Sarah might have overheard it. Such an occurrence seems the only counter-argument to the remarkable case of Sarah Gideon, and thus I find it important to try to sort that out. Can you help?

Hamilton then responded with a message that for me was totally unexpected:

Sarah Gideon is an amalgam of three different patients. It would be unlikely in these cases that the recovery room nurses could have reported the conversation from the OR in any detail unless it was somehow relayed in great detail. It would seem odd that an OR nurse would report such an unrelated conversation to a patient emerging from anesthesia.

First, about Hamilton's second point: It doesn't seem odd at all that an OR nurse would recount Rita Hightower's story to a recovery-room nurse. If Barrow operates at all similarly to the hospital where my sister-in-law works, then these nurses interact frequently and might well want to share such an intimate, touching, and humorous story. Additionally, the story is unusual and worth repeating, especially the part about the waiter falling into the wine case. (By the way, I could find no evidence of any "Johnston Fellows" jewelry store or jewelers in Phoenix.) Second, I did not mean to suggest that a nurse would report this story to the patient; that might be odd. I suggested that Gideon overheard the story as she came out of the anesthesia. But the stunning revelation from Hamilton was that the Sarah Gideon case is an amalgam of three cases. This, it seems to me, totally alters the circumstances and renders the case almost useless. We can't sort out what happened to whom. We don't have any evidence that what appears in the amalgamated case actually happened as described. Indeed, we can infer that events did not unfold in this way, since Hamilton felt compelled to combine elements from three different cases. Which elements belong to which cases? Putting three cases together into one case does nothing, as far as I can see, to advance the idea that there is veridical evidence that consciousness operates independent of the brain. So I asked Hamilton in another e-mail:

If the Sarah Gideon case is an amalgam of three patients, then does that not create doubt as to what happened? With three different patients, the details did not happen to any single patient. Her case, as a single case, seems almost fool-proof, but if it's an amalgam, then the very aspects of it that make the evidence compelling now come into question, because they are scattered across three patients. Don't you think so?

Hamilton then responded in the following way: "Three patients with excellent recall despite electrocerebral silence (cooling and barbiturate coma) with recall seems unlikely that all could be related to overheard conversations. One recalled comments shared between myself and a resident at the microscope. I doubt anyone else could have even heard it."

All of what Hamilton says may be so, but it undercuts the evidence in the case. Maybe all three patients, of whom Gideon is the amalgam, had excellent recall, but recall of what? Documented how and by whom? What was the conversation between Hamilton and the resident? Where was the patient? Did anyone in the room hear that conversation? Could and will the resident verify a) that the conversation took place and b) that the patient was in electrocerebral silence at the time? Can that be verified? If so, why make up an amalgam and not use the three individual cases?[45]

There are NDE cases that produce veridical evidence—Lloyd Rudy's case and the denture case are two examples. But the putative white crow of Pam Reynolds's case still has issues. And the Sarah Gideon case, so promising in its details, does nothing to settle those issues.

Indeed, the studies undertaken so far that might provide compelling, systematic evidence seem a mixed bag. Are they sufficient for demonstrating consciousness independent of the brain?[46] In his article, "The Science of Near-Death Experiences," Gideon Lichfield (2015) reports that all of the studies designed to demonstrate veridical evidence have failed to do so. The studies involved placing a sign, symbol, number or set of numbers, or an electronic display in a high location that could only be seen from close to the ceiling. The researchers made certain that no one involved in the patient's treatment, and most of the patients were cardiac-arrest patients, would know what had been placed in the location. The test was to see whether any patient's consciousness floated out of the body and to the ceiling where the sign, numbers, or symbol could be seen. In Sam Parnia's "Aware" study only one patient out of 2060 cardiac cases studied remembered an out-of-body experience in which he could discuss instances related to his care that he could not have known because they occurred as late as three minutes after his heart stopped (Lichfield, 2015). There were no reports, however, of numbers, signs, or symbols displayed near the ceiling.

But Parnia's study is not all studies designed to demonstrate veridical evidence. To be sure, Parnia designed his study to *elicit* veridical evidence, and it failed. *Demonstrating* veridical evidence, however, is different, and we have a mixed bag of results. The "mixed-bag" result means for us that there are some clear veridical elements in these cases, but also many promising elements that cannot be verified. As one final example of the mixed bag, consider the case of Irene Badini. Blind at the time, Badini was in a car accident that put her in a coma. While in the coma, she claims that she perceived her mother come into her room and stand at the foot of her bed. Her mother exclaimed, "What's to become of a blind girl" whose brain has now been damaged because of the accident? This later turned out to be true.

Also, while still in the coma, Irene claims that she perceived that the staff dropped her on the floor when they moved her onto the x-ray table. One staff member took off her jewelry and said to the other staff member that he had placed the jewelry in his coat pocket and told the other staff member not to forget that. When Irene regained consciousness, she told the nurse that she would like the two men to return her jewelry. Irene told the nurse that the two staffers had dropped her and taken her jewelry. She remembered that the one who took her jewelry was "Caribbean or dark-skinned," remarkable given that Badini was blind. When informed of this, the hospital administrator investigated, found the two staffers, who verified the drop and returned Irene's jewelry immediately. It had been in one of their coat pockets.

Dr. Jean Pierre Postel, an anesthesiologist who treated her, contacted Irene's ophthalmologist who confirmed her blindness. But no one confirmed the extent of her coma and whether she could have been conscious during both her mother's visit and the episode in the x-ray room. A suggestive story, therefore, remains largely anecdotal, since no one was interviewed to confirm the depth and duration of Irene's coma.[47]

Perhaps when considering all of the cases together, the evidence—despite some flaws in the seminal cases—seems compelling, because there is more than one instance of veridical evidence, more than one white crow. Nevertheless, let us consider, on the other hand, another kind of paranormal phenomenon that might be more promising. Let us consider reincarnation and, in particular, a case from the voluminous work of Dr. Ian Stevenson. If there is strong, even compelling, evidence for reincarnation, then as reported such a case would show the continuation of consciousness after death and into a new life.

Reincarnation

The most systematic study of cases of reincarnation comes from the ongoing work at the Division of Perceptual Studies (formerly the Division of Personality Studies) at the University of Virginia. Dr. Ian Stevenson founded the Division as a research unit in the Department of Psychiatry and Neurobehavioral Sciences with a grant and subsequent million-dollar bequest from Chester Carlson, the inventor of the photocopying process that became the basis for the Xerox Corporation.

Since their founding in 1968, and despite Dr. Stevenson's death in 2007, the Division has amassed over 2500 cases of reincarnation from around the world. What seems especially important about the methods used by the investigators is their attempts to reason away reincarnation as an explanation of the events or phenomena presented. After extensive interviews with subjects and their family, friends, and neighbors and after exhaustive investigations into possible corruption or contamination of evidence, researchers are often left with reincarnation as one, if not the only, satisfactory explanation.

From that daunting number of cases, I am drawing on one as illustration. It seems to be in the eye of the beholder whether the evidence in these many cases is suggestive or strong or even compelling. I find this one compelling, and so it is for me a possible white crow. It is the case of Gnanatilleka Baddewithana.[48]

The Case of Gnanatilleka Baddewithana

Gnanatilleka was born near Hedunawewa in Sri Lanka in 1956. From the age of two she reported to her parents that she had a mother, father, and two brothers in a town, Talawakelle, that was some 16 miles away from Gnanatilleka's own town. The little girl said that she wanted to go to that town to visit her parents.

A couple of years later, with the stories from Gnanatilleka not having subsided, a neighbor wrote to a journalist, Mr. H.S.S. Nissanka, who had written about some cases of reincarnation. The neighbor conveyed what Gnanatilleka was saying. Nissanka decided to interview Gnanatilleka and accompanied by a Buddhist monk, Venerable Piyadassi Thera, who had also heard about Gnanatilleka's story, traveled to her village. When interviewed, Gnanatilleka described incidents from life in Talawakelle, including seeing Queen Elizabeth of England traveling by train.

Nissanka then wrote two journalistic articles about Gnanatilleka's tale. A resident of Talawakelle confirmed that the incidents described in the articles matched the life of a teenage boy from the village who had died in 1945. The boy's name was Tillekeratne.

Gnanatilleka's family took her to Talawakelle where the child correctly identified several of the buildings. Gnanatilleka's father had visited Talawakelle only once, some 20 years earlier; her mother had never been there before. The house that Gnanatilleka directed them to as hers had been torn down. But the location proved to be accurate, and the family of Tillekeratne had moved (Stevenson, 1974, p. 132).

Shortly after this visit, one of Tillekeratne's teachers and two men who had been unknown to Tillekeratne went to see Gnanatilleka. Each of the men asked Gnanatilleka whether she knew him. She said, "No," to both. But to the teacher she said, "Yes, you are from Talawakelle." She acknowledged that this person had been her teacher and never punished her. Gnanatilleka also correctly identified two other of Tillekeratne's teachers (Stevenson, 1974, p. 132).

Gnanatilleka was especially affectionate with one of the teachers, Mr. D.V. Sumithapala. This, Stevenson commented, seemed appropriate, since Sumithapala had taken a special interest in Tillekeratne and had managed his pupils without harsh punishment (Stevenson, 1974, p. 135).

Gnanatilleka also showed greater affection for one of Tillekeratne's sisters, Salinawathie, than for the other sisters, and this Stevenson commented also seemed appropriate given their relationship. Gnanatilleka was also especially cool toward Tillekeratne's brother, Buddhadasa, with whom Tillekeratne had a strained relationship. When asked initially, "Who is this?" Gnanatilleka denied knowing Buddhadasa, but then later conceded that he was his/her brother (Stevenson, 1974, p. 135).

The following day, Nissanka and the monk arranged for Gnanatilleka to travel to an inn in Talawakelle to meet members of Tillekeratne's family, but they did not tell Gnanatilleka the purpose of the trip. "Gnanatilleka sat in a room with her mother, the monk, and Dr. Nissanka, who recorded the events with a tape recorder. Gnanatilleka's father and Tillekeratne's teacher stood near the door" (Tucker, 2005, p. 152).

Tillekeratne's mother entered the room. Gnanatilleka was asked whether she knew her. "Gnanatilleka, after making sure that her own mother could not hear her, whispered to Tillekeratne's mother (and to Dr. Nissanka's microphone), 'Talawakelle mother'" (Tucker, 2005, p. 153).

Gnanatilleka then correctly identified in succession her Talawakelle father and one of Tillekeratne's sisters. Next entered a man who had moved to Talawakelle after Tillekeratne had died. When asked whether she knew him, Gnanatilleka replied, "No." When asked by Nissanka to reconsider, Gnanatilleka said, "I don't know him."

Three women entered next, and Gnanatilleka correctly identified them as Tillekeratne's sisters. When one of the sisters asked, "Who am I?", Gnanatilleka said, "The sister who lives in the house below ours," which was true (Tucker, 2005, p. 153). Gnanatilleka's mother asked her who the third woman was, and Gnanatilleka said, "The sister to whose house we go to sew clothes." That, too, was accurate.[49]

In total, Gnanatilleka correctly identified seven members of Tillekeratne's family, as well as two persons from the village. No one in the room knew the relationships to Tillekeratne of the people who walked in, and so the repeated accurate recognitions are significant, as are the tests to identify people Tillekeratne could not have known. Later on, many days later, Gnanatilleka, walking in Talawakelle with one of Tillekeratne's teachers, pointed to a woman in the crowd and said, "I know her...She came to the Talawakelle temple with me" (Tucker, 2005, p. 154).

This was later confirmed to be so.

Ian Stevenson came to conduct an investigation of his own in 1961, when Gnanatilleka was five. He determined that while the distance between the two towns was not that far, movement from one to the other was difficult, for Talawakelle is in the highlands, and Hedunawewa, in a deep valley. Gnanatilleka's family lived in the jungle, their house accessible only by footpath some half mile from Hedunawewa. "Nobody would reach the house of Gnanatilleka's family unless they were intent on visiting them...I am confident therefore that no one from outside the village of Hedunawewa itself...could have reached the home and talked with Gnanatilleka without her family knowing of the visit" (Stevenson, 1974, p. 133).

Stevenson also commented that the emotion that Alice Nona, Tillekeratne's mother, showed toward Gnanatilleka and about her various identifications "certainly suggested strongly to me that [Nona] was acting quite spontaneously and was not a party to any contrived drama" (Stevenson, 1974, p. 142).

Having interviewed all of the relevant parties, often more than once, Stevenson concluded that he could find no motive for fraud among them (Stevenson, 1974, p. 144). There was no remuneration for anyone for anything, and the publicity generated by the case proved to be "more vexatious than welcome" (Stevenson, 1974, p. 144). Only a conspiracy of many persons could have succeeded in the fraud, and such a conspiracy would have to involve not only coaching participants on their stories, but also evoking at the right time the proper emotional responses, including tears. Gnanatilleka was only two when she began her "tale" and was five when Stevenson interviewed her. That is quite young for memorizing and rendering consistently the same story and details. Moreover, could a toddler of this age be coached to deliver the proper emotional reactions, especially to "strangers" from Tillekeratne's family?

Most powerful to Stevenson (1974, p. 145) are the recognitions made by Gnanatilleka. She achieved these without any hints from the adults with her. She was asked simply, "Do you know this person?" "Who is this person?" and "Do you know me?"; she was not given clues about relationships or identities. Plus, she failed to identify three "blanks" who were presented to test Gnanatilleka. And, remember, she correctly picked out two women from crowds.

Conclusion

In Stevenson's and Tucker's work on reincarnation we have, again, a murder of white crows. When the evidence of reincarnation is combined with the incidents of veridical evidence both from near-death experiences and from medium readings, the murder seems expansive, and the evidence, in total, compelling. As Mark Leary himself concluded:

> The research evidence in support of psi (parapsychological phenomena) is stronger than I had ever imagined, with the support for anomalous precognition and telepathy being strongest...findings so strong that they would be widely accepted with little debate if they involved phenomena that were less strange (2011, p. 275).

My point in writing these first two chapters has not been just to show skeptics and doubters that there is strong evidence showing that consciousness is independent of the brain. My point is also to convince them, especially scientists, to look at the scientific research on the paranormal, because, at the very least, there is evidence that demands attention. I am arguing that there is no good reason to dismiss and ignore that research and very good reasons for attending to that research.[50]

Too often, however, within the discourse that constitutes and reinforces the materialist paradigm one is applauded not for arguing against the paranormal but for dismissing it out of hand. Scientists, whose *modi operandi* are to investigate claims, are too often content to disregard phenomena that run counter to their own views. In short, they fall back within their discourse on the very claims that they pride themselves on opposing—faith and assertions without evidence. The result: The scientific materialist worldview limits our knowledge by a discourse that frames the social constructs of life and death. Scientists can't pursue the paranormal without risking ridicule not for what they might find there and how they might go about finding it, but for even venturing into that domain—that is, venturing beyond the conventional discourse into a research domain that, ironically, uses the same experimental apparatus. Scientists thereby suffer from a professional panopticon, which exists not as institutional checks but as a discourse that reposes within themselves, where it is so much more difficult to recognize and oppose.

Sam Harris, best-selling author and well-known atheist, is also a neuroscientist who states that the one significant area of what we take ourselves to be as human beings that science has yet to prove is the origin and existence of consciousness in the brain. And yet he also states that views about consciousness existing independent of the brain, stories of souls ascending to the light or seeing dead relatives, as claimed in many (if not most) near-death experiences, are "profoundly naïve."[51]

This he states with the certainty for which he criticizes many (if not all) religious believers. How can he be so certain? He can be so certain only because he adheres, stringently it seems, to the idea that consciousness must exist exclusively in and be produced by the brain. But other ideas are also plausible, as I hope to have suggested. Since we know that science has yet to measure consciousness, because it can't measure what it doesn't know, and since science has yet to offer us any explanation of how the brain produces consciousness, we can offer a different idea: Consciousness is reflected in and through the brain but is itself independent of the brain. That is, to manifest, consciousness needs the brain and its complexity of neural pathways, but consciousness does not depend on the brain for its existence.

This could explain why brain damage can result in various diminished capacities—speech, sight, movement, and the like. If I damage a microphone, you might still be able to hear my muffled voice, but that doesn't mean that the voice itself is damaged. If the microphone is destroyed, we seek another microphone; the voice itself continues to exist. Consciousness, after the brain dies, can continue to exist. It is only the amplifier or transmitter that is destroyed.[52]

Of course, I don't know enough to state this proposition with any confidence or with any certainty. It is just one way to attempt to integrate the veridical evidence into a picture of how consciousness works in the living. Another attempt is to suggest that the brain does not simply reflect consciousness, but also participates in some way in developing consciousness. Rather than being only a vessel for consciousness, the brain serves some interactive or creative capacity yet unknown. A third attempt is to suggest that consciousness is an emergent property of the brain that arises when the neural complexity of the brain reaches a certain level. This attempt is less satisfying. How do we explain how the emergent property—consciousness—once brought into existence, continues to exist independent of the physical and chemical properties that created it?

All of the above is speculation, some of it more aligned with the veridical evidence than others. Still, I don't think that Harris or any other scientist can speak at this point with certainty about what people can experience at near-death (and even beyond). There is simply too much anomalous experience to examine scientifically and too much veridical evidence for anyone to issue such pronouncements with any certainty and absent any serious study of the parapsychological research presented here (at least).

Harris does admit that he cannot categorically dismiss the

contents of such books as Ian Stevenson's *20 Cases Suggestive of Reincarnation*. Yet "[t]he fact that I have not spent any time on this should suggest how worthy of my time I think such a project would be."[53] But how can this project not be worthy of his time? If the parapsychological experiments and studies presented in these first two chapters follow rigorous scientific protocols, as seems the case, then how can the project not be of paramount importance to Harris? The eminent biologist and captain of the new atheists, Richard Dawkins proclaimed, as I quoted earlier, that the existence of phenomena such as telepathy would "turn the laws of physics upside down." We have the studies. Why won't they look? So much is at stake, and perhaps, as I discussed in Chapter 1, too much is at stake: their entire scientific worldview, including the nature of consciousness. The presence of so much anomalous experience and evidence mandates, however, that the proper attitude toward parapsychology should be now and for the future that of scientific inquiry itself: skeptical, as in open-minded, and humble in the ongoing possibilities of evermore unfolding evidence.

Chapter 3

Morality Without God: Does Science Inform Our Moral Codes?

"Without God and the future life? It means everything is permitted now, one can do anything?" "Didn't you know?" he said. And he laughed. "Everything is permitted to the intelligent man," he said.
Fyodor Dostoyevsky *(The Brothers Karamazov)*

What is the result if you find the evidence in the first two chapters compelling? That is, if you now think that personal consciousness might well be independent of the brain, and not the brain's product, what follows? Foremost, I think, is that that new viewpoint calls into question not just what neuroscientists might be telling us, but also what religionists preach. Almost all of the reports from "heaven" or from "the other side" are subjective tales. The personal experiences of those visited, for example, by their recently deceased grandmother or of those undergoing a near-death experience when they meet their long-dead relatives are significant for those individuals, but not so much for those of us who don't participate in the experiences. To be convinced, we on the outside need something veridical. Unfortunately, we don't have much veridical evidence to substantiate most of the stories from the afterlife, and so each person must decide for himself/herself where to draw the line. Just which of these tales—and which parts, if any—will you accept and on what grounds?

Surely one casualty from experiments with the paranormal is our conventional, theistic understanding of God. This understanding must undergo a transformation, and I'll address in the next couple of chapters what form(s) that transformation can take. In this chapter, however, I want to consider a preliminary concern: Could we have a moral system without our traditional God? If so, what might that system look like?

So, if God is dead, then, as Dostoyevsky queried, is everything permissible? That is, do we lose morality if there is no religion? Of course not, or so I'll argue in this chapter.[54] But religionists like William Lane Craig[55] argue that if God exists, then we have a sound foundation for objective morality and moral duties; if God does not exist, then we have no such foundation. But this assumption seems questionable and feeble from the outset.[56] First, even if God exists, how do we know, how would we know, what moral precepts he espoused for us all? Through our holy books? And what do we do when those books contradict internally, to say nothing of contradicting among one another? So even if God exists, we have no way to know with any certainty, and certainly without any objective evidence, whether God espoused any moral views for us or, if He did, what they might be. Indeed, perhaps God is a Deist who built the universe, wound it up to tick away through the slow process of evolution, and left us sentient creatures to fend for ourselves. What moral source, then, do we look to? Nature?

Second, why does God's absence indicate no sound foundation for objective morality? I'm going to argue the opposite: That the existence of God is unnecessary for a sound moral foundation. Indeed, I think that we can have or can come to or can move toward objective morality. Such a morality is not given to us by anyone; it is constructed as all valid epistemology or justified knowledge is constructed.

Thus, even if God is Goodness Itself, by His nature perfectly loving, generous, and kind, we cannot really know this in any objective way, and thus we cannot know what God expresses or commands since we do not know Him. To say we know Him is to ask how we know Him, and that knowledge is either through a personal, and perhaps direct, experience, which is subjective, or through His holy writings, which again contradict and offer us no objective evidence.

There is nothing wrong with basing one's actions and outlook on personal experience. The problem is that experience is subjective until it is discussed with others in order to establish its epistemological validity—that is, until we share with others what we have experienced to help us determine through reasons and evidence the nature of that experience. It is the basis in evidence that is missing for most religionists.

The sharing is key, for this is how we put together an objective morality. Sharing and comparing subjective experiences turns those experiences from subjective into inter-subjective experiences. When those inter-subjective experiences have sufficient overlap across time, place, reason, and evidence, then I think that we can say that those inter-subjective experiences are inter-objective.[57] Hence we are on our way to creating an objective morality, and it rests on what people experience and on how they reason together and not on the source of that experience. This is a bold claim, and it is one that I hope to substantiate moving forward in this chapter.

So what does this claim amount to? It means that we don't have to accept—indeed, we cannot accept as objective—the commandment, for example, to love thy neighbor as thyself because it represents God's view, edict, or will. This brings us back to where we began: How do we *know* that the commandment does represent God? Because it says so in the Bible, which is offered to us as the word of God. This, of course, is perfect circular reasoning. This provides very little, if any, epistemological justification, which is the sesquipedalian way of saying that we can't use this position to paint our action as good or right, because it has no foundation in reason or evidence that others who don't believe in that book can accept.

Instead, we should examine why we should love our neighbor as oneself, what that means, what is involved, what the demands and detriments to doing so are, and why such a precept might be good or result in positive outcomes.[58] Having had this discussion, then, we might well conclude that ways of life that undercut loving our neighbor can be evaluated as pernicious, even evil, if they purposefully undercut these goals and values. Likewise, ways of life and philosophies that enhance or enact this goal and its values can be shown to be beneficial, even good.

In brief, we build our objective moral values out of the many ways that humans have over time tried to institutionalize the flourishing of life, especially of human life, by weighing reasons and evidence; that is, by deliberating together. We want the lives of people to go well, and that well-being includes helping ourselves and fellow creatures meet basic needs, including food, shelter, clothing, warmth, loving relationships, self-determination, exercise of talents, and even levels and forms of transcendence and self-transcendence. To understand what those terms mean or amount to, to see how lives go well, requires that we spend time examining our own beliefs and actions in accordance with those around us. We need and deserve such conversations and deliberations, because we owe it to ourselves and to those with whom we interact, especially intimately, an honest accounting and assessment of what we believe, seek, value, fear, and don't know.

Morality and making mature moral decisions often depend upon this kind of deliberation—that is, reasoning within ourselves and with others. The best testing ground for that reasoning is to think about moral dilemmas where there is no clear answer as to the right thing to do. The word "dilemma" comes from the Greek term meaning to seize or take two positions. A dilemma is, therefore, a situation in which one must choose between two equally strong positions. The Greeks used "dilemma" when someone had to take or seize (*lembanein*) one of two (*di*) choices, neither of which was an advantage. That isn't to say that every choice was a bad one. Instead, this means, as philosopher Alasdair MacIntyre put it, choosing one option over another leaves undone what still ought to be done.

A *moral* dilemma adds the dimension of our conduct toward others. That is, a moral dilemma places us in a situation in which two (or more) values, obligations, or commitments to others conflict, and there seems no right thing to do.

A classic example of such a dilemma is the trolley problem. British philosopher Philippa Foot created this dilemma as a thought experiment: The driver of a runaway trolley, barreling down the tracks, sees five people ahead on the tracks. The driver, unable to stop the tram, can either proceed and kill all five people (who cannot get off the track), or he can steer the trolley onto a sidetrack where it will hit and kill only one person. So, should he kill one person or all five? Another philosopher, Judith Jarvis Thomson, later modified the dilemma by adding this twist: You are standing by a switch next to the tracks as the runaway trolley approaches. If you throw the switch, the tram will be diverted to a sidetrack where it will kill one person. If you do nothing, the trolley will hit and kill five people. Unlike the driver of the trolley, you as a bystander have no professional responsibility in this situation. Nevertheless, you are in a position to take action to save five lives and kill one person or, by omission, kill the five. So, should you do nothing, or should you pull the switch?

Thomson then altered the dilemma once again: You are standing on a pedestrian footbridge that crosses above the tracks. You see the runaway trolley approaching. Only a very heavy object could stop the trolley from hitting the five people on the tracks. The only object around of sufficient weight is a very fat man who is peering over the edge of the footbridge on the opposite side from you. Should you push the fat man to his death (from the fall or from the trolley) and save the five people? For those who are squeamish about physically pushing the fat man to his death, there can be yet another twist: There is a switch on the footbridge that will open a trap door through which the fat man will plunge to his death. Unlike diverting the trolley by pulling the switch, your action here will have an immediate effect on the fat man, though you will not touch him physically.

One can readily see in the trolley dilemma and its offspring that choosing any action, including inaction, leaves undone what should also be done—saving a life or lives. The factors involved need to be discussed and debated. I taught an undergraduate course on moral dilemmas over multiple semesters. I found that most of the students were willing to throw the switch to save five lives at the cost of one life, but were unwilling to push the fat man. Many but not most were willing to throw the switch to open the trapdoor, and the students who would throw that switch but not push the fat man struggled to explain the difference. My job was always to press their thinking by adding new wrinkles to the dilemmas and probing the students for arguments in defense of their positions. For example, does it make a difference—and if so, why does it make a difference—if the one person on the track is a five-year-old and the five persons are all retirees? Does it make a difference if the one person on the track is a young Einstein? A young Hitler? What if the five persons are all the world's greatest opera singers?

In the course we discussed dozens of moral dilemmas. Doing so required students to listen to the viewpoints of others, to move beyond opinions into arguments, to examine two sides (at least) of every dilemma, and to try to persuade others to take one of those sides or move away from some particular side(s). The impetus behind the course was not to try to anticipate the kinds of social, political, and personal dilemmas that the students might actually face in the future. It was to have students deliberate together about seemingly unsolvable problems.

One social fact that confronted my students as it confronts us is that we live in an environment of plural perspectives and competing conceptions of what is good. That is, we are surrounded by beliefs, values, goals, ideas, and practices that differ, if not conflict, with our own. Within this possible miasma of conflict and difference, we must make decisions and choices that may well affect our individual and collective lives. Simply living in our current cultures necessitates confronting all sorts of moral dilemmas and differences that require deliberation and critical thought. Chief among those differences and dilemmas will often be clashes of religious outlook.

Religion, of course, continues to be a significant source of morality for many people, and it often seems as if the goal of religion is to disavow, more than move through, moral dilemmas to provide followers with ready-made rules for proper behavior. Some of those directives—such as stoning adulterers and killing those who work on the Sabbath—have fallen out of favor in the West. Others, such as Islam's mandate to kill apostates, still hold influence. But if we get our moral rules from the holy texts and those anointed to teach them, then, I think, we do ourselves as self-directing humans a great disservice. We deny ourselves autonomy or self-direction by short-circuiting one of our greatest strengths: the ability to deliberate individually and with others.[59] My argument is that, that is how we really establish morality—by building it deliberatively—and we need not rely upon religion for that.

That isn't to say, however, that religion plays no part in our deliberations. Clearly religion for many often plays a significant part. But where we need to look for guidance and even inspiration is not to the texts or to their interpreters, but to the experiences of the founders of those religions and to the millions of followers who experience those religions today. Hence, mysticism, which is a form of religious experience, will play an important role in my view on morality and, later, on spirituality.

Going back at least as far as Plato, philosophers and researchers of all sorts have proposed that there are three ways of knowing—through the senses, through thought, and through the soul or spirit. These are known more colloquially as the eye of flesh, the eye of reason, and the eye of spirit or contemplation.[60]

Each of these ways of or processes for knowing is associated with its own realm of examination: The eye of flesh is associated with the material world and thus with science; the eye of mind or reason, with thought and, more broadly, with culture; and the eye of soul, spirit, or contemplation, with religion.

Of course, each of these domains—science, culture, and religion—corresponds to one aspect of our being, one aspect of our selves. Each domain is discrete, is real on its own terms, and pertains to an aspect of our human nature: body, mind, and soul or spirit. Each domain also has associated with it a particular kind of knowledge, so that we can *know* these domains to be real and know what we find in them to be real. Although the methodologies for knowing each realm are different, the process for validating this knowledge—that is, the epistemological principles or steps—are identical across the three domains. I enumerate below the elements in this process.

Bear in mind that in the realm or domain of religion we are not talking about the institutional structures or the diversity of scriptural interpretations that often constitute the religion. We are talking about that which is experimental within religion: the experiential aspect of religion called mysticism.

Because the processes for knowing are identical across the three domains, knowledge in one realm or domain is as real as knowledge in the others. Thus knowledge of mysticism or the spirit world is no less real than knowledge of the physical world. Yet each domain has its own particular way of being seen or examined. So when any pair of eyes invades the domain of another and seeks to dominate that other domain, then we have problems. For example, idealists, who only use their rationality or eyes of the mind, claim that only ideas are real; logical positivists argue that only statements grounded empirically have any meaning; and fundamentalist Christians declare that the earth is 6000 years old.

Each set of eyes has its own domain to examine, and yet

what is seen with each set is validated identically in all three domains. How is that done? It is done through following the same set of steps as described by Ken Wilber for establishing epistemological validity in all domains:

1. An instrumental or injunctive step: "a set of instructions, simple or complex, internal or external" that one must undertake to see anything in any realm. "All have the form: 'If you want to know this, do this'" (Wilber, 1983, p. 31);

2. An illuminative or apprehensive step: Having followed the injunction(s), one then looks. When one looks, one sees—or does not see—something. What, precisely, has one seen; what has one experienced? Determining that leads to

3. A communal-validation step: This is the sharing of what one has seen, of one's experience in this realm, with others who are using the same eyes. When the sharing leads to agreement as to what has been seen, then we can conclude that we have "a communal proof of true or real seeing" (Wilber, 1983, p. 32).

The epistemological situation can be complicated, as when the eyes of reason look into the domain of science and of spirit. This is, after all, how we generate hypotheses and theories (theologies) in those realms. But, as I hope to show, even in these cases true knowledge depends upon following these three steps. And while the first two steps may seem straightforward, especially for the scientific realm, the third step requires far more explanation. Conferring "communally" may result through inter-subjective communication in agreement, even in a consensus, but how can this be construed as evidence of true or real seeing? That would seem to attach validity to applause: What is true is what we agree on; our agreeing makes it true. But, in truth, the issue isn't *that* we agree; the issue is, rather, *why* we agree.

But of course there is not always agreement. When there is agreement, however, the knowledge generated, whatever the nature of that knowledge, rests on following these three enumerated steps. The Yeats scholar T.R. Henn, for example, observed when helping Cambridge University science students with their writing that "...what the biologist does is comparable to what the poet does...close looking in the lab is like close reading of a complex poem."[61]

Through an exposition of the first two of these three domains, I hope to show that establishing a moral system or moral code does not depend on our acceptance of God or of religion. Later on, in Chapter 4, I will use this exposition as well to gesture toward a different understanding of God and thus of religion. If we demonstrate the epistemological validity of higher states of consciousness in the same way that we validate scientific knowledge, then the knowledge of higher states of consciousness, seen as valid as any kind of scientific knowledge, can serve as a new foundation for our connection to the divine and to one another.

The Three Domains of Knowledge: 1 The Scientific-Empirical World

Because the epistemological principles operating in each domain are identical, knowledge of the spiritual world attained through mysticism should be no less real than knowledge of the physical world attained through science. At the same time, though the principles are identical, each domain has its own particular way of being seen or examined. To see these domains persons must use the different eyes mentioned earlier: Our physical eyes examine the material or empirical world and, with it, factual truth; our second or mental eye—eye of the mind or reason—examines rational truth; and to those sets of eyes we add what St. Augustine called the "eyes of the Heart" or contemplation to examine the world of spirit, the mystical world.

Examination in all of the domains requires following the three epistemological steps. First, you follow an experimental or test procedure: You do something. Second, you mark what you experience in or through the procedure. Finally, you report what you did and experienced. For example, if you come into the room where I am sitting and declare, "The sun is shining," and I counter you, "No, it is not," your response should be, "See for yourself." If I get up and head to the window, then I have taken the injunctive, the first, step. Looking out the window is the illuminative step: The day is sunny or not. When I return, I say, "You are right; the sun is shining." My report back to you provides us with inter-subjective validation. This epistemological process is available to anyone who wants to know whether the sun is shining.

Notice, of course, in this prosaic example, that very little is required: The instruction is simple to follow, the illumination is easily available and non-controversial, and confirmation is without problems, in large part because we bring to this "experiment" so much in common. In particular we share the same language. We do not have to quibble over what we mean by "shining"; it is part of the background that we share. So what we find already in this form of epistemological validation is a hidden assumption: We must share the same language. This is what philosopher Charles Taylor calls being members of a "language community," and it is among such members that confirmation takes place.[62]

The idea of a shared language community underscores the idea that participants in the third epistemological step, the communal-confirmation step, must speak the same language. If they do not, then they cannot participate in the confirmation (or refutation). But speaking the same language does not simply mean, say, speaking English. It means that one has been adequately trained not only to articulate what one has seen, but also to be able to see in the first place. Thus, for example, "if you want to see a cell nucleus [and comment on its condition], then learn how to take histological sections. Learn how to use a microscope, learn how to stain tissues, learn how to differentiate cell components one from the other, and then look."[63]

In other words, in whatever realm one is looking, the eyes must be trained until adequate to the illumination. Thus, communal confirmation is among those who have *adequately* completed the injunctive and illuminative steps, and that may involve training (Wilber, 1983, p. 44). But "adequately trained" can be subjective and biased, for it might mean being trained until one adopts the prejudices of the group or community providing the training. This is why science requires replication of experiments: to see whether others using controlled settings are getting the same results. Replication is the way scientists try to minimize, if not eliminate, any prejudice resulting from the presence of norms, ideals, or biases inculcated during training. This is also why there must be inter-subjective validation. You can see the importance, therefore, in having more scientists replicate, for instance, the mediumship experiments of Julie Beischel.

One who refuses to be trained has not completed the illuminative step; one who refuses to look has not completed the injunctive step. So if someone refuses to learn geometry, she cannot be allowed to judge the truth of the Pythagorean theorem; if Cardinal Bellarmine refused to look through Galileo's telescope, he was not eligible to judge the truth of Galileo's observations.[64]

In the realm of the physical world where illumination is seen through our natural eyes, there is little training involved. But science is the realm of *empirical* illumination, empirical data, and that stretches beyond our "natural eyes"—our five senses—to their extensions: telescopes, microscopes, sonar, and the like. The data we apprehend or experience with our five senses or their extensions are objects that are separate from us. Even so, to avoid particularistic biases, science demands testing and replication of findings. We have an excellent example of the importance of replication in the cases of cold fusion and bubble fusion. In 1989 two researchers at the University of Utah claimed to have generated energy through a form of fusion at room temperature, hence "cold" fusion. In 2002 Rusi Taleyarkhan claimed that he had created a small-scale kind of fusion by collapsing bubbles of acetone, hence "bubble" fusion. Unfortunately, no other scientists around the world have been able to replicate the fusion successes originally claimed.

The data that scientists gather—the facts, observations, and experiments central to science—are not like rocks that scientists just happen to stumble over. They are selected according to a theory or hypothesis that motivates the scientist and that is itself not sensory data. So while truths about the physical world rest on sensory data, there can certainly be disagreements about and controversies over the nature of the data or what they "mean." Meanings are not given by nature; they are the product of interpretation. That is part of communal confirmation, but the realm that generates interpretations, meanings, and theories is not the sensory world, the world of empiricism, but the world of the mind. In that realm the appropriate eyes are not the eyes of the body but the eyes of reason, of the mind.

The mind's eye can, and must, look into all three domains. Scientists, like philosophers and mystics, need to explain what they have seen. They need to fit their seeing and their explanations into a context of what has come before them, of how what they have experienced is different from or similar to what others have seen. All of that requires interpretation. In all three realms someone can rightly ask, "What is the meaning of this?" Meaning, or interpretation, depends on the mind's eye.

Remember, the domains and the eyes appropriate to each are interrelated, even integrated. So we want science to investigate mystical phenomena and parapsychological phenomena, where that investigation is appropriate. Indeed, all confirmation—the third epistemological step—in whatever realm, proceeds through deliberation, inter-subjective communication, which requires the "mind's eye." The use of language central to mental work "enables us to put things in public space," as Charles Taylor phrases it. "Public space" means "that it [whatever is put there] no longer is just a matter for me, or for you, or for both of us severally, but is now something for us, that is, for us together" (1985, p. 259). The speech of deliberation is not a series of monologues, but a series of responses to what the speakers say. Thus, public space is created in any deliberation, because to deliberate speakers must join their perspectives. In this way every deliberation creates a "space" that is neither yours nor mine but ours, and we see our views as one perspective among others. This is a public realm of inter-subjectivity.

Language enables us to create a public space or a common vantage point from which we determine jointly and inter-subjectively the truths in the world, whatever world, or domain, we are surveying. This includes science. Anyone adequately trained, who follows the epistemological steps—which must involve inter-subjective communication to confirm or refute the illumination—is privy to that public space. The community is not public in that *anyone* is eligible, but it is public in that *anyone following the epistemological steps* is eligible. No one can be excluded, for example, simply because of political ideology, because, as the Nazis did, he or she is Jewish. That is a position whose basis would be refuted either in the sensory realm or in the mental realm. What both realms, what all realms, provide is public knowledge—evidence that must be available to anyone capable of looking properly.

As I said, in the scientific realm data do not interpret themselves. The mind's eye must be used in that realm as part of inter-subjective validation. Thus we have in the academic world the emphasis on peer reviews for communal validation of one's work. Peers are scholars whose eyes are trained adequately to confirm or refute what another scholar has written.

The Three Domains of Knowledge: 2 The Mental-Moral World

Sometimes the evidence about which we confer and which we discuss is "inconclusive." Thomas Kuhn points out that for those set in a particular paradigm—that is, those immersed in "the entire constellation of beliefs, values, techniques, and so on shared by the members of a given community" (1962, p. 175)— evidence that undercuts or contradicts that paradigm is almost always thought to be inconclusive. As we saw in Chapter 1, such a conclusion rests on the assumption that those in the scientific or materialist paradigm will consider any contradictory phenomena. So, the question to ask, then, is this: To just what are scientists committed? Are they committed to the scientific method—the three epistemological steps where the evidence, the "experience," is empirical? Or are they committed to certain central beliefs or values—perhaps security or prestige— that come from another realm? These beliefs and values are themselves "testable"; they are themselves evidence, but not of the empirical kind. They are data for the mind's eye, for testing in the mental-moral world.

Validation of moral claims differs from validation of scientific claims in that confirmation of "moral data" calls into question the very nature of what is seen. In the moral realm the question is not so much "Is it there, or isn't it?" or "Did this work, or didn't it?" The questions are, rather, evaluative and interpretive: "Is this practice right and good? What does it mean?"

Communal confirmation in the mental-moral world involves validating the *meaning* of what is seen. It is not enough simply to see that a certain culture has an incest taboo and adheres to it. Required in knowing a moral practice is also understanding its meaning—why, when, and how it is held and followed.

Furthermore, to know the moral practice requires confirming whether it is true; in the moral world that means not only whether it is supported by the reasons offered for it, but also whether it is right and good, whether it should be held and practiced.

The criteria that we use to judge morality are not so readily agreed upon as they are in the empirical world. In the sensory world we confirm theories and hypotheses—the mind's eye looking at the physical world—in terms of empirical data. In other words, a proposition about the physical world is true if it matches or conforms to empirical data, gathered many times through replication of observations (experiments). In the mental-moral world both the propositions made and the data on which they rest are symbolic. Both involve meaning. A scientific theory, to be true and scientific, must rest on or refer to sense data—something we can "check and see." A philosophical moral theory, to be true, must rest on or refer to arguments or reasons— also things we can look at, that we can "check and see."

But reasons are not things "out there"; they are themselves symbolic or mental constructs. So how do we validate them? And who is in *this* "community of inquirers"? In brief, we validate them by seeing whether the reasons offered are *good* reasons according to some inter-subjective structure of meaning. Those properly trained to look at and to see those reasons and who "speak the same language"—those, for instance, at a minimum, who can give reasons and follow reasoning—can be in that community. They may not accept the reasons, but they must understand them.

Seeing in this realm doesn't necessarily require any special training. There is only the ability to reflect, to use and identify reasons. But isn't smuggling in the idea of needing "good" reasons a way to influence the community of inquirers to accept a certain preconceived idea of what "good" means? How does someone know what is a good reason? Likewise, how does someone know that she has the "right" values?

How does anyone know what is right and good? She is convinced by it. Reasons and values must be articulated, interrogated, and defended, and one must do so publicly, in the public space, before a community of inquirers. In other words, we know that reasons are good and that moral values are right because we have deliberated about and validated them inter-subjectively. We have introduced and examined all available evidence, and we have listened to, criticized, and rejected or accepted the reasons offered.

When those within a given community have differing views among themselves on what counts as a reason, let alone a good reason, or when in one culture what counts as a reason differs radically from what another culture accepts, then in both instances we want to know what counts as *their* reasons. Reasons themselves will be subject to scrutiny and deliberation. We want, and need, to understand how those in the culture or community view the world, how they construct their worldview. To do so we need to step inside, we need to see inside, their world. Then we need to join the community of inquirers to deliberate about their worldview, including what counts for them as reasons. When we talk about the moral goods of a person or a culture, to see those goods, we must "see" what it is that he sees or they see and how this moves him or them. Those not in the culture may not see the goods in the same light, but they must see them in the same way. That is, they must publicly articulate what they see. Those unwilling to publicly articulate their reasons and positions cannot expect to gain understanding, sympathy, or converts among those outside their worldview.

To articulate the goods of a society, and the rules and roles that govern those goods, requires an understanding of them sufficient to express the goods accurately. So one must be able to express the ideas, ideals, purposes, norms, and customs important to that society and that serve as a background for the society's way of life. This expression or articulation also presupposes some level of "experiential meaning." That is, inquirers into a society's worldview or goods need to have sufficient life experience—they have lived long enough or interacted enough with the society or community—to understand the purposes of and feelings associated with those societal or communal practices, behaviors, and outlooks. In short, members of the linguistic community understand in general the motivations of others and the meanings of circumstances for those living in the community that they are exploring. Members of the linguistic community, therefore, can put themselves in the place of the others. To understand those experiential meanings, to know how to respond appropriately— whether to laugh or to listen seriously—is already a sign of being within the linguistic community. Putting oneself in the position, or shoes, of another does not mean interpreting the world of that other in one's own terms. Instead, the interpretation must restate to the satisfaction of the other the nature of the other's practice. This is to understand that practice as if from the inside.

Bear in mind that the requirement presented here for communally confirming the meaning and truth or goodness of a moral practice is to understand the nature of, reasons for, and importance of that practice. It is not necessarily to *accept* that practice or to accept the reasons for it. One must be able to share the common public language, to use it properly, and that includes understanding what Wittgenstein called the "inherited tradition" necessary to make sense of talk of truth or falsity. Part of arriving inter-subjectively at the truth may well include scrutinizing that inherited tradition. As a result, communal validation cannot simply be an adoption of or conformity to traditional rules or practices.

So people in a culture, from this perspective, continue to define themselves and their moral goods in conversations with others, presumably inside and outside that culture, but the community by which and through which they define themselves is not necessarily the given historical community. They define themselves by the linguistic community. As I have been describing it here, the linguistic community is open to all who can and will share the public language. This community is therefore more inclusive than what might be described as an "identificatory community"—a community in which the inherited tradition in part defines who one is. In that kind of community identity is secured by social solidarity and conformity to social norms (as I shall show in more detail in Chapter 5). Because dissension can lead to doubt and thus to insecurity and instability in such communities, members might have to be brought into line with what the society or group expects one to believe.[65]

But communal validation cannot simply be an adoption of or conformity to traditional rules or practices. The deliberation that serves as the setting for that validation consists of many voices, as many voices as there are available in the linguistic community. Again, the linguistic community is an inclusive community open to all who can share the public language. That community wishes to adjust to or adopt only those norms and standards, values, and outlooks confirmed in inter-subjective communication—that is, confirmed in deliberation among persons.

This line of argument underscores that knowledge is not so much discovered as constructed in dialogue by the linguistic community. Knowledge, then, is not lying "out there" waiting to be found.

Because the linguistic community includes all those who "see" these concepts, patterns, and linguistic constructs, and yet is not limited to those who accept these as good and true, it would seem that a clash is inevitable between those who speak the same language but are from different communities, whose knowledge constructions are different. Indeed, those from another community may well attack my standards *because* they are from a different community. When two different cultures have two different ways of describing and understanding the same phenomenon, then what we see is not simply a difference of vocabulary, but a difference of social reality. Sunni and Shia Muslims, for example, are surely divided on who should be or should have been the caliph to succeed Muhammad. This division, centuries old, paints a different reality for these conflicting sects and keeps many Sunnis and Shias from using their linguistic community for dialogue on multiple issues.

Of course, both Muslim groups connect in how reality is negotiated. Social reality consists not simply of *what* is constituted but also of *how* it is constituted. Thus, social realities are "practices" and not independent of the vocabularies that describe them. Language is constitutive of the reality. So, when important issues are at stake for communities, when their social worlds collide, then we examine together the part or parts of those social worlds that reflect disagreement. We do that by taking up and facing the particular positions or critiques involved in the disagreement. We can do so because we are part of the same linguistic community. In deliberation we express thoughts and reasons to others and gauge their reactions to what we have said. In the same way, we also listen and react to their thoughts and reasons. This is an inter-subjective exchange. Different persons or groups, our Sunnis and Shias, share language and meaning and make their reasons and interpretations "public" between them so that each group or person can see and understand the moral constructs of the others.

Yet, if morality is tied to language, and if language rests on and expresses an "inherited tradition," then how can there be anything but a relative reply: What works for us is good for us; what works for you is good for you?

If the purpose is to overcome or reconcile disagreement, then we assume that both groups are open to deliberation and thus open to an avenue for figuring out together how they differ. Step one is to demonstrate to the other that each group has "seen"; that is, understood the meaning and importance of the other's practices or positions.[66]

Step two: our clashing groups or cultures are looking for the same thing: evidence that supports the theory or the practice. The evidence for scientists is empirical facts and whether one of the theories better fits those facts. For cultures the evidence is arguments or reasons for believing in and following the practice.[67] This brings us to step three: Once we have the evidence, we then need to weigh or evaluate it. We need, in short, the third step in our epistemological sequence, the communal validation step.

As a test case of this process, let's consider the moral practice of witchcraft of the Azande of Central Africa, made famous by anthropologist E.E. Evans-Pritchard. Are their beliefs in and practices of witchcraft irrational? Are they therefore "bad" practices, practices to be condemned?

To know that, we must get inside the Azande's system of beliefs. We must see the practice as they see it. In other words, we must fulfill the first two epistemological steps and follow the third: enter the community of inquirers. Once inside we can apply rules of reasoning to see whether the Azande made any mistakes in logical consistency and logical reasoning. But we also need to get inside their system of rationality.

There are two implications here. The first is that the Azande do reason about witchcraft; that they think about why they do it, what it is, how to do it, when it is proper to do it, or when it has been improperly done. This they must do to give any kind of account of their lives in which witchcraft plays an important part. To know that it is a moral good requires articulating the good and thereby subjecting it to public—communal—scrutiny. The second implication is that the Azande reason as we modern Westerners reason. While what counts as a reason is relative, *that* they reason and *how* they reason are not. Logic is about the propriety of relational statements in moving from premises to conclusions. Rationality requires at least self-consistency: that propositions are consistent with related ideas simultaneously held. For an act to be considered rational it must at a minimum conform to the norms of the community and fit in without contradicting those norms.[68]

So if we examine the reasoning of the Azande and find no logical mistakes, then we can conclude that their beliefs are rational on that account. We may also find, however, that their premises are false and that we can argue epistemologically by offering counter-evidence, or even facts. Are these reasons that the Azande would accept? Perhaps not, for they might well reject *our* premises. Perhaps they practice witchcraft because they believe it makes their crops grow and heals the sick by appeasing the spirits. This we reject, but they reject the basis of our scientific evidence. Perhaps they practice witchcraft because it is symbolic, a series of social ceremonies and beliefs essential to community cohesion. This we could accept, because we can see the consequences in this situation of their practice. Depending on the reasons that both sides offered, and depending on other or further consequences of their beliefs and practices, then we might not come close to any reconciliation; we might not change any minds. But if we are going to do either, this is how we must proceed.

Are both accounts, both the practices of witchcraft and our arguments against it, therefore true? Where witchcraft relies on empirical statements or facts, then we conclude that it is not true.[69] But where it may be a practice for social cohesion, one that works, we would have to conclude that it is true and for that purpose is perhaps even good.

Looking at the Azande in this way helps us determine the nature, the moral nature, of their practice of witchcraft. But what if we have already made up our minds, through the epistemological steps, that a practice is immoral? Different cultures have different moral traditions, practices, ideals, and beliefs. But that diversity in no way excuses us from criticizing those that undercut or prevent the well-being of persons. Someone might argue that we need to respect different cultures and their different choices, even moral choices. But if those cultures choose practices that jeopardize the well-being of others—say, throwing battery acid into the faces of girls who want an education, thereby both scarring them physically and hampering their development— then how can we argue to protect that practice? Isn't showing respect for that culture to argue with that culture, to point out as forcefully as we can through reasons and evidence why the practice is deleterious to the health and well-being of the people involved? Their response might well be that failing to throw the acid undercuts the well-being of others in the society. The girls must be considered within the context of the entire social and religious structure. We want to know how and why. In this way the inter-subjective exchange unfolds.

If we have concluded through our three epistemological steps that a practice is immoral or bad, then it is bad for all those who practice it. If somehow there are mitigating circumstances that single out a need for this practice or its variations, then those circumstances must be adduced and put through the process of epistemological validation. Sam Harris introduces this example of the Islamic practice of forced veiling of women. After running through a series of reasons, Harris concludes: "Given the challenges that face society, this is a bad practice in almost every case" (2010, p. 223, n. 17). Notice that he says, "in *almost every* case," and that phrase is the key. We can imagine a situation in which it might be preferable to dress your daughter in a burka, if she happens to be traveling in rural Afghanistan and wants to avoid the attention of "thuggish men."

As I have been saying, determining whether one value or set of values is better than another requires dialogue and deliberation (the weighing of evidence, whether empirical, rational, or, as we'll see, mystical). The point of this dialogue is a "public" presentation to show that one's claims are grounded in reasons and evidence that others can accept as reasons and evidence even when they disagree with them. Some of these reasons might be "bad" reasons, ones that can be shown logically or through evidence to be wrong. For example, it cannot be demonstrated scientifically that human intelligence can be measured by head size. So, any argument for justifying academic tracking on the basis of such measurements can be proved to be without evidence and unreasonable. There are "good" reasons, therefore, for rejecting such claims.

Reasons and evidence are good relatively; that is, they are relative to the context that itself can change. New reasons and new evidence can be introduced that alter the initial reasons and evidence. But the fact that in science, morality, and mysticism we hold open the possibility that new reasons and evidence can alter our view is no reason to refrain from holding to the conclusions that come from the three epistemological steps. Open-mindedness does not mean empty-headedness. Is it possible that there could be unknown reasons and evidence that show us that cannibalism is a life-enhancing practice? It's possible, but highly unlikely, and the existence of that possibility is no good reason for abandoning a strong condemnation of cannibalism, given our current evidence and reasons. Our conclusions on the matter are firm but always open to alteration. Thus, as I said at the outset, our morality and moral codes are relative, but they are relative to reasons and evidence, not to cultures or levels of applause, even if unanimous.

How could we prove to a culture that its annual sacrifice of humans does not protect their crops? We can't introduce Western empirical evidence, because in the context of this particular culture such evidence is irrelevant. We might present our reasons and evidence, but these are reasons and evidence as we and our culture see them. What we can do is engage in dialogue with this culture. We try to establish a commonality of language and concepts, the most important of which is what the culture counts as a good reason and what counts as evidence. If there is no agreement on that, then further discussion is pointless. At that point, we can only conclude that there are two incommensurable systems. Yet we don't also conclude that this culture's practice of human sacrifice is good and true for them. We have concluded on the basis of reason and evidence that it is wrong and immoral for any culture to practice it. The culture in question rests its reason for human sacrifice on the empirical claim that the sacrifice protects their crops, but they do not perform any experiments to test whether the claim is true.

Moral goods only exist for us through some articulation; they take place in the "space," the public space, between us. What is made manifest in that public space is a world not only seen by but also constituted through language. Morality in the narrow sense of the term—how humans find or determine what conduct among themselves is good or bad, right or wrong—is the product of language of meaning and interpretation. Actions take on moral attributes depending on what we take in our language to be suitable or unsuitable behavior: good or bad for what? In regard to what? Our cultural conversation provides such questions, and our actions and these questions are "directly available for all to see"—that is, are made public—through our language.

It may seem as if I am insinuating that participants in the epistemological inquiry must reason according to formal logic, that any moral conclusion can only follow from a major premise about values and a minor premise about facts. But what we are after in our third step of communicative or inter-subjective exchange is the meaning of propositions more than the relationships among them. So while there must be reasoning within the deliberation, much of the dialogue is not just reason-giving. Participants are not trying to speak from an impartial perspective. They are not just searching for reasons that all participants will find compelling. They are also sharing their perspectives and experiences.[70] Bear in mind that sharing perspectives and experiences is not just about giving reasons.

It is also about telling stories. People provide testimony as to why they see the issue in a certain way and how it affects them. Someone might say, "Here is what I have seen in our neighborhood. Here is how your proposal hurts my family and my neighbors."

"Experiments" in the mental-moral domain are designed to reveal reasons. Stories can provide reasons, even if in a form that requires us to do some additional examination and probing. But this kind of deliberation and inquiry does not demand practices in formal logic. Rather, the deliberation requires what Aristotle called *sumbouleuesthai* or "reasoning through consultation with others" or talking things through with others. It is sharing, comparing, and contrasting reasons with others where ethical or moral choices have to be made.

Ideas such as courage or dignity or honor might become through history and ongoing practices real parts of our cultural world. But are those ideas true, right, and good? Determining that is not a factual matter relating to the physical world; we cannot cut open a soldier and see his courage. It is a hermeneutical matter: Is what you mean by courage truly courage? If so, is it a virtue we ought to encourage?

Moral truth is not mere opinion, for then it would depend on who agreed or how many agreed. Those who agreed might decide by caprice that tomorrow they believed something else, making *that* true. If truth rests on agreement alone, then no challenges, whatever the basis, which undercut the agreement could themselves be true. Truth rests not on agreement, but on reasons and evidence, not on *that* we agree but on *why* we agree. We examine the reasons and evidence with the mind's eye; those reasons and that evidence are what we seek communally to confirm or refute.

All moral truths must be affirmed through communal validation. That is how we establish their truth. But such truths must also be open to new deliberations, to renegotiation. They

105

are not fixed, but rest on reasons and evidence in a context in which new reasons and evidence can come to light. In that sense moral truths are open to ongoing discussion and evidence, just as science is. Likewise, what counts as truth, reality, and knowledge in the spiritual domain depends no less upon the three steps of experiment, evidence, and communal validation than do science and culture. I shall discuss this idea in the next chapter.

Yet all knowledge begins with some sort of faith or metaphysical assumptions. We cannot prove the assumptions, premises, or assertions with which we begin, but we must begin somewhere. Perhaps Karl Popper said it best:

> Science does not rest upon solid bedrock. The bold structure of its theories rises, as it were, above a swamp. It is like a building erected on piles. The piles are driven down from above into the swamp, but not down to any natural or "given" base; and if we stop driving the piles deeper, it is not because we have reached firm ground. We simply stop when we are satisfied that the piles are firm enough to carry the structure, at least for the time being.[71]

In short, the basis of empirical science is not itself absolute, which I take to be a good thing. If there were an absolute to it, then its enterprise might at some point end. But its dedication to understanding, inquiry, and skepticism (in the positive or open-minded sense) permits and requires an ongoing process. Its basis is reason and evidence, which is the same for finding knowledge in all three domains, and that basis itself must be open to continuous questioning. Whatever our bases and our claims, they should be tested. Nowhere is this testing more significant than in the face of evidence that contradicts or points out exceptions to the rules—our white crows. Such evidence is, of course, veridical evidence that materialists need to confront and examine. Such evidence is also empirical evidence that undercuts religionists' historical claims that they wish to treat as facts.

The focus of this chapter has been to remove the idea that we must have religion or some belief in God in order to have morality or moral systems. Moralities are mental constructions created together through language, deliberation, and lived experience within groups and communities. That is, moralities are made through thought and feeling and then confirmed, rejected, modified, or reinforced in our cultural conversation. They do not rest or depend on belief but on knowing.

In examining the nature and basis of morality, we've moved into a second idea: That it is time to move our view of spirituality from belief and faith into experience and evidence. In other words, it is time, as the mystic Meister Eckhart observed, for us "to leave God for GOD," to return to that which we truly are. We'll begin that conversation in the next chapter by examining the scientific evidence for spirituality and by delving into the third eye of knowing: the contemplative or spiritual eye.

Chapter 4

Divine Knowing: Experience-Based Spirituality

Religion exists to protect us from a direct experience of God.
Karl Jung

For this I taught you, not to believe merely because you have heard, but when you believed of your own consciousness, then to act accordingly and abundantly.
Buddha (the *Dhammapada*)

Why should our views of spirituality rest on certain holy texts? Why do those texts—the Koran and the Bible in particular— serve as the basis for our religious views and beliefs? Why the New Testament and not *A Course in Miracles*, a text also said to be the word of God (Jesus)? Why do we reject J.K. Rowling's stories about Harry Potter but accept the fantasies of the Old Testament?

There is enough metaphysical, even mystical, evidence in the paranormal phenomena of mediumship, near-death experiences, and reincarnation—to say nothing of such other phenomena as materialization and electronic-voice activation—to occupy the most ardent transcendentalist, in the generic sense, in the pursuit of the numinous and ethereal. I have argued that science can help us establish and evaluate evidence of the paranormal. If you are moved to accept my arguments about the need for veridical evidence to support the claim that consciousness is independent of the brain, then the call should be to see more, and even better, evidence and more science. That consciousness is independent of the brain would not free us from the need for evidence, but instead would reinforce that need.

On the other hand, one does not need scientific evidence of consciousness's independence of the brain or of death to free an adherent from the absurdities found in most religions. Did Adam really live to be 930 years old, and was Noah 500 when he fathered Ham, Shem, and Japheth? Was Jesus really born of a virgin? Did Mohammad fly from Mecca to Jerusalem, to heaven, and back to Mecca on the winged steed Buraq? If any such claims, and myriad others in these texts, could be substantiated, then we would confront a murder of white crows.

But, alas, there is, of course, no evidence for any of these, and the claims violate everything we know about science and that we see in our own world (now and in the past). Yet each of the three Abrahamic religions relies on such absurdities to advance significant beliefs within and practices of the faith. But why are such beliefs and practices necessary? Why must anyone believe any of this? There is, as I said and hoped to have presented, sufficient miraculous phenomena in the paranormal to satisfy the seeker, and that phenomena can be documented through veridical evidence.

The absurd tales of Judaism, Christianity, and Islam detract from what these faiths might otherwise offer. All three religions claim historicity for their sacred scriptures, thus advancing the position that the absurdities are historically accurate and real. This makes the absurdities not just unnecessary distractions; it makes them dangerous. When people believe that the absurdities actually happened, then those who deny them—those who demand evidence that they did or could happen—threaten the beliefs of adherents. Those "deniers" must be punished into silence. Thus, as Voltaire said, believing in absurdities can lead people to commit atrocities.[72]

Stripping the texts of the literal readings, stripping away entirely the literalness of the tales, enables the adherent to see the power of the psychology underlying the stories. In short, there are better ways to read the texts than to accept as real even an inkling of the absurdities. The books of the Bible, for example, reveal to us, or can, the psychological states of those living millennia in the past, as I'll discuss in the next chapter.

From such a perspective on psychology, we do not have to wonder how a perfect divinity could be the author of works fraught with contradictions, to say nothing of absurdities. By adopting a psychological perspective, to rework Voltaire's apothegm, we do not then have to worry that those who can be led to believe in absurdities can further be led to commit atrocities in the name of those absurdities, as the faithful, believing in literalness, have shown us over the centuries a willingness and even an eagerness to commit.[73]

We don't have to believe in these absurdities. The fundamentalist, literal reading of the Bible is the least significant and least satisfying approach to understanding that text. Let's explore that idea: Given the number of internal contradictions and inconsistencies in the Bible, the notion that an infallible God and not men wrote the text is absurd. Better because less absurd is the idea that men experiencing altered or higher states of consciousness—that is, direct experiences of the divine— wrote the Old and the New Testaments, but in the years that separated those two texts men had learned a great deal about human nature and human behavior and had learned how better to integrate divine insights into daily life.

So the New Testament describes human experiences and psychology from a level of consciousness different from because higher than the level of consciousness underlying the Old Testament.[74] The New Testament writers were, say, far more experienced contemplatives than the Old Testament writers. One time-tested method for educing such altered or higher states of consciousness is meditation and/or contemplation, which our ancestors clearly practiced. "Time-tested" in what ways? First, there is the historical record, found in multiple texts,[75] of thousands of years of meditative experiences of both

Eastern and Western mystics. Second, the West over the past several decades has focused laboratory experiments on studying the physiological changes of meditators and contemplatives.

Every religious tradition is based on somebody's spiritual or mystical experience, and that somebody is most often the religion's founder. Although the founder's own experience—as, for example, in the case of Christ or Muhammad—is often taken as unique and therefore worth forming a following around, every religion also has some tradition of mysticism within it. This includes the Kabbalah of Judaism, Sufism in Islam, and the Prayer of the Heart in the Eastern Orthodox Christian Church.

In the East, however, mystical or meditative practices—practices that induce spiritual or mystical experiences—are often the principal focus of the religions. This is so much the case that we might describe Eastern religions as developmental psychologies, since they examine systematically the realms of being and becoming that all humans are capable of experiencing—that is, experiences that all humans can have and grow into. These spiritual psychologies offer meditative techniques or practices to induce and stabilize those experiences. They can be stabilized to such an extent that two psychologists, Dan Goleman and Richie Davidson, argue that the experiences through extensive meditation can become "lasting traits" that affect how we behave, think, and navigate in the world (Goleman and Davidson, 2017, p. 6.).

Additionally, we know from over 40 years of Western scientific investigation that meditation offers psychological and physiological benefits.[76] Over the past few years, as scientists have begun investigating changes through meditation of brain structure and function, a new kind of science has emerged, which some are calling "the cognitive neuroscience of religion."[77] For example, Andrew Newberg at the University of Pennsylvania—the head of Penn's Center for Spirituality and the Mind—has been using a brain-scanning machine on meditators to measure what happens in the brain during spiritual experiences and meditative practices. Using single-photon-emission computed tomography or HMPAO-SPECT imaging, Newberg injects a radioactive tracer into the meditators as they are meditating. The active parts of the brain absorb the tracer. At that point the meditators enter the scanner, which can show where in the brain the tracer has settled. Through this technique, Newberg found that the meditators' brains showed heightened activity in their frontal lobes, which relates to focused attention or increased concentration, and decreased activity toward the back of the brain, the area of space and time orientation. Thus there seems to be a biological correlate, as Newberg phrases it, to spiritual experiences.[78] Perhaps not surprisingly, the meditators said that during their meditations they experience unity with everything and everyone.[79]

Nor are biological or brain correlations surprising. As I noted at the end of Chapter 1, the brain is clearly necessary for reflecting or projecting consciousness. Changes in brain physiology will affect that reflection or projection, just as changes of consciousness will alter brain physiology. There is an interactive effect that occurs. Yet such interactions do not imply that consciousness is produced by the brain.

In another study Mario Beauregard and Vincent Paquette used functional magnetic resonance imaging (fMRI) and quantitative electroencephalography (QEEG) to record the brain states of 15 Carmelite nuns during their prayers.[80] Collectively, Beauregard writes, the 15 nuns had spent about 210,000 hours in prayer (2006, p. 187). Beauregard and Paquette found that mystical experience is not located solely in the temporal lobes, but involves many brain areas, including the inferior parietal lobule, the visual cortex, the caudate nucleus, and the left brain stem. Such regions of the brain are associated with perception, cognition, emotion, body representation, and self-consciousness. Finally, they found an "abundance of theta activity during the mystical condition"

(2006, p. 189), the same kind of activity found in Zen Buddhist meditators and practitioners of Sahaja Yoga. This theta brain-wave activity demonstrates a marked shift in consciousness.

Further, at Wisconsin, Richie Davidson and his colleagues used both EEG and MRI scans to examine the brain functions of highly-trained Tibetan Buddhist meditators. In a paper in 2004 they concluded that long-term meditation can lead to measurable improvement in attention. Their meditating subjects showed the highest level of synchronization among neurons ever reported for healthy humans: "the highest reported in the literature in a non-pathological context."[81] They also found high activity in the prefrontal cortex, which equates with feelings of happiness, compassion, and joy.

Although Davidson et al. studied highly-trained Tibetan Buddhist meditators—those with tens of thousands of hours of meditation practice—other research, such as the extensive research done on Transcendental Meditation practitioners who meditate twice each day for 15 to 20 minutes each session, shows benefits for more "casual" meditators. Sara Lazar and her coauthors looked at subjects who meditated six hours per week. They found that even among these "casual meditators" there are some important findings. One is that these meditators, in comparison with a control group, had thicker brain regions associated with attention and sensory processing. This cortical thickness was most pronounced in the older meditators, which suggests that the cortical thinning associated with aging may be reduced through meditation. Cortical thinning is implicated in the slowing of emotional and cognitive processes.[82]

Of course, people in religious traditions don't usually undertake prayer or meditation techniques simply to relax, feel better, or improve their health. They are after, and claim to find, higher states of consciousness, connection to God, or a sense of oneness with the universe and all in it.[83] Those experiences cannot be empirically verified. A neuroscientist can correlate a meditator's claim of experiencing the oneness with all of life with the meditator's brain changes or neural activities, but she cannot corroborate what the meditator is experiencing. That same neuroscientist sees the cortical activity but not the content experienced during that activity. She knows that something is going on, even something unusual, but not what is going on. To know that, then, the neuroscientist would have to ask the meditator.

That "asking" brings us to how we can validate the content of the meditator's experience and how that validation connects with establishing scientific knowledge and with building a moral system or moral view, as discussed in the previous chapter.

In the West the mystical or contemplative side of religion is often underplayed. Instead, religion in the West *is* largely its history. Judaism, Christianity, and Islam are religions established on the historical existence of sacred persons and/ or covenants with God. The center of these theistic systems is the clergy, sacred texts, and sacred practices sanctified by, if not derived from, the historicity of the founding and of the teaching. The history justifies or legitimizes some ecclesiastical hierarchy while condemning other such hierarchies. These ecclesiastical hierarchies are then used to instill and reinforce the faith and are bent on saving souls through the one true way. The basis of the faith is theological, and that theology, using categories from the previous chapter, is epistemologically mental-moral, and only epistemologically mental-moral, because the theology presents for interpretation theories and histories of the acts and the nature of God and His kingdom. Where theologies remain mental only, mystical and contemplative experiences might well offer valid spiritual epistemology that clergies will often combat, condemn, or ignore.

To be epistemologically sound, we want to see evidence, demonstrable and replicable evidence, which is most often scientific evidence. Yet, as I have argued here, scientists can verify the neurological or physiological correlates of meditative states, but cannot verify the content of what is experienced in those states. Still, what scientists seek to do is what mystics have been doing for millennia: Creating experiments that can be replicated and validated. Whereas scientists measure their results empirically, yogis and mystics and monks measure theirs inter-subjectively. As you may recall, that inter-subjective measurement is also central to the work of scientists. This brings us to the third eye of knowing: the eye of the soul or the eye of contemplation.

The Three Domains of Knowledge: 3 The Spiritual World

When people report that in a rapturous state they were spoken to by angels or felt one with the universe, how do we know whether these experiences reveal something of an expansive or higher consciousness or whether these experiences are simply indicative of a commonplace subjective phenomenon—a delusion, an emotional effusion, or the product of one's creative imagination?

Those on the esoteric or mystical side of the world's sacred traditions argue that there is a way to know. That knowledge, they claim, is as real and true as any scientific discovery or philosophical syllogism and follows the three epistemological steps that I discussed in Chapter 3. Yet what makes such claims difficult to fathom is that what we experience spiritually, what we apprehend directly, is beyond logic, beyond reason, beyond the empirical world. And the method we use for seeing in this realm is contemplation.

Contemplation, the eye of the heart or soul, cannot be reduced to or derived from reason or the five senses. This is why, in part, contemplation is dismissed. Philosopher A.J. Ayer concluded, "the fact that [the contemplative] cannot reveal what he 'knows' or even himself devise an empirical test to validate his 'knowledge,' shows that his state of mystical intuition is not a genuinely cognitive state" (1952, p. 118). Yet mystics and contemplatives do not claim that their intuition—their insight—is empirical. They claim that their insights are "trans-empirical" and "trans-logical."

They do claim, however, that their insights are public; they are available to anyone who undertakes the proper training, follows the proper instructions, and discusses what he or she sees with the community of inquirers.[84] In short, knowledge of the spiritual domain follows from exactly the same broad epistemological principles as knowledge of the physical or mental realms. Philosopher W.T. Stace argued this point in *Mysticism and Philosophy*:

> We should believe in the existence of a newly discovered mountain in the Antarctic even though only one competent [trained] and reliable explorer had seen it. This is because we think there is good reason to believe that all normal men could observe it if they took the proper steps. Not all men perceive the mountains at the South Pole...but all men could perceive them if they would carry out certain instructions which might in most cases and for most of us be so unenduringly rigorous and time-consuming as to be practically impossible. In like manner it may be held that any normal man could verify the experience of the mystic if he would...subject himself to a long and rigorous course of physical and mental discipline... And this means that mystical experience is just as "public" as sense experience, since to say that an experience is public only means that a large number of private experiences are similar, or would be similar if appropriate steps were taken (1960, p. 139).

An example of how esoteric or mystical knowledge is determined might help solidify the point. Zen Buddhist meditation takes the form of an injunction (our first step): "If you wish to know whether there is Buddha nature, you must sit." "Sitting," or *zazen*, is the term for Zen meditation, and it often requires years of practice and discipline to see or experience the transcendental sphere. That sight—"looking" and "seeing for oneself" is our second step—can result in a form of "intuitive apprehension" known in Zen as *kensho* or *satori*, both meaning a "direct seeing into the spiritual world." This looking, Ken Wilber observes, is "as perfectly direct as looking into a microscope." But, he adds, "only a trained eye need look" (1983, p. 60).

This perception is called intuition to differentiate it from sensory experience and from thought. It is beyond both. But how does a Zen practitioner know that what she has experienced, what she has seen, is "a direct apprehension of spirit, by spirit, as spirit"? That must be confirmed by both a Zen master and the community of inquirers—fellow meditators. This is our third epistemological step, and it is a

> vigorous test…Both in private, intense interaction with the Zen Master (*dokusan*) and in exacting public participation in tests of authenticity (*shosan*), *all* apprehensions are struck against the community of those whose cognitive eyes are adequate to the transcendent, and such apprehensions are soundly non-verified if they do not match the facts of transcendence as disclosed by the community… (Wilber, 1983, p. 61).

In these contemplative or mystical paths no one is asked to accept any belief or anything on faith. Pascal Kaplan studied as a representative sample of esotericism six spiritual teachers from different traditions, all offering contemplative injunctions to contemporary Westerners.[85] He concluded that all of these spiritual teachers separated esotericism from any belief or belief system. Inayat Khan, for example, representing the Sufi tradition of Islam, declares that the true Sufi teacher "never asks his disciples to accept any doctrine on mere faith. 'My work is only to tell you in what way the faculty of revelation can be awakened. Do this practice, and this faculty will be awakened; you will then see for yourself.'"[86]

There does still seem to be an element of faith involved in what Inayat Khan asks of us. He is after a "faculty of revelation," which seems attached to a practice of faith. Those who come to the practice of Sufism might well be looking for something like this faculty. However, the only "preaching" involved here is to "do this practice" and "see for yourself." Yet the idea of faith is found in all three domains. It seems unavoidable that there must be some acceptance "on faith" of certain starting assumptions. We have faith that when someone of greater experience, and wisdom, tells us to do something, to train adequately to see, and also to participate in the validating community, we have faith that in following that program, whatever it is, we shall be able to determine epistemological validity. The initial faith exists to get us to the requisite experience; it is not to substitute for experience.

Within the spiritual domain especially, the goal is to avoid being mired in subjectivity, prisoners of the limitations of our moral imaginations. If personal visions come to define the world, then subjectivity is all we can know because that is all that there is. But when the mystic tells us to turn within to find God, Spirit, Being, or Reality, he is not thinking that that discovery is the result of our subjective visions, sentiments, or phantasms. Instead, the discovery is preceded by an injunction— "If you want to know God, look within in this way"—and after the discovery, the validity of what is discovered depends on the inter-subjective exchanges within the community of inquirers.

If contemplatives did no more than tell us to look within and gave us nothing but descriptions of transcendental states, then perhaps we could conclude with A.J. Ayer that "the mystic...is unable to produce any intelligible propositions at all" (1952, p. 118). But contemplatives provide injunctions, or meditative practices, for looking into the spiritual realm, for seeing the transcendental. And they insist that what is seen is public. What is seen can be and *must be* communally verified. Thus contemplation renews our spiritual aspects and does so not through belief but through experience. If we want to know whether something is real, then the experience must be beyond *my* experiences, my *personal* vision. It is experience available to anyone willing to follow the procedures and to look at the evidence and then to seek interpersonal validation through the public dialogue among the community of inquirers.

Let us say that a friend comes to you or to a Trappist monk and says that during deep prayer she was visited by Jesus, who instructed her to quit her job, leave her family, and preach his gospel. Presumably, if she is coming to you or to the monk for conversation, rather than simply to inform you of her decision to follow or not follow the visitation's directive, then she is not quite sure whether the message is authentic. Can you or the monk tell her that it is? I doubt it, because this visitation is personal. Jesus came *to her* and instructed *her* on what to do. It was not a transcendental awakening to a transpersonal level—that is, going beyond personal and individual identity. Was that really Jesus who visited? Who knows; who can tell? Whatever there is to discuss about this personal experience is to be taken up on the moral-mental level: What follows if you quit your job? Leave your family? Preach his message? What is the *meaning* of what you experienced? That belongs to the moral-mental domain.

Is it possible that someone who claims to have had transpersonal or spiritual experiences has merely memorized the language and internalized the concepts of what contemplatives report and thereby is faking his/her knowledge? This certainly seems possible, though surely not for all contemplatives. The communities that confirm such knowledge have long histories and high reputations. I am thinking here of contemplative

Christian brotherhoods such as the Trappist Order, of Tibetan Buddhist lineages, and of the Zen tradition about which I have already spoken.

Validation of contemplative experience seems confined to one's own contemplative tradition. That is, a Zen Buddhist master will be able to read the experiential state of a Zen student. So, too, presumably, will other Zen Buddhist masters. But can a Christian contemplative read the awakening of a Zen student? A student of yoga? A Sufi?

My own sense, at some distance from any level of expertise, is that one—master or novice—looks to see how the awakened person lives in the world, acts in the world, and interacts with others. Let us see the results of the awakening in behavior and attitude and temperament. Let us see whether the experiences have led not simply to knowledge of the divine but to a transformation of consciousness in thought and action to a higher, more integrated, more harmonious level of being and well-being. As Socrates says, show us in your life that you know not just beautiful things but also Beauty itself (*Republic*, 507b1-6 or 476c2-4).[87] Let us see not only how Truth, Beauty, Goodness, Nature, Essence, and Reality are explained or presented, but also how they are lived out.

There is another test as well: Can the person who claims to have awakened communicate that experience consistently? Socrates addresses this point as well: "And is not this true of the good likewise—that the man...who cannot, as it were in battle, running the gauntlet of all tests, and striving to examine everything by essential reality and not by opinion, hold on his way through all this without tripping in his reasoning—the man who lacks this power, you will say, does not really know the good itself..." (*Republic*, 534b8-d2).

A person might have an experience that is real to her, but it is not verified. Imagine that she has a dream in which she solves the Riemann Hypothesis in mathematics. However great the dream accomplishment might make her feel, until she can demonstrate the mathematical proof, there is no real epistemological knowledge to what she dreamt. As long as the content of the dream is unverified communally, then the content of the dream remains only personal.

Spiritual knowledge is not personal but is interpersonal and even transpersonal. But that must be demonstrated. Spiritual knowledge gleaned from public confirmation of direct experience is evidence, the same kind of evidence we get from public confirmation of a scientific experiment or a moral conclusion.

Is confirmation enough? How, for example, do we confirm that the Bible is the word of God with our knowledge that the gospels were written decades after Jesus's life (if he lived)? We have no gospel written earlier than that. Indeed, we have no original copy of any gospel. Instead, we have copies of copies of copies that started in Greek and ended up in Latin and English and German and on and on. Well, someone might say, the New Testament was God-inspired. But which parts? Was all of it God-inspired? And what of the gospels like Thomas's that were purged or discounted? Were they not God-inspired? Who judges and on what basis?

The search for confirmation must continue, and the continuation needs to take the form of investigating alternative explanations. An experience that others have also had is not conclusive of epistemological validity. We need to take into account the possibility of confirmation bias and the applause of a self-congratulatory group that trumpets any example that reinforces their teachings and practices.

There are in spiritual experiences aspects to be explored further. One that I have already raised is the effect of the experience on the practitioners. Spiritual or religious experiences can have and often do have deep psychological effects, a transformative and lasting effect on the practitioner's life moving forward. The consequences, therefore, are evidence of something profound happening to the person and are worth paying attention to. Spiritual experiences seem different from hallucinations and unconscious breakthroughs. Hallucinations are unpredictable and short-lived. Yet I can imagine that it could be difficult to differentiate spiritual visions from hallucinations. Surely this is why Buddhist teachers discourage students from clinging or attaching to visitations, signs, symbols, or images that occur through meditation. Still, spiritual experiences, as I suggested earlier, can be life altering and often lead to permanent changes in consciousness, which hallucinations do not seem on their own to do. I shall have more to say about this in Chapter 6.

When the Zen master slaps his student on the side of the head with his sandal, he is not trying to bring the student to realization of the knowledge found in the koan, "Show me your original face." He is bringing him to an awakening, an awareness, of his true nature. The koan is the vehicle of awakening; it is not the source of awakening itself.[88] There is no truth in a hallucination, and any truth that comes through a spiritual symbol or holy visitation is not in the symbol or visitation itself, but in what is conveyed through that symbol or visitation.

Awakening will bring the practitioner knowledge about herself, but it is knowledge that leads the student to see life and live life in a different way—to awaken to one's true nature. This is knowledge about who one is as a being, not who one is in this particular life; for example, what hobbies or career to pursue, the best partner for this life, or where to live. Those are issues to be discovered or resolved in another domain. Likewise, physical laws and moral dilemmas do not then dissolve in the face of this kind of knowledge; the student is not now suddenly capable of following the mathematics of String Theory. That is not the kind of knowledge that we are talking about, for those laws, puzzles, and dilemmas remain to be dealt with by the awakened student in the same way that you or I deal with them.

Therefore, the knowledge now seen or learned is about Being,

Reality, or Consciousness. The practitioner knows the essence or nature of everything, including her own nature. She knows that she is not separate from anything, that all is one. She knows, in short, the true nature of reality and of one's Self. This is lived.

Yet if this is such a powerful insight that it transforms lives, why must it be validated at all? Perhaps it doesn't need to be, but to avoid confusing the insight with delusion or psychosis, to verify what one has seen as part of the ongoing life experiences of contemplatives, one brings that experience before the community. At the very least, the communal confirmation provides guidance for integrating this and other such authentic experiences into one's life.

Where, then, does this view of the contemplative spiritual domain leave our faith, our theistic forms of religion as currently practiced, where there is little if any emphasis placed on spiritual experience? Can we expect anything different from our theistic forms, because theists, whether Judaic, Christian, or Islamic, hold that God is forever separate from the world and thus from us? We might have a personal relationship with God, or God might do things *to* us. But we could never become God. Can orthodox theistic traditions do anything but emphasize moral passion not just before experience, but in place of it?

I am not suggesting that conventional theistic religions today have no part to play in the lives of modern selves. They can certainly contribute to persons' emotional uplift; they can make us feel good. They can offer ecstatic experiences, but are those experiences brought forth to be validated by the community? Or are they left to each person to serve as a personal gift, a mark of being singled out, and to be used and interpreted as one sees fit? Worst of all, does such ecstasy underscore one's special relationship to God and reinforce how special, even unique, the religion is that provides such pathways? In short, does this kind of religious experience further distance practitioners from followers of other religions, or does it bring people together in seeing the oneness of all of life and all of creation?

Our theistic religions continue to offer solace to millions; they continue to lead many societies in non-governmental organizations that do good works. Yet those good works are social, emotional, and psychological expressions. Those expressions miss what seems unique to religion: spiritual knowledge through direct experience.

Something like theistic good works can exist through groups like Sunday Assembly, an organization founded in Britain by comedians Sanderson Jones and Pippa Evans. But Sunday Assembly is no joke. These two have created a "service" of sorts, replete with music, readings, contemplation, and even sermons. T.M. Luhrmann (2014) estimates that there are almost 200 Sunday Assemblies worldwide.

So it seems that theistic religions could retain their buildings, holidays, beginning-of-life and end-of-life rituals, and all the rituals and rites of passage in between. They could even keep the hymns. If Samuel Francis Smith could translate "God Save the Queen" into "My Country, 'Tis of Thee," then someone can further translate that song, and many hymns, into celebrations of life, community, and humankind without the reference to a God always other to and ultimately separate from us. That's the God of theism. Those religions could and should jettison the distant God, as well as the histories and sclerotic hierarchies, while adding a focus on each person's spiritual experience to be confirmed as genuine spiritual experience. Perhaps even Christmas can continue with Santa Claus and without Christ, with the message and power of giving, sharing, loving, and celebrating the seasons of life past, present, and future.

People find significant in their lives expressions of gratitude, celebration, and fellowship. Organized meetings and rituals help us form and mark such feelings and occasions. But why must they be built on or around theism? Indeed, meetings and rituals can serve as transcendent and divine expressions without theistic religion. Such meetings can and should focus on actually experiencing the transcendent and not center on clerics and their homilies, sermons, and disquisitions on what the Transcendent is about.

To paraphrase philosopher W.T. Stace, God is not to be found at the end of a telescope or the end of a syllogism but in the experience of our own consciousness. Having come to know through science the nature and the limits of the empirical world, having come to know through reflective introspection the nature and limits of reason and creative imagination, we are poised, as the twelfth-century Christian mystic Meister Eckhart said, "to leave God for GOD," to escape the constraints of institutionalized religion and look within, past the internal to the eternal. That is, we are poised to implant in our culture a new focus in our spirituality, a focus on experiencing God as GOD directly through the eyes of our own souls.

Before discussing the GOD of spiritual experience, I want to consider one version of the God that we will be leaving. This is the God of much of the Bible, both the Old Testament and the New Testament. As I mentioned at the outset of this chapter, the Bible is a book full of fantasies or fables or literary creations of various sorts, all to be taken as imaginative and most of which are not to be taken historically. I doubt that a Christian mystic, regardless of denominations, would declare after a direct spiritual awakening that the Bible is the inerrant word of God. Still, the Bible is also a book with some significant insights, and in the next chapter I'll explore a few of them by proposing a better way to read the Bible. At a crucial juncture, that reading will be able to do without God, and perhaps Jesus, at all.

Chapter 5

A Devil's Advocate for God: A Better Way to Read the Bible

But above all these things put on love.
Colossians 3:14

We too are to write Bibles.
Ralph Waldo Emerson

In 1861 Thomas Huxley, the British biologist, was invited by the University of Edinburgh to give a series of lectures on comparative anatomy. Huxley took the opportunity in the lectures to defend Darwin's theory of human evolution—that is, that humans, as with all other animals, evolve through natural selection. His audience and those who read reports of Huxley's lectures followed the logic and concluded, quite correctly, that Huxley thought that all humans were descended from apes. This thinking appalled many. One critic called his conclusions the most "blasphemous contradiction to Bible narrative and doctrine" (Kaag, 2016, p. 134). Not to be cowed, Huxley recapitulated his lectures the following fall and then compiled them in a published volume, *Evidence as to Man's Place in Nature*. If you honor evidence, suggested Huxley, you are not going to traipse through the books of the Bible to find human origins. You are going to search out the fossil records in nature.

If we are going to be led by evidence, as I have argued throughout that we should, then let me spend some time discussing what not to follow or believe: faith-based religions. Perhaps it is okay to think that religions' metaphysical claims are not the same as empirical claims, and with this I agree. But, as I argued in the preceding chapter, when religions base their claims on historical fact, then they need to produce evidence to support those claims. Here is the key to understanding why these religions should not be believed or followed, for they lack this evidence across the board.

Without the empirical evidence to provide a basis for their claims, the religions of Abraham reduce to superstitions, fantasies, and myths. But if practitioners of these religions acknowledged that they lacked evidence and, indeed, that theirs were books of myths, then we would be making progress. I say this because myths offer a view of the world that has nothing to do with historical fact and everything to do with interpretation. Myths are stories, parables, and allegories that point to something significant about human origins, human being, and even human destiny. But they repose on a bed of interpretation, not on literal claims about historical facts. When readers recognize that interpretation and not recourse to nonexistent facts is the required *modus operandi*, then we can judge the reading of the text on the basis of the coherence and consistency of that reading. In short, viewing the Bible as allegorical narrative can provide a coherent and consistent reading of the text and, thus, a better way to read the Bible. In this chapter I am going to offer such a narrative, what my friend Rory Varrato calls "an allegory of development."

You may also recall from the previous chapter that I mentioned that the religions of the East placed such great emphasis on meditative and spiritual practices that we could refer to the texts that explored and illuminated these practices as psychologies, even developmental psychologies. The authors of these texts, and the religions affiliated with them, systematically examine the realms of being and becoming open to all of us, and they do so through their own mystical experiences. Thus the writings are spiritual psychologies that offer both techniques of exploration and explanations of what is experienced through these techniques. Their purpose is to help us induce and stabilize the experiences. So, too, is the Bible a narrative on developmental psychology and moral imperatives, or so I shall argue in what follows.

Moral Development and the Bible

Moral development necessarily entails how we interact with others and what we think that we owe to others. In that sense, then, I want to focus this discussion on our sense of identity—of who we are and how identity connects to the obligations we owe to others. When I speak of moral obligations, I am talking about what duties we owe to others—that is, what we *ought* to do for them, even if we don't want to.

Within Western psychology the most famous theory of moral development is surely that of Lawrence Kohlberg. Following Piaget's schema of cognitive development, Kohlberg argues that there are three predominant stages of moral thinking that all persons go through sequentially and manifest to one degree or another. These three stages, in order, are abbreviated as "pre-conventional morality," "conventional morality," and "post-conventional morality."[89]

Pre-Conventional Morality: Edenic Consciousness

Egocentrism characterizes the pre-conventional, or first, stage of development. Here the person has little in the way of a code for moral behavior other than to avoid personal punishment or to seek reward. Therefore, the extent of one's behavior is determined solely by the physical consequences of one's actions. At this stage the person's sense of moral obligation extends largely to oneself; that is, the person asks, "What's good for me?" Morality, then, is highly egocentric.

The temptation at the pre-conventional stage, which I am calling "Edenic Consciousness" or "Consciousness of Eden," is to save oneself from retribution. Most often, but not always, persons act in the Book of Genesis, the first book of the Bible, to save themselves from God's retribution. The extent of one's moral obligation begins and seems to end with oneself. That extent would also include God, if people could figure out what God wanted. I discuss this problem below, but for now, consider these examples of egocentrism from Genesis:

When Abraham (Abram) and his wife, Sarah (Sarai), travel to Egypt because of the famine, Abraham is frightened that the locals, enticed by Sarah's beauty and their desire to possess her, will murder him because he is her husband. Therefore, to protect himself he tells Sarah to lie and say that she is Abraham's sister. As predicted, the Egyptian princes espy Sarah's beauty and inform Pharaoh who then adds her to his harem. But God is unhappy with Pharaoh's actions and unleashes plagues on his household. When Pharaoh learns that Sarah is actually Abraham's wife, he chastises Abraham for the deception and banishes the two of them from Egypt (Genesis 12:10-13). Despite Abraham's scurrilous behavior, it is the king/tyrant—Pharaoh—who behaves with more moral restraint than God Himself. Surely Pharaoh is not culpable for Abraham's lie and thus not deserving of God's harsh punishment of plagues.

Abraham's sense of moral obligation was not for Sarah's well-being but rather only for his own. Perhaps his actions were simply prudent, and yet he did not attempt to disguise Sarah to protect her. Abraham knew what would happen to Sarah, and he was morally limited, if not weak, for not attempting some action that might have protected her from the abuse and sexploitation that awaited her.[90]

Later, when Abraham and Sarah journey to Gerar, the same scenario unfolds. Abraham, having learned no lesson, again hides the truth: "Now Abraham said of Sarah his wife, 'She is my sister,' and Abimelech king of Gerar sent and took Sarah" (Genesis 20:1-2). When God then comes to Abimelech in a dream and threatens to kill him ("Indeed you are a dead man because of the woman whom you have taken, for she is a man's wife."), Abimelech assures God that he did not touch her. Besides, he says, "Did he not say to me, 'She is my sister'?" God then acknowledges Abimelech's integrity, which seems totally unnecessary since God knew all along what was happening. God explains to Abimelech that Abraham is a prophet who will now pray for Abimelech.

So Abraham in this account amounts to little more than a spoiled child whose Father protects him, excuses his actions, and allows him to escape with little punishment (Genesis 20:4-6). Moreover, why punish Pharaoh in the earlier account so much more harshly than Abimelech, when both committed the same crime? There appears to be no explanation for what seems to be little more than divine caprice.

When confronted by Abimelech and asked to explain his deceit, Abraham says that he did not think that the people in Gerar feared God, and thus those people would not refrain from killing him. Moreover, it seems that Sarah really is Abraham's half-sister: "She is the daughter of my father, but not the daughter of my mother" (Genesis 20:11-12). This revelation makes the entire episode more, not less, demoralizing.

Finally, in a similar vein but later in Genesis, Isaac, too, ventures to Gerar. Accompanied by his lovely wife, Rebekah, and worried for his own safety, Isaac tells the locals that Rebekah is his sister "lest the men of the place kill me for Rebekah, because she is beautiful to behold" (26:6-7). Abimelech the Philistine, perhaps now experienced in the lies of Jewish patriarchs and fearful of the Lord, catches on to the ruse and castigates Isaac for the deception. But rather than acting vengefully, Abimelech commands that anyone who touches either Isaac or Rebekah "shall surely be put to death" (26:11).

Both Abraham and Isaac feared the punishment from others and thought egocentrically of saving only themselves. They did not think about the fates of their wives, both who seemed expendable. Their actions served themselves in avoiding punishment and death and showed little regard for the outcomes of others.

The early books of the Bible reflect little but this pre-conventional morality. God wants to be obeyed, and for that reason there is some, but not frequent, reward for good behavior, because that is simply what one ought to do. On the other hand, failure to obey God results in punishments of various kinds and in great numbers. For example, God tells Abram (before he becomes Abraham) that he shall inherit land. Yet Abram is not confident about this. He says to God, "How shall I know that I will inherit it?" (Genesis 15:8). God then commands Abram to sacrifice a three-year-old heifer, a three-year-old ram, a turtledove, and a young pigeon (Genesis 15:9). Abram does as commanded, but he fails to split the birds into two pieces, as he did the other animals. For this infraction what is the punishment? God tells Abram, "Know certainly that your descendants will be strangers in a land that is not theirs, and will serve them, and they will afflict them four hundred years" (Genesis 15:13).

Unfortunately, it is not easy to obey God, since it is not easy to discern just what God wants us to do or even to refrain from doing. Why, for example, is sacrificing animals to God an answer in any way to Abram's question about inheriting land? Perhaps the sacrifices are additional tests of Abram's level of fear. But why such a harsh punishment for failing to split the birds into two pieces? These events seem merely to be more signs of God's caprice.

Along similar lines, consider what God does to his creation when he detects wickedness among humans. The Lord is apparently disappointed with his human creation, for humans are iniquitous and degenerate; "every intent of the thoughts of [a human's] heart was only evil continuously" (Genesis 6:5). So God decides to destroy humans. Yet, he chooses one human, Noah, who through his sense of justice "found grace in the eyes of the Lord" (Genesis 6:8) and will therefore live on with his family.

What, then, is the punishment for God's disappointment in and displeasure with humans? Utter destruction through the flood of *everything* alive, save those creatures entering the ark two-by-two: "So he destroyed all living things, which were on the face of the ground; both man and cattle, creeping thing and bird of the air" (Genesis 7:23). But what wickedness had all "living things" done, and why include them in God's displeasure with humans? What possible justification could there be for such a petulant overreaction to initial divine disappointment?

"In the beginning," therefore, what do we see? We see God creating the heavens and the earth. God is creative, but as Genesis and other early books of the Old Testament unfold, God is also repeatedly vengeful, petty, angry, vain, jealous, conniving, vindictive, dictatorial, and even homicidal and genocidal. He seeks obedience above all, and the motivating force behind almost every action is to induce fear. Fear, too, is the primal motivation of the pre-conventional stage, fear of punishment. Indeed, in the desire for obedience God seems little different in his petulance and caprice from the tyrants and kings of the Bronze Age, except that God has far more power.

Consider, for example, God's demand—for no apparent reason—that Abraham sacrifice his only son, Isaac, as "a burnt offering" (Genesis 22:2). God is testing Abraham's obedience. Abraham does not seem hesitant, for he ties up Isaac and lays him on the altar to be sacrificed. At this point, even Isaac must be clear on what is about to happen, though Abraham has told him—as either a lie or as a profession of perfect faith—that God will provide a lamb as the burnt offering. God then intercedes and says to Abraham: "...[F]or now I know that you fear God, since you have not withheld your son, your only son, from Me" (Genesis 22:12). Surely God knew Abraham's mind and heart, and so he must have known, given the level of appropriate fear of God expressed by Abraham, that the man would have killed his only son. Was acting out that fear necessary? Abraham considered only what the punishment would be if he had withheld Isaac from God.

The basis of obedience throughout the Old Testament is fear of God: "Do this and live, for I fear God" (Genesis 42:18). It is, therefore, fear of what God will do, what punishment He will mete out, that drives action. So an act is committed, avoided, or rebuked because doing it may result in God's wrath and punishment. But God's retribution or punishment is rarely explained. God acts, but do we know why? There seems little understanding of why actions are right or wrong. They are described only in terms of what might or might not bring forth God's anger. All moral thought is outside of the individual in the form of an absolute authority. Why not do X? I cannot, due to fear of God's punishment for doing so.

Throughout Genesis we see a paucity of actions taking into account the consideration of others. Most actions are undertaken, as said, because God said to do so. "If I do this, what will God do to me?" seems more likely than "If I do this, how will it affect others?" Morality early in the Bible is centered on the individual. It is pre-conventional, both egocentric and selfish. Whereas "self-interest" can take into account the well-being and interest of those others important to oneself—especially family, friends, colleagues, and neighbors—the "selfish" person thinks only of himself or herself. That thinking emphasizes fearing God and avoiding His punishment. But such punishment is unpredictable, because God's behavior, as we saw with Pharaoh, Abimelech, and Noah, seems capricious.

Perhaps there is within the Bible no greater example of this caprice than that of Job, who is described as a man "blameless and upright and who feared God and shunned evil" (Job 1:1). Surely Job is the kind of man whom God would reward. But no. In a game with the devil to test Job's righteousness, God permits Satan to visit on Job every kind of horrendous misfortune. If God is willing to permit this to happen to Job, then how can anyone know how to fear God properly; that is, how do we obey him to receive the reward of plenty or to avoid torture and abuse? Job asks God, "Have I sinned? What have I done to You, O Watcher of men? Why have you set me as Your target, So that I am a burden to myself?" (7:20). Job knows, as does God, that he has done nothing to warrant such punishments. But Job receives no adequate answer.

Conventional Morality: Mosaic Consciousness

Job deserves an answer from God, because before Job's trials there was Moses, the lawgiver, who brought a clear set of rules or laws to be followed to honor the Lord. Job must have followed these laws to be judged upright and blameless, and so God owes Job an answer. Job, however, is a mere pawn, a plaything, in the contest between Satan and God and as such apparently deserves little.

Mosaic rules and laws, or commandments, were not just guidelines for Job or any other discrete pawn to attain and sustain righteousness (and, let's face it, to gain protection against caprice); they were guidelines for the entire tribe, clan, or community. Knowing and following the laws was not to distinguish oneself, but to identify oneself as a member of the tribe, clan, or community. Because one seeks to be a member in good standing, that desire leads one to conform to the expectations and to the moral conventions—the rules and roles and commandments—of the community. Such sets of rules or laws establish conventions for all to follow to be members in good standing of the community. This describes conventional morality.

Identity under conventional morality is conjunctive; unlike earlier or pre-conventional morality, perspectives broaden beyond the individual, beyond egocentrism. One's identity and morality now rest on formative interaction with others recognized as members of the community. Sharing in common or conventional practices, rules, and values with the entire group makes the group integral to one's identity—that is, to the sense of who one is and what one owes to others. Those "others" are now one's fellow members of the community.

As you can imagine, from the perspective of moral development this move is significant, because morality expands as it shifts from egocentrism to ethnocentrism (also referred to as socio-centrism)—that is, to a focus on the tribe, clan, or group that constitutes not just one's community but also one's identity. Moral obligation now extends beyond one's self or beyond one's close familial ties to the "ethnic" group with whom one shares a life.

In the Bible the foundational move to conventional or ethnocentric morality is through Moses. Personally, Moses does not know why God has chosen him for the task of freeing God's people from oppression by the Egyptians—"Who am I that I should go to Pharaoh, and that I should bring the children of Israel out of Egypt?" (Exodus 3:11). Still, God reveals himself through the burning bush to Moses and tells Moses to inform the people that "I AM" has sent Moses to the people. What is the phrase "I AM" but a reflection of that which we all are at our highest or in our deepest consciousness?[91]

By Chapter 12 of Exodus God is providing the children of Israel with practices to follow and to avoid. For example, "whoever eats leavened bread from the first day until the seventh day [of Passover], that person shall be cut off from Israel" (12:15). Here God informs the people that all those of the congregation must follow the proper rituals "whether he is a stranger or a native of the land" (12:19). Implied here is that blood or kinship ties are no longer adequate for binding the collection of people now within the congregation. The people need rituals and tribal rules as the community grows and diversifies: "And when a stranger dwells with you and wants to keep the Passover to the Lord, let all his males be circumcised, and then let him come near and keep it;

and he shall be as a native of the land...One law shall be for the native-born and for the stranger who dwells among you" (12:48-9). One law shall pertain to and bind native-born and stranger alike. That law is not just for those who already dwell together, but also for those who wish to join the tribe, the community. Diversity adds a level of complexity in living that requires rules for all to follow to provide order and continuity, and to define and thereby stabilize the community and the identities of those members within it.

The Biblical community at that point had grown to a scale where Moses sees the need for communal leaders to teach the people "the statutes and the laws and show them the way in which they must walk and the work they must do" (18:20). So he selects "able men such as fear God" to be "rulers of tens, hundreds, and thousands" (18:21).

Again, fear continues to be the principal motivation: "Thus Israel saw the great work which the Lord had done in Egypt; so the people feared the Lord and believed the Lord and his servant Moses" (Exodus 14:31).[92] Without the numerous plagues and miracles would the people have feared the Lord and been in awe?

In the beginning individuals fear the Lord; then their families or kin fear the Lord; and now the tribe of Israel, with its ever-expanding congregation, fears the Lord. And with the coming of Moses there need be no guessing as to what the Lord wants; caprice should be eliminated: "If you diligently heed the voice of the Lord...[by giving] ear to His commandments and [by keeping] all His statutes, I will put none of the diseases on you which I have brought on the Egyptians" (15:26).[93]

Moses is the divine conduit. He says, "I make known the statutes of God and His laws" (18:16). There is no clearer rendering of this than Moses's descending from Mount Sinai with the 10 Commandments. These laws and ritual practices are what will create a sense of membership among the congregation. In presenting the Commandments to Moses, God says, "Now these are the judgments which you shall set before them" (Exodus 21:1). But these are God's judgments presented to the people. When Jesus comes, he will demand of the people that they judge for themselves. That demand represents a paradigm shift in moral and spiritual behavior. But for now the commandments, rules, laws, and ordinances are what God commands: "You shall not add to the word which I command you, nor take from it, that you may keep the commandments of the Lord your God which I command you" (Deuteronomy 4:2).

The judgments given to Moses are not just the 10 Commandments but a whole series of laws to govern different aspects of ethnocentric living and behavior, many of which if not followed will result in harsh punishments; as examples: "And he who strikes his father or his mother shall surely be put to death...And he who curses his father or his mother shall surely be put to death" (Deuteronomy 21:14, 16); "You shall not permit a sorceress to live...You shall not afflict any widow or fatherless child. If you afflict them in any way...My wrath will become hot, and I will kill you with the sword" (Deuteronomy 22:18, 24); and "[w]hoever does any work on the Sabbath day, he shall surely be put to death" (Deuteronomy 31:15).

Such commandments, along with the commandments that Moses himself issues (See Exodus 36:6 as one example.), are ready-made rules to follow. Just as in the specifications for building the tabernacle to glorify and serve God, the rules for good behavior and for avoiding bad behavior—to distinguish between holy and unholy, clean and unclean, for instance—within the nation of Israel are laid out with specificity. Such behaviors circumscribe membership with the community and its moral boundaries. Even when abroad, the children of Israel must follow the rules and laws of proper behavior: "You shall observe My judgments and keep My ordinances, to walk in them" (Leviticus 18:4). Persons who fall away from the path and who commit sins related to these judgments will be "cut off from among their people" (Leviticus 18:29), if they are not put to death.

At the conventional stage of moral development the basis of moral thinking and behavior is set by valued role models and by the rules that those models follow. Boundaries of behavior are set by the roles and rules of the group to which one belongs. One's sense of moral obligation at the conventional stage extends, then, to the boundaries of one's group. Those obligations are set and bounded by ethnocentrism. This sense of ethnocentrism does not always mean that your group is necessarily superior, though that bias often tags along with the definition, but it does mean that your sense of identity and morality is shaped by and limited to your group or "ethnos" — people, caste, class, tribe or clan. Here persons ask, "What's good for us (for our clan, kin, or tribe)?"

The extent of one's ethnic group or "people" was first established through bloodline or blood ties more than beliefs. The early books of the Old Testament are full of genealogies, lists of who married whom and who begot whom. The lists are accounts of kinship — who composes which families and how are they related? Even as God clears the way for adding new members to the tribe soon to be known as the nation of Israel, we return in First Chronicles, for example, to the importance of blood ties for the genealogy of the Family of Adam, of Ishmael, of Keturah, of Isaac, of Seir, and so on. In the Book of Numbers the lists comprise the first and second censuses of the children of Israel, the census of the Levites, gifts from the heads of the tribes of Israel. All such concrete lists solidify and clarify who belongs where in the community.

All kinship ties are personal ties, flowing from familial and personal relationships and descent, rather than, say, from territory. Our word "kin" derives from the Old English cynn, which means family, kind, sort, or rank. From "kin" we derive the term "king," and so it is not surprising that kings first ruled over people in kinship villages, with an easily demarcated sense of family and rank. Later their rule stretched beyond the village to territory where kin lived outside of it.

One's sense of obligation, therefore, extended as far as the extent of one's blood ties to others. In short, one's moral obligations to aid or assist another were determined by one's kinship to that other. Thus kinship represents a step in moral development beyond one's own egocentric boundaries—oneself—and into obligations to blood relatives. This we might describe as the beginnings of the widening of morality into ethnocentrism. This is a narrow ethnocentrism, as our morality relates only to those who share our bloodline. This is the first level of tribalism, and it is based on separating out those who are different from those who are family.[94]

When beliefs, rules, and roles more than kinship become the focal point of the boundaries, then there is a shift from who ethnically constitutes the group to what the group believes. In short, the emphasis shifts from a focus on the members of the group to the values and traditions that one must accept to become part of the group. Strangers, then, could accept the rules, roles, and beliefs—the conventions—and thereby join the group. In this way groups become ethnically diverse.

We see an opening for such diversity in God's renaming Abram as Abraham. He did so, because God has "made you a father of many nations" (Genesis 17:5). The many nations are multiple clans or tribes that might move the community beyond blood ties.

One example for moving beyond blood ties, and already mentioned, is the requirement of circumcision as the sign of membership (Exodus 17:10-12). Even earlier in the Bible, we see the following example: After Jacob's daughter Dinah is raped, her brothers confront Shechem, the rapist, and his father, Hamor the Hivite. The brothers insist that Dinah should become

Shechem's wife, given the violation, but only on the condition that all the Hivite men now and in the future "become as we are. If every male of yours is circumcised, then we will give our daughters to you, and we will take your daughters to us; and we will dwell with you, and we will become one people" (Genesis 34:16-17). Shechem and Hamor readily agree, and in this way the tribe could encompass new members. Unfortunately, though this is one path by which clans or tribes might be joined, it does not happen in this example, perhaps because we are so early in the Bible and steeped in egocentric behavior. And so, still outraged by the rape of their sister, even after concluding their agreement, Simeon and Levi murder all of the Hivite males, including Hamor and Shechem, bring Dinah back to Jacob, and plunder the city.

The egocentrism of the earliest book of the Bible is difficult to escape. In true egocentric fashion Jacob is angered because Simeon and Levi have made him "obnoxious among the inhabitants of the land, among the Canaanites and Perizzites... [T]hey will gather themselves together against me and kill me" (Genesis 34:30). Simeon and Levi point out that their action might well have endangered their father, but they acted out of regard for their sister. This, too, has an egocentric ring, expressed as the brothers' personal anger, because there had been an agreed-upon alternative. Giving Dinah as a bride to Shechem and joining the tribes together seemed a sensible solution and arrangement—"sensible," of course, except to Dinah herself who, not surprisingly, is not consulted about a prospective marriage to her rapist.

Another opening toward a boundary marked by the acceptance of values over blood ties is found in Leviticus. After yet another list of rules and laws to follow, God says that no Israelite shall mistreat a stranger living among them. Indeed, such a stranger shall be "as one born among you" (19:34). New members, of course, are required to follow the commandments and to conform to and fulfill the set roles; doing so will reinforce the bonds and connections among diverse people. "And what great nation is there," Moses observes, "that has such statutes and righteous judgments as are in all this law which I have set before you this day?" (Deuteronomy 4:8). "Therefore be careful to observe them; for this is your wisdom and your understanding in the sight of the peoples who will hear all these statutes" (Deuteronomy 4:6). This is the new covenant made not simply with "our fathers," but with all who are gathered together today—all, that is, who now constitute this community (Deuteronomy 5:3).[95] The people with whom one interacts most frequently are those who are following the same laws, behaving in much the same way, and fulfilling the roles necessary to and important in the community. These interactions give shape and expression to one's identity, and that membership identity and its concomitant conventional morality are reinforced and secured through the communal life.

Post-Conventional Morality: Christic Consciousness

To break free from the communal ends, practices, and rules that bound and identify persons would require them to step back reflectively from those ends, practices, and rules. That can only be undertaken from a perspective that is higher than or different from the community's own ends, rules, and practices. If such a perspective were higher, then presumably it would also be better, because it would encompass the ends, practices, and rules of the community but in addition would add something unavailable to the community—in brief, it would add a principled position beyond the community from which to judge and act. When a person's identity is embedded in the community, one cannot step into that principled perspective. This post-conventional perspective is precisely what Jesus brings forth.

At some point within a conventional-moral community, people of different backgrounds and practices may test and even question the rules and roles of the group. That testing creates the space for greater accommodation of differences and for justifications of moral actions beyond simply accepting what the community demands. In other words, people begin to judge moral thought and behavior on the basis of moral principles that could underlie and inform such rules and roles and that currently may be absent from the community.

Such moral principles constitute the post-conventional stage of development, so-called because the principles extend beyond group or community boundaries and thus beyond the conventions found within those boundaries. Instead, the principles and the moral obligations attendant on them pertain to all persons in all sorts of communities. If need be, the person following moral principles is willing to adhere to her positions even if those positions transgress the rest of what society believes and accepts. We can refer to this level of moral development as *"ethos-centrism."* Here the person asks, "What do we need to institute within our society in order to make the lives of diverse people within it good lives?"

Ethos-centrism is the idea that what constitutes moral obligations is neither kinship nor territory as much as a spirit or ethos. Ethos-centrism is therefore more expansive, certainly more far-reaching and encompassing, than ethnocentrism, which still has marks of kinship. The ethos or spirit that unified a community heralded and reflected the need for increased integrative mechanisms such as governing rules and regulations. Herein arises the opening for the codification of rules, laws, or commandments to live by. But these codifications went beyond what the tribe needed. They recognized that diverse perspectives had to be integrated into the society, because people from different backgrounds and experiences were now joining the community. This necessitated a move from ethnocentrism—what worked for the original clan or tribe—to ethos-centrism, what could work as a foundation for harmonious life among a diverse population. In short, in the face of diversity what are the values, goals, ideals, customs, and beliefs that hold the community together? All of those factors are compiled into guiding principles, and those principles constitute the character or ethos of the community.

The idea of principles that can hold a diverse population together is different from principles that serve as a moral foundation for *all* peoples in all places. The first level of principles, which Kohlberg identified as the "social contract" form of principled thinking, pertains to ways to bring the greatest good to the greatest number of those in society. The second level of principles is considered universal—pertaining to all persons at all times in all places. Thus, moral obligations under "social-contract" principles extend to the boundaries of the principled society—*ethos-centrism*—whereas moral obligations based on universal principles extend to everyone, everywhere—"world-centrism" or "cosmo-centrism." At this stage of universal principles people ask, "What is good, not just for me or for my community, but for all persons?"

Jesus demands that we operate according to such a stage and according to the universal principles that underlie it. Furthermore, Jesus demands that we exercise our own reflective judgment and trust our own experiences,[96] as we attempt to bring those experiences into accord with the reflective judgments and experiences of others.

The emphasis here is on individual judgment, to be sure, but it is a judgment that takes into account not just one's own community members, but all persons in all communities. This is possible because now the person can step back reflectively to see that she *has* rules and roles that she might live by; she is no longer constituted by those rules and roles. The community's rules and roles no longer form her identity, since she can separate herself from them, just as Jesus will demand that she separate herself from the very embodiment of those rules and roles and the duties attached to them—her family, friends, relationships, and attachments.

In summary fashion Jesus tells us how demanding this detachment will be: "Do not think that I came to bring peace on earth. I did not come to bring peace but a sword" (Matthew 10:34). This sword is not physical; it is an emotional, psychological, and spiritual sword to cut the cords of connection to one's family, traditions, relationships, beliefs, and attachments to this way of life. To follow Jesus, that way of life and all that constitutes it must be renounced:

> He who loves father or mother more than Me is not worthy of Me. And he who loves son or daughter more than Me is not worthy of Me. And he who does not take his cross and follow after Me is not worthy of Me. He who finds his life will lose it, and he who loses his life for My sake will find it.[97]

Only a willingness to surrender one's life and the actions taken in surrendering that life will bring one into harmony with the mission and consciousness of Jesus. One's parents and family represent a different kind of life, a life built around being a good member of the family and of the community. That life and membership require good standing, which is constituted by following conventions, fulfilling one's roles and duties, and living up to community expectations. Jesus asks that you renounce the hold that that life has on you and on your identity. By doing so you receive a new and eternal life, not just a new way of thinking but also a new level of consciousness from which to view and interact with the world and those within it, including your loved ones.

Here we see the demands of Jesus not simply to love but to love in a new way. We can love our father and mother and honor them, we can love our neighbors and not bear false witness against them or covet their spouses or act on that covetousness. And yet the love that Jesus demands seems beyond this love, and it is. Sacrificing all that one holds dear for the sake of a stranger, who is no less our neighbor and no less than a loved one (as we shall see below), expresses the love of Christ or Christic love.

One of his disciples told Jesus that he would come with him, but first "Lord, let me go and bury my father." To this Jesus replied: "Follow Me, and let the dead bury their own dead" (Matthew 8:21-2, Luke 9:60). Those "dead" are dead in spirit. When another of his disciples points out that Jesus's mother and brothers are standing outside waiting to speak with him, Jesus responds: "'Who is My mother and who are My brothers?' And he stretched out His hand toward His disciples and said, 'Here are My mother and My brothers! For whoever does the will of My Father in heaven is My brother and sister and mother'" (Matthew 12:46-50).

When one's soul is cleansed, when it is "empty, swept, and put in order" (Matthew 12:44), by the spirit of love and the love of Spirit, then from that level of consciousness one looks differently but lovingly on one's relationships and attachments. One now sees in these persons and these relationships the living Spirit and the love of God. For the first time a person knows herself to be a spark of the Divine and thus simultaneously knows for the first time the persons in her relationships—for these persons can now be seen without expectations, prejudices, past experiences, and one's own projections. Now one sees them as persons in their own right and sees them, too, as sparks of the Divine. She knows now, also for the first time, how to serve those persons. She sees from a more encompassing perspective how best to help and embrace them, for using principled thinking permits one to step into the perspectives of those within community but also of those outside the community. One's consciousness is then expansive like the mustard seed that grows through multiple perspectives into a tree so mighty "that the birds of the air come and nest in its branches" (Matthew 13:32). But that level of consciousness can only be achieved through the renunciation of the prior life—the conventional life and the relationships and attachments that defined it—and a focus on spiritual love.

This principle of service to others is akin to Kant's principle never to treat others as a means to one's own ends, but always to treat others as ends in themselves. One might well be willing to serve as a means to another's ends, but never to treat others as a means to any end, even one's own. This might come close to what we think of as unconditional love, a love that opens to and trusts in the person regardless of what he or she does. That doesn't mean that we honor everything, every end, that a person chooses. We don't honor their drug addiction or adultery. But we see the humanity of the person behind or beneath every choice and action, especially when we disagree with what he chooses or how she acts. This is a reflection of love from the Christic level, from Christ consciousness, where we are always aware of and sensitive to the humanity of the person in his or her circumstances.

So when Jesus challenges his followers by telling them to separate from (even renounce) their mothers and fathers and come with him, he is challenging them in two ways. First, they must break with the traditions and customs, the rules and laws, that underscore and bind the family; that is, the conventional level. Those things that they believe and follow must be left behind when joining with Jesus. His principles of action are of a higher order. Second, those aspects of their lives that might be most significant—family and friends—must be left behind if they are to make a commitment to Jesus and his teaching. Only by doing so can they attain the consciousness that will permit them to transcend the particular, the circumstances of the community and family, and live from the perspective of the universal.[98]

Transforming to this "universal perspectivalism" requires the stripping of familiar attachments in order to see and know yourself in a new way. You need to drop, give up, surrender, and renounce the need to read your own life through how others, especially those most intimate with you, see you. Drop their expectations of you; forget their desires and images of you. Empty yourself of their visions of you and for you. Empty yourself of your own dreams and visions. Walk in the moment, and be willing to walk without the comfort of those closest to you. In short, be willing to break from the cocoon where you feel safe and protected, from the shell of the family and of the familiar.

Yet Jesus's demands such as these do not abandon the 10 Commandments; instead his commandments build on or off of them. His commandments transcend but include those Commandments.[99] One continues, as Jesus tells us, "to keep the commandments" (Matthew 19:17). We should "not murder...not commit adultery...not steal...not bear false witness"...[and we should] honor parents (Matthew 19:18), because these are ethical ways to behave with any persons and in any community. Jesus reminds us that he came not to destroy the Law, as he tells us, but to fulfill it (Matthew 5:17).[100] To do so requires, however, moving beyond the original rules. Should we keep the Sabbath? Yes, and Jesus says that he is "Lord even of the Sabbath" (Matthew 12:8). But when Jesus is accosted by the Pharisees because he healed on the Sabbath, Jesus issues the higher law: Do good on the Sabbath (Matthew 12:9-12).[101]

Notice here that Jesus is critical of the Pharisees for mere rule-following instead of appreciating and following the higher principle of doing good, regardless of the setting. In this way, the Pharisees miss the message entirely. They may follow the letter of the law and "make the outside of the cup and dish clean," but they have missed the essence: "your inward part is full of greed and wickedness." As a result, their adherence to the rules—say, tithing mint and rue and other herbs—leads them to "pass by justice and the love of God" (Luke 11:39, 42).

Again, Jesus is not suggesting or demanding that the Pharisees ignore the rules or laws. On the contrary, principles supersede but do not entirely abandon the rules or laws; as said, the principles transcend but include the laws. One must step back reflectively from the communal context and then judge which action, done under which circumstances, and for what reasons must be undertaken. Sometimes that action will be to follow the commandments; sometimes, not. Of course, the Pharisees as strict rule-followers feel threatened by the demands of such higher-order thinking, of principled thought. So, this action by Jesus precipitates their "rage" at him (Luke 6:11) and leads to their plot to destroy him.

When Jesus demands that we "do good" even on the Sabbath, what does he mean? He does not provide a ready-made course of action that is supplied or prescribed by a law or rule. Instead, we must undertake action that we have examined and that we know within our own hearts. And so Jesus emphasizes two commandments as principles: 1) Love the Lord thy God with all thy heart and soul and strength and mind and 2) Love thy neighbor as thyself (Matthew 22:37-9; Mark 12:30-31).[102]

Both of these commandments, so often associated with Jesus, appear first in the Old Testament. In Leviticus (19:18), we see one of the few references to love in the Old Testament: Love thy neighbor as thy self. But after this one reference, God quickly recurs to His main theme: "...fear your God; I am the Lord" (19:32). Likewise, immediately after Moses declares that we should love the Lord with all of our heart, soul, and strength (Deuteronomy 6:4), he tells us to "fear the Lord your God and serve Him...for the Lord your God is a jealous God among you, lest the anger of the Lord your God be aroused against you and destroy you from the face of the earth" (Deuteronomy 6:13-15). By now, this much we know with certainty.

Commandment One: Love the Lord thy God with all thy heart and soul and strength

How do we "love God with all [our] heart, soul, and strength"? First, recall that as a principle there are no ready-made behaviors that we can undertake to follow that commandment. Principles need to be interpreted according to our own experience, judgment, and knowledge. Jesus is here demanding that we love God with our entire being. But how can we do so, when we do not see and in that sense do not know God? How can we know God and love God with all that we are? Perhaps this is what is intended in the First Letter of John (4:20), even as it seemingly contradicts what Jesus said about following Him: "If someone says, 'I love God,' and hates his brother, he is a liar; for he who does not love his brother whom he has seen, how can he love God whom he has not seen?" We do not have to see God to feel God within. That feeling is our unconditional love. Such love for one's brother would be a love without expectation.

Second, note that whereas the Old Testament emphasizes fearing God, Jesus emphasizes love. Again, how do we love God unseen, especially with all that we are? We do so by linking the love mentioned in the first commandment with the love in the second. That is, we love God by loving with our whole being, with every resource available to us, all those whom we see—that is, we see that all persons are reflections of God. Our brothers and sisters, husbands and wives are such reflections. Equally among these reflections are more exacting challenges of our love: 1) our enemies and 2) the poor. Loving them is loving God, and the commandment is to love them fully without exception and without pulling back.

1) Love your enemies. We may rightly judge someone to be an enemy, a person who curses us, hates us, uses us, and persecutes us (Matthew 5:44). This person we do not punish or shun or even resist. Instead, "whoever slaps you on your right cheek, turn the other to him also."[103]

But first you must judge and act on that judgment. Jesus does not command that we not judge, as if that were a rule or law to follow: "Never judge!" Instead, he tells us to judge only if we ourselves can withstand a similar judgment in this situation about ourselves. Judge, in other words, as if everyone looking at this situation would likewise judge this way...even about you. Therefore, "judge not lest you be judged." That is a principle about judging, not a proscription or rule against judgment itself: "For with what judgment you judge, you will be judged; and with the measure you use, it will be measured back to you" (Matthew 7:1-2). This, then, is a universal principle to be used by all persons in any situation.

According to Jesus, judgments should be made from that place inside of you that is the will of the Father; that is, for my purposes here, the will of all persons equally situated looking for what is right and good for all persons. This might be called judgment of the heart or "righteous judgment."[104] Here one uses his/her critical faculties in taking up the perspectives of others, but also acts from a felt need, from an abundance of the heart. This abundance is the flow of love, which comes in the form of radical openness to another. That openness is itself an expression of one's presence so much so that one opens to another as if empty oneself. This is not just empathy, but a selfless act, almost in the literal sense, of being fully present for and fully attentive to another.[105]

2) Love the poor. Jesus may tell us to feed and shelter and clothe the poor, and these may seem like commandments or rules to follow. Yes, go and sell what you have and give it to the poor (Matthew 19:21, Mark 10:21), but for Jesus the point is to do so out of love in your heart. Look within to make sure that your motives for helping are to do good, not to receive reward. Again, one must judge the nature and depth of one's motivations. "Take heed that you do not do your charitable deeds before men, to be seen by them...[D]o not sound a trumpet before you as the hypocrites do in the synagogues and in the streets" (Matthew 6:1-2). Therefore, "do not let your left hand know what your right hand is doing" (Matthew, 6:3). Keep confidence with yourself and know in your heart what you have done and why

you have done it.

The poor are those who are downtrodden, shunned, exploited, and in need. To them we do good: "...[F]or I was hungry and you gave Me food; I was thirsty and you gave Me drink; I was a stranger and you took Me in; I was naked and you clothed me; I was sick and you visited me; I was in prison and you came to Me" (Matthew 25:35-6). Why the capitalization of "Me" in the text? Because the Christ is in all of us, as we are in Him:

"Assuredly, I say to you, inasmuch as you did it to one of the least of these My brethren, you did it to Me" (Matthew 25:40). We are all reflections of God.

Often the poor are those poor in spirit, those attached to the materials of this world and to the relationships in it. Those relationships, even with one's family, can hold a person back from moving to the higher consciousness, the spirit-rich consciousness, that then permits one to return to those familial relationships to think first, foremost, and always of others and not of what the relationships can bring oneself. In brief, in relationships we serve others, not ourselves.

Commandment Two: Love Thy Neighbor as Thyself

With the coming of Mosaic law, the community had to tolerate anyone following the rules, doing his or her duties, and living according to expectations. Toleration extended to all community members, whether kin or strangers. Christ's injunction to love our neighbor went well beyond simple toleration. Rather than merely putting up with a neighbor's behavior, which might be within the laws but still odd (say, wearing flamboyant clothing), Jesus tells us to be open to and accepting of such behavior. Rather than "live and let live," we owe our neighbor our attention and compassion, our aid and embrace. We need to expand our reach of compassion and to widen our embrace of difference—to allow others to remain themselves and to accept what in them makes them the persons, the unique individuals, that they are. We don't leave people alone to do "their own thing"; we embrace them with all their differences. Indeed, their differences may well be their gifts.[106]

None of this suggests, however, that we ignore the laws and statutes of our community or nation. Recall that Jesus tells us that he has come to fulfill the law, and that fulfillment includes Mosaic law. When those laws conflict with our obligations to other human beings, then we must hold in mind that our foremost obligation is always to love all humanity and never to treat anyone as a means to our own ends.

Yet there is an even deeper interpretation of this commandment. Jesus is instructing us not simply to love our neighbors, including strangers and thus including all persons, as much as we love, and regard, ourselves. We should love others as if they were actually us, ourselves. Others are an extension of you, an aspect of yourself. You would not think of leaving your broken arm unattended. Likewise you would no more leave a neighbor in distress than you would ignore your broken arm. It is not that your neighbor is little or no different from you. It is that your neighbor *is* you. Treating your neighbor is treating yourself. If there is suffering in the community, in the nation, or in the world, you act, however you can or must, to end that suffering, because anyone else's suffering is your own.[107]

Who does the God of the Old Testament think constitutes "thy neighbor"? Given the emphasis on the rules, laws, and ordinances that pertained to the children of Israel (speaking of "all the congregation of the children of Israel" [Matthew 19:1]), we can suspect that one's neighbors were literally those who lived near you in your community or congregation. Jesus, on the other hand, is clear that he has a different concept in mind.

That concept is found in the story of the "Good Samaritan." A scene from the Gospel of John provides the context: As I have already mentioned, Jesus journeyed to Sychar, a Samaritan town. While waiting for his disciples, Jesus sat by a well and asked a

Samaritan woman to draw him a drink of water. She queried him: "How is it that you, being a Jew, ask a drink from me, a Samaritan woman? For Jews have no dealings with Samaritans" (John 4:9). His request, of course, shows us that Jesus is more than a Jew. He is first and foremost a child of God, as are all humans.

We learn from this incident that Jews did not interact with Samaritans, whom Jews considered inferior. Though many Samaritans came eventually to worship the God of the Jews, they continued with some of their own customs and worship practices that Jews found not just different but also offensive. This helps explain why Jesus's request of the Samaritan woman was startling and why the following story from the Gospel of Luke (10:29-37) is so challenging:

A lawyer—actually a Biblical scholar of Mosaic law— interrogates Jesus about getting into heaven ("inheriting eternal life"). Jesus interrogates in return: "What," he asks the lawyer, "is written in the law?" The lawyer responded that we should love God and love our neighbor. Then the lawyer asks Jesus: "Who is my neighbor?"

The question seems straightforward and easy enough to answer. But Jesus tells a story: A "certain man" goes to Jericho and is set upon by a band of thieves, who steal his belongings, strip him naked, and beat him senseless. So the man, unidentified and, because naked and speechless, unidentifiable, lies unconscious by the road. By chance "a certain priest" happens by, sees the man, crosses the road to avoid him, and keeps moving. The priest here is undoubtedly a rabbi. For the rabbi to aid the man if the man were a non-Jew would be to risk defilement. The priest does not check to ascertain whether the injured man is a non-Jew, but keeps moving.

Next comes "a Levite." Levites, from the Hebrew tribe

of Levi, helped the rabbis, the descendents of Aaron, in the temples. Presumably also worried about defilement, the Levite, too, crosses the road and keeps walking.

Then comes a Samaritan. Recall from the earlier episode that Samaritans and Jews each thought the other to be vile, corrupt, and venal. Regardless, this Samaritan does not know whether this injured man is a Jew. He does not know where the man is from. It is a good bet, however, that this man is not literally his neighbor. Nevertheless, when the Samaritan sees the injured man, he feels compassion, caring not about whom the man might be. The Samaritan goes to the man, binds his wounds, places him on his beast, and leads him to an inn. Finally, the next day, the Samaritan gives money to the innkeeper and says to him: "Take care of this stranger and, when I return, if I owe you more money for what it cost you to care for him, I shall repay you."

Jesus then asks the lawyer, "Now, which of the three is neighbor to him who fell among the thieves?" The answer is, of course, "all three," though only one of the three recognized that. Jesus is pointing out that a neighbor cannot be defined by propinquity of place or relation. A neighbor is **anyone** who needs help or assistance, regardless of status or circumstance. The Samaritan didn't know the man lying in the ditch, other than to recognize him as a fellow being in need of aid. His "love" for this neighbor was not born of language, religion, history, proximity, or any other kind of relationship. It was born only of fellow feeling, born solely of compassion.

So do we owe aid to anyone in need? We do, and the basis of that obligation is not legality, but compassion—our sense of being-to-being connection. So how could the priest and the Levite, both ostensibly compassionate men, not provide aid? They did not feel the need to do so; their compassion could not override their concerns about laws of ritual purity or whatever else stopped them from helping. Their sense of obligation ended with the boundaries of the community and the extent of the law. Notice that the lawyer whom Jesus addresses is a scholar of Mosaic law and, based on the story, steeped in and bounded by that law. The beginning and the end of Christic consciousness, however, is that everyone matters; how another person's life goes, and how the person says his life is going or how she wants it to go, matters to me.

With the coming of Moses and the 10 Commandments there doesn't have to be any guessing about what God does or does not bless or condemn. Here are God's commandments; follow them. But do they make sense? At this stage, does it matter? The commandments are presented as if they are self-evident; to be a good Jew one must follow them. Behaviors that accord with the commandments are good; those that do not are bad. Be good by following the commandments. Since in conventional morality people want to be accepted as good members of the community, they strive to obey the commandments, just as authorities strive to apply and enforce them.

Do people readily come to understand on their own, internally, why *these* commandments are the central, or only, ones; why, that is, some actions in accord with these rules are good and those that violate them are bad? At the membership level there is reasoning, but it is mostly instrumental: What are the best means for achieving the end of following this rule, being good, exhibiting good behavior? Absent here is reasoning that also involves the ends themselves toward which we direct our behavior. Absent here is any stepping away from and interrogation of the laws or commandments themselves.

The teachings of Jesus provide a high-order reasoning, and so they represent a step in moral development or moral improvement. Though the rules or commandments do not disappear, and though Jesus tells his followers to obey them, the laws are superseded by a higher moral principle: Love

God and love your neighbor. So the old rules or laws remain, but the greater task is to try to adhere to the principle of love that Jesus preaches. Why is it greater? Because it includes the 10 Commandments but adds principles—and concomitant reasoning and judgment—not found in those commandments.

Jesus's principles require more than simply following rules and commandments. Persons are required to exercise their own judgments in deciding when to act and how to act, to take into account the people involved, the circumstances involved, and both the motives for acting and the consequences of those actions. In other words, Jesus is asking you to be a white crow, to push for and into those exceptions that may contradict or undercut society's rules, beliefs, and norms.

What Would Jesus Do?

What does Jesus teach us, then, about moral obligation? First, he offers us a higher form of morality, because his is based on moral principles and not simply on moral rules or laws to follow, rules or laws that stipulate content about how to behave, or not behave, and under what circumstances. Moral principles throw us back onto our own thinking, intuition, and compassion.

Second, Jesus teaches us to recognize the humanity in all persons and to honor that humanity. As such, our sense of moral obligation extends to all humans and not just to those who share our particular set of values or even our particular location. We still owe our actual neighbors, as we owe our actual families, certain moral obligations. But from the Christic level our first obligation is to all humans simply because they are human.

An image might clarify this idea. Imagine that our moral identities are like a set of *Matryoshkas,* Russian nesting dolls. The innermost and smallest doll represents our egocentric self, highlighted in the Book of Genesis, and egocentrism is our notion of moral obligation. The next doll, which houses our egocentric self, is that of our families and relatives. The next larger doll in line contains the first two dolls but also our friends and fellow community members. These two dolls I described as the Mosaic or membership self. Here moral obligation is larger, as it expands and extends to those who share rules, roles, duties, and expectations with us as codified in our laws, statutes, and governing or founding documents.

The final and largest doll, because it contains all the other dolls, and which seems most remote from our egocentric center, is the doll of all humanity. Here we owe moral obligations to all persons, even to strangers, because they share our common humanity. Jesus urges us, even requires us, to feel this connection in our hearts and to act on it as our foremost obligation. This means that we support rights, duties, values, ideals, and the like that respect, honor, and aid all persons, irrespective of who they are and where they reside.

How do we change moral identities?

How do we move from Mosaic consciousness to Christic consciousness, from ethnocentrism to cosmo-centrism? Using the *Matryoshka* metaphor, how do we make the largest and outer doll our center — the tightest, smallest, and most intimate doll? In such movement there seems to be an interactive effect between consciousness and identity; as we change one, we change the other. But bear in mind that we don't lose access to those different dolls. At times, our moral focus will shift from ourselves to our friends and family if they are in crisis. Likewise, we may well love all humans as ourselves, but when our survival is in jeopardy, then our focus will return to our own safety and well-being. The dolls, then, are not so much nested and isolated, as they are housed on a moral spiral, where our attention can move up and down that spiral as circumstances warrant.

The key to changing identity is the ability and the willingness to step into the perspectives of others — that is, to exercise empathy and thereby appreciate the plight and circumstances of others, even of strangers — those seemingly farthest from the center.[108] As one grows psychologically, the ability and the willingness increase. When we pay attention, the world offers us constant moral challenges and choices. Those challenges confront our thinking, feelings, and imagination. Through this interaction between the world's challenges or conflicts and the organism—ourselves—we move historically from an egocentric perspective, where the focus of attention is predominantly on oneself; to an ethnocentric perspective that includes perspectives of those others who share our rules, roles, and values; and then into and through an "ethos-centrism" that leads to a world-centric or even a cosmo-centric perspective that potentially brings any human perspective into our moral ambit. In short, persons move from an orientation on "me" to an orientation on "us," and that notion of "us" expands as we move toward or into a world-centric perspective. Thus one with a world-centric orientation can take up multiple perspectives all at once, not just "my group" but any group, even *all* groups. In his poem "An Essay on Man," Alexander Pope encapsulates the transformation of moral obligation:

> God loves from Whole to Parts; but human soul
> Must rise from Individual to the Whole...
> Friend, parent, neighbor first it will embrace
> His country next, and next all human race.

The broader our perspective, the wider and deeper the relationships we create and the wider and deeper the moral obligations that ensue. This is simply another way of describing what we have been discussing in this chapter as moral development, the widening of our relationships and obligations. Concomitant with that development is also the widening and deepening of what we value and of who we are. Such development, this advance in taking up different and differing perspectives, expands one's capacity for care and compassion, which is Christic love.

What Jesus taught is not simply an extension of the moral perspectives offered in earlier books of the Bible. What he taught transcends, even as it includes, those earlier moral perspectives. Jesus demanded adherence to moral principles over the codified laws of any particular society or tradition, especially where those laws did not reflect a foundation of universal principles. Sadly, though not surprisingly (given the cultural climate in the United States), many staunch Christians, usually of an evangelical variety, argue vociferously for placing the 10 Commandments in some, many, or even most of our government buildings. This, presumably, is to remind all of us of the basis of our morality. Few of these same Christians—and perhaps none of them— argue for placing a sculptured version of Christ's Beatitudes in those same buildings.

The principled behavior that Christ introduces, however, does not rest on principle alone. Adherence to principle might not always differ appreciably from actions that flow from adherence to rules and roles. Adherence is not the point; judging and acting on the basis of principle is. WHY do we do as we are doing? What are the reasons? If there is a default position within Christic morality it is to be openhearted and compassionate. The love that moves us is the foundation of our principled behavior. It will be on this level that we undertake to examine and judge what is required of us and what we are asked to do. Our foundation for proceeding is to ascertain what is best for all of us: for ourselves, for our community, and for all of humanity. Love is the action that makes the outer doll our center.

So if one argues as a good Christian that she must follow the word of God, Jesus is laying out in high relief just what that word is—to wit, base your actions on love and justice for all humans and form your moral obligations around the recognition of and commitment to the humanity of all persons, even to strangers who are non-Christian.

Notice, however, that the expansion of one's consciousness and the development of love and compassion do not necessarily require God. To love all of humanity as yourself, to treat persons always as ends in themselves and never as means, to view life from a world-centric perspective, and to embrace difference in all its forms can all be found in other religious traditions. They can also all be achieved through secular means and expressed in secular terms. I have simply used the language of the Bible and the teachings of Jesus as one expression of this moral development. So follow Thomas Jefferson's advice and action: Strip the Bible of its absurdities and of the miraculous and accentuate the moral guidelines. View the Bible as one expression, one account, of humanity's moral growth.

What Jesus asks of us is demanding, even daunting. Jesus is, perhaps, the embodiment of a white crow: testing every rule, norm, custom, belief, and even commandment. He demands of us that we do the same; that we, too, be white crows. Exceptions to all that we hold dear, including the need for a theistic treatment of God, can abound when we interrogate, when we probe, and when we thereby risk undercutting what we have used as a foundation for our community and our identity.

My own research has shown me that the level of consciousness that Jesus demands is not beyond our reach as human beings and is certainly not peculiar to Christians. Of course, we don't need the Bible in any way to achieve Christic consciousness, despite the label. We have plenty of evidence in the world today of egocentric, ethnocentric, ethos-centric, and world-centric behaviors; evidence of the levels of consciousness that reflect those behaviors; and evidence of ways to move toward those levels. We can avail ourselves today of the practices that can transform our consciousness and behavior. Some of those are Christian practices; many are not.

Yet didn't Jesus declare: "I am the way, the truth, and the life. No one comes to the Father (God) except through me" (John

14:6)? This suggests that one can realize God only through Jesus; that is, only if, as born-again Christians say, one has accepted Christ as her personal savior. But immediately before this passage Jesus says: "In My Father's house are many mansions." This can imply, I think, not only that there is ample room in heaven, but also that there are multiple paths to the Divine. No one comes to the Father, however, except through Christic consciousness, which despite the labeling, is not the domain or property of any single religion. That consciousness resides in or through all of us, regardless of our spiritual beliefs or outlook.

So, what if Jesus never lived? What if Jesus did not die on the cross? Is Christianity thereby rendered meaningless, even useless? It is not. Christic love is, for me, both the centerpiece and the bedrock of Christianity. We no more need an historical Jesus than we need an historical Athena to talk of love, an Eleos to talk of compassion, or Homer's Hektor to show us courage. We still read Greek myths because they inform us about human capacities for love, honor, courage, and other virtues. The myths have something specific and significant to teach us about human relationships, virtues, and behaviors and do so in ways that enliven these subjects. We can read the Bible and the parables of Jesus in just the same way and for the same reasons. More important than thinking of Jesus as a person is to recognize Christic consciousness that reflects openness, forgiveness, compassion, and love. The message about Christic love and Christ consciousness is no less significant had he never lived. Christ's method of righteous judgment, exercised from the perspective of Christ consciousness, is the white crow. Jesus himself, an historical Jesus, to contradict what I wrote earlier, is not.

Transcendental or Christic consciousness is not a product only of devotion or of moral imagination, though those can certainly help boost or color it. Instead, it is a level of development—psychological and spiritual development—that all of us can pursue and that many of us can attain. As I discuss in the next chapter, there are myriad spiritual teachers today exploring and explaining this state of consciousness and in some cases offering practices to help us attain it. I discuss three of these teachers— Eckhart Tolle, Gangaji, and Bernadette Roberts—and I do so in the context of Existentialism. Early Existentialists, and I focus heavily on its philosophical progenitor, Friedrich Nietzsche, offer insights into this level of consciousness. These insights, alas, have too often been overlooked. I hope to resurrect them.

Chapter 6

Happy Existentialists: When Every Moment Is Delicious

...[T]he infinity of the ocean — [T]hat liberates us.
Karl Jaspers (quoted in Bakewell, p. 303)

A certain kind of literature makes the mistake of believing life is tragic because it is miserable...Life is tragic precisely because it is overwhelming and magnificent...[T]he affirmation of life's absurdity cannot be an end, but only a beginning.
Albert Camus

In the previous chapter I described myths as stories, parables, and allegories that point to something significant about human origins, human being, and even human destiny. Ancient civilizations, especially the Greeks, wove their myths deeply into their social fabric as expressions of, guideposts for, and sometimes even as counter-examples of proper beliefs, practices, and behaviors. Myths as stories did for the ancients what they do for us today: They explain and inspire. Myths offer some of the best stories in human history, and evidence of that is their historical and continuing influence in our art, literature, and culture.

One of those myths with staying power and influence is the myth of Sisyphus, whom Albert Camus saw as representing the plight of modern humans. In Greek mythology Sisyphus, a mortal known for his guile, repeatedly irritated some of the gods, especially Zeus, with his tricks. On several occasions Sisyphus was hauled down to Hades to be punished for various scams and infractions, but he always figured out clever ways to deceive and escape. At last, he was captured and issued a hideous punishment.

The Judges of the Dead ordered him to push a gigantic boulder up a slope, only to have it roll down when almost at the top. Thus, each time he neared the pinnacle, the boulder would roll back down the slope, and Sisyphus would have to start over. As Camus writes in his essay "The Myth of Sisyphus," the gods thought that "there is no more dreadful punishment than futile and hopeless labor" (1991, p. 119).

The Judges stripped Sisyphus of what we might find most meaningful in life; for example, friendships, family, intimacy, conversation, choices, changes. He still has his thoughts, especially, say, of revenge, and his feelings, perhaps of sorrow and self-pity. Thus, the torment for Sisyphus lies not in the hard work of pushing the boulder. It lies in the endless repetition of a meaningless task and the removal of every aspect of his life that we might find worthwhile. And it lies in Sisyphus, as Camus comments, being conscious of both the task and the absurdity of it (1991, p. 121).

Camus, the Nobel-Prize winning Existentialist writer, refers to Sisyphus as "an absurd hero." That is, in the face of a world that doesn't care about what Sisyphus has to do—a world that is indifferent and that renders our experiences meaningless—Sisyphus perseveres. Absurdity lies in thinking that life should amount to something.[109]

Sisyphus perseveres in the absurd action in this absurd universe. Camus sees Sisyphus resigning himself to the absurdity of his condition and thus to the absurdity of life. But what does such "resignation" mean? Would Sisyphus refuse to be freed from his burden of pushing the boulder, because any other life would be just as equally absurd? Any life will be one filled with distractions—from sporting events to café conversations, from cleaning streets to writing sonatas, from the bachelor life to having a family—to avoid confronting the only significant question: How can we continue to live?

To resign oneself is to acquiesce, to give up, to submit. In other words, to surrender to circumstance, to acknowledge that one is captured by the situation, controlled by it, and unable to affect the outcome. Yet in this resignation, if this is what Camus means, Sisyphus offers us, in Camus's words, "a lucid invitation to live and create, in the very midst of the desert" (1991, Preface, p. 1). This, Camus concludes, renders Sisyphus happy (1991, p. 123). Yet how can Sisyphus be happy when he has no control, no choice, and thus no freedom? And create what in this circumstance? Can we, how can we, make this move with Camus and imagine Sisyphus as happy?

He can be happy because Sisyphus, according to Camus, is free. Sisyphus lives in the ultimate absurd circumstance: utter meaninglessness. A world of meaning always implies "a scale of values, a choice, our preferences," but a world that is absurd "teaches the contrary" (1991, p. 60). The meaninglessness therefore emphasizes quantity of experience over quality of experience, since there is no scale by which to assess or evaluate anything. Therefore, "what counts is not the best living but the most living" (p. 61). Whether you are Bill Gates or Sisyphus, your life is measured by how long you live, not what you do. In that circumstance, the absurd circumstance, it doesn't matter what Sisyphus does as long as he can do it. And Sisyphus will do this for eternity.

Camus is challenging us to see how Sisyphus can be happy. To do so surely requires that we step out of our usual perspectives, to rethink our ways of viewing life and living it. He can be happy because resignation can also connote "giving oneself over to" something. This is a form of surrender that is almost spiritual in that it is an opening of oneself to the world, even a world that is absurd.

Yet Sisyphus, Camus says, is driven by anger at the gods and resentment for what they have done. "There is no fate that cannot be surmounted by scorn" (1991, p. 121). But those emotions — anger, revenge, scorn, and resentment — are products of our thinking. What Sisyphus can do through his absurd plight is shift his emotions into or back into the body, to trust his body wisdom and not get caught in the web of angry, vengeful, resentful thoughts. His body wisdom rests simply in the functioning of his body, the movement of his muscles, the strain of his limbs. Whatever he does with his body in this movement and strain is a sign that he is alive. In that exertion there is joy and relaxation, effort and peace. Sisyphus is happy. "All Sisyphus' silent joy is contained therein. His fate belongs to him. His rock is his thing…Each atom of that stone, each mineral of that flake of the night-filled mountain, in itself forms a world…The struggle itself toward the heights is enough to fill a man's heart. One must imagine Sisyphus happy" (1991, p. 123).

Why **must** one imagine him happy? [*Il faut imaginer Sisyphe heureux.*] Can't we more easily imagine him miserable, frustrated, angry, and forlorn? We cannot, if we understand Camus's Existential view of Sisyphus. What makes Sisyphus's plight tragic is that, unlike many assembly-line workmen of Camus's day (p. 121), Sisyphus is fully conscious of his endless torment and his wretched conditions. This consciousness brings to Sisyphus the futility of his task but simultaneously a lucidity about that task, his fate, and himself. The lucidity explodes in Sisyphus as the realization that he lives and expresses that life in the touch on the stone, the strain against the stone, the push of his feet against the earth. There is after all only this world, and he is fully alive in it. The task of pushing the boulder endlessly up the hill represents frustration and futility only for those trapped in their thoughts about the world and how it should be, not for those fully in the world, who love living and say "yes" (p. 123) to all that life brings.

According to Sarah Bakewell, Simone de Beauvoir, Sartre's long-term lover and fellow Existentialist, viewed Sisyphus's state as a "bland…affirmation of cosmic flux and fate" (2016, p. 226). Such affirmation is little but a shallow recognition that his situation is beyond his control without any possibility of change and that his only recourse is to relax into his plight. I think, instead, that Sisyphus glimpsed and even lived a state of radiant expansion of consciousness. Sisyphus's heart, Camus tells us, is full, because Sisyphus, through his wisdom rooted in the body, is fully alive in every moment of pushing the boulder. Sisyphus has dropped the scale of "best" and "good"; he lives instead in the world of "most" and "longest." He can say, "yes," to every moment, because every moment, whatever the moment, is itself full.

Perhaps Camus didn't see and mean that, but he does describe Sisyphus as "happy" and loving life enough to say "yes" to all of it. One Existentialist, or a progenitor of Existentialism, who did mean it, I think, was Friedrich Nietzsche. Life affirmation and the very phrase "say 'Yes' to life" are central to Nietzsche's philosophical outlook and underscore a life that is joyous ("gay" in one of Nietzsche's terms) and happy, even to an extreme. Nietzsche sets life affirmation in the context of "self-creation" and dramatizes our saying "yes" to life through his concept of "eternal recurrence."

Stalking Nietzsche

The spirit of Existentialism is captured for me in a phrase attributed to and used by Jean-Paul Sartre: "Existence precedes essence." First we live (existence); then we become (essence). Who and what we become (our essence) as individuals rest on and are determined not by nature (existence) but by the choices that we make. We are free to become who and what we want to be. In short, we make our selves up as we move along through life; we "self-create." Sisyphus at the end, of course, has no opportunity to self-create or to make choices that determine who he is. He is obligated, without rest or any alternatives, to push the boulder up the hill. Yet Camus sees in Sisyphus's situation the very heart of his Existentialism: Life is not about "the best living"; it's about "the most living." Existence thus not only precedes essence, but in an absurd world existence trumps and even negates essence. As Camus tells us through *The Stranger*, living, however one lives, is itself the meaning of life.

Nietzsche, on the other hand, seems all about self-creation and making choices. For Existentialists the fewer encumbrances we have on our choices—that is, the more that we can eliminate or overcome barriers such as socio-economic conditions, habits, unconscious drives—the freer our choices are. The freer our choices, the more authentic our lives. To an Existentialist like Jean-Paul Sartre we always have a choice in how we face the circumstances and "situation" (Sartre's term) of our lives. Not surprisingly, Existentialists emphasize such ideas as "choice," "freedom," and "authenticity."[110]

For Sartre, for example, we are ultimately and truly free because we have no traits, habits, inclinations, memories, or identity—we have nothing—that ineluctably define us. We are free, therefore, to change or to keep all of our characteristics, as we choose. Indeed, for Sartre we are nothing but what we choose to do or be. So, the actions and experiences that we put into the world amount to who we are. To know who you are therefore means to reflect on those actions and experiences. An example of self-creation through choice and freedom might be found in the life of de Beauvoir who sought to define herself through the completion of her formal education and through her struggles to remain unfettered by career, by children, or in her sexual relationships.

Nietzsche, too, sees self-creation in our choices, but how we choose is different for him from how Sartre and even Camus saw choice. But first the context in which Nietzsche understands choosing: In section 125 of Nietzsche's *The Gay Science* a madman announces to those gathered in a marketplace that "God is dead." If God is dead, then where do we find a source of morality, where do we look for meaning, how do we know right from wrong?[111]

What or who guides us in our choosing? Without God it appears that events once full of meaning are now seen as arbitrary and without ultimate justification.[112]

Nietzsche appreciated the concern, if not the fear, that the madman's announcement heralded for people: Is there even "still any up and down? Are we not straying as through an infinite nothing? Do we not feel the breath of empty space?" (1974, p. 181). We had poured our humanity into God, and if God is dead, then we are tossed back onto our own frail, limited human resources.

Relying on our own resources is precisely where Nietzsche thinks that we ought to be. In his view, through religion we had falsely emptied ourselves of our natural inclinations and motivations, fearing that they represented the beast within us that if unleashed would make life a living hell. For Nietzsche, with God now dead we can find ourselves and express our true natures, for meaning is not found, it is created. We can see here the difference between Nietzsche and Sartre: Unlike Sartre, Nietzsche sees that humans do have innate traits and inclinations that arise out of our physiology. Again, it is our biological existence that is important; what we choose to create with that biology will determine the kind of persons we shall become. And so, for Nietzsche, we can always make something of ourselves, do something with what we are born with and born into...or do something against what we are born with or born into. Use what you've got; in Pindar's phrase (one of Nietzsche's favorites) "become who you are." That is, you must choose to cultivate and develop some capacities, ignore or fight against others. These are your choices; these are your responsibilities. Do you have enough will (willpower) to make the choices and live up to them?

But where do we look for guidance, according to Nietzsche, in how to create meaning? We look to those who live "dangerous lives" (1974, p. 197), those whom Nietzsche calls "the free spirits." These spirits are those who will break from the old rules, the old norms, the old ideals; who will "build your cities on the slopes of Vesuvius...[s]end your ships into uncharted seas...[l]ive at war with your peers and yourselves," and, above all, seek knowledge (1974, p. 197). Stand on your own; deny those ideals, habits, and goals that the crowd acclaims; seek out contradiction and criticism; and have the courage "to say of morality what Master Eckhart said: 'I ask God to rid me of God'" (1974, p. 235). Be prepared, therefore, to risk everything and to find in your suffering the opportunity to grow, invent, create. "Ask yourselves," Nietzsche intones, "whether a tree that is supposed to grow to a proud height can dispense with bad weather and storms..." (1974, p. 91). The answer, of course, is no. We need adversity to achieve "great growth."[113]

In short, treat life as your canvas or your marble; be the poet of your life (1974, pp. 239-40). Letting loose, striking out on one's own "for undiscovered worlds and seas" (1974, p. 242), leaves one vulnerable to being thought mad. But better to be mad than great, for greatness is an ascription of the herd, the mob, the *canaille*. Yes, Nietzsche says, "for an individual to posit his own ideal and to derive from it his own law, joys, and rights—that may well have been considered hitherto as the most outrageous human aberration...The wonderful art and gift of creating gods...was the medium through which this impulse could discharge, purify, perfect, and ennoble itself." This impulse is "to have an ideal of one's own," which was formerly the center of all morality (1974, p. 191). But we ceded this impulse to sacred texts, priests, and their institutions.

It is not simply through the creation of art, philosophy, or experiments in living that we explore meaning. It is also through establishing, even inventing, new moralities that we do so. "And whoever must be a creator in good and evil, verily, he must first be an annihilator and break values. Thus the highest evil belongs to the highest goodness; but this is creative" (1982, p. 228).

Our power to create meaning and to create values prevents us from falling into, or falling back into, nihilism—that all values and morals are baseless and ultimately meaningless. Nietzsche argues that each of us is responsible for creating our morals, for "transvaluing our values." He tells us to "stand all valuations on their head" (1982, p. 265). There are new values to create, new moral standards, and these are found for Nietzsche in aesthetics and in our individual strength, vitality, and health—all found in and through our physiology. Unlike Camus and his view of the absurd world, Nietzsche is not arguing for no morality; he pushes for "higher moralities" (1992, p. 305). But what are these moralities?

Here is one principle of morality for Nietzsche: Become strong and express that strength (1982, p. 542). That principle reflects a higher morality: We must exercise our instincts and impulses, deep within our physiology, to destroy the values and idols of society, replace them with new values only to destroy those values when they lock us into norms and manners—always to defeat what is built that society, you, and I establish as true and untrue (1982, p. 579).

The free spirit "spits on the contemptible type of well-being dreamed of by shopkeepers, Christians, cows, females, Englishmen, and other democrats. The free man is a *warrior*" (1982, p. 542, emphasis in the original). For Nietzsche one person who embodied this morality was Goethe. "Goethe conceived a human being who would be strong, highly educated, skillful in all bodily matters, self-controlled, reverent toward himself, and who might dare to afford the whole range and wealth of being natural…the man for whom there is no longer anything that is forbidden…" (1982, p. 554).

Above all, Goethe no longer negated. Instead, he said "yes" to life, and, above all, "he *created* himself" (1982, p. 554, emphasis in the original). This, too, is a higher morality, for Goethe like Sisyphus says "yes" to everything in this life and thereby affirms life, honors it, even loves it. To build the "yes" of life, to affirm it, one must destroy what negates life including, and especially for Nietzsche, Christian morality. Yet isn't negating Christian morality to say "no" to an aspect of life? It is a "no" that leads to the affirmation of "yes": Destruction is negation but underscored by a monstrous "yes." When life, growth, and health are thwarted, one must say "no" to get to "yes."[114]

Eternal Recurrence
I am content to live it all again,
And yet again...
I am content to follow to its source
Every event in action or in thought;
Measure the lot; forgive myself the lot!
When such as I cast out remorse
So great a sweetness flows into the breast
We must laugh and we must sing,
We are blest by everything,
Everything we look upon is blest.
W.B. Yeats "A Dialogue of Self and Soul"

For Nietzsche the result of philosophizing must be "the revaluation of all values" (1992, p. 782), including the values that we ourselves create. How seriously should one take these existential creations and destructions? Profoundly seriously. Nietzsche captures this seriousness in his idea of eternal recurrence: Imagine that

[t]his life as you now live it and have lived it, you will have to live once more and innumerable times more; and there will be nothing new in it, but every pain and every joy and every thought and sigh and everything unutterably small or great in your life will have to return to you, all in the same succession and sequence...This eternal hourglass of existence is turned

upside down again and again, and you with it, speck of dust! (1974, p. 273).

If you are Sisyphus, your life will eternally recur just as it is and has been in every moment. Can you love that?

Can you affirm all that has happened to you, is happening to you, and will happen to you, including, and especially, suffering? As Nietzsche said, "I do not want in the least that anything should become different than it is; I myself do not want to become different" (1992, p. 711). This is also Nietzsche's *amor fati*, loving one's fate or all that happens to you: "My formula for greatness in a human being is *amor fati*: that one wants nothing to be different, not forward, not backward, not in all eternity. Not merely bear what is necessary, still less conceal it—all idealism is mendaciousness in the face of what is necessary—but *love* it."[115]

To welcome the idea that we are fated to live the same life over and over again, exactly as it is now lived, means that we affirm our lives just as they are. Eternal recurrence, then, challenges us not simply to accept but also to embrace—to love—every aspect, large and small, healthy and harmful, of our lives. Nietzsche's formulation is not like the movie *Groundhog Day*, where Bill Murray lives one day over and over again and yet can change the circumstances within that one day so that the following day is not exactly the same—where Murray can learn, for example, a foreign language or to play the piano, since he can carry over from one version of February 2 (Groundhog Day) to the next what he has learned from the prior versions. In Nietzsche's rendition every moment from this life will be lived again and again, without variation, just as it has happened and is happening.

This idea ties in with the plight of Sisyphus, or rather with seeing Sisyphus's ostensible plight as something else: a new moment at every moment. In eternal recurrence everything in our lives—including, Nietzsche tells us in *The Gay Science*, even our watching the spider in the moonlight (1974, p. 273)—will be lived and seen in the same way, from lifetime to lifetime. Yet when reborn, our events from the past lives, which will unfold and lead to other events exactly as before, will be lived as fresh moments. But as Sisyphus demonstrates we do not have to live from lifetime to lifetime to live fresh moments. Every moment, including and especially every moment involved in pushing the boulder, can be lived fresh. Every time Sisyphus approaches the rock, feels the rock, and strains against it are all new moments never lived before. When the bell chimes noon, when we eat from our plate of linguine, when caressed by our partner, each chime, morsel, and touch is heard, tasted, and felt anew. Nowhere are we regretting yesterday or dreading tomorrow. Instead we are fully present in this moment, this Now.

For Sisyphus the recognition of physical living is the center of life, not the thoughts, feelings, or actions that one experiences in that life. Everything reduces to Now, to this moment. The task isn't so much to ask ourselves whether we are doing in every moment what we want to do or think that we ought to do. Instead, the task is to focus on living fully in each moment, regardless of what we are doing. To look back at one's life and regret a choice—or a seeming choice; from this perspective it seems irrelevant whether all of our life is predetermined or freely selected—is to focus wrongly on the choice itself or the planning behind it and not on the moment in which the choice arises. See each moment, as Nietzsche tells us, as a chance to destroy or create, create to destroy, destroy to create. In each moment we "are new, unique, incomparable, the self-legislating, the self-creating" (1974, p. 266).

The happiness we experience then is that of Zarathustra who is "himself the eternal Yes to all things, 'the tremendous unbounded saying Yes and Amen'" (1982, p. 762). What an injunction! Say "yes" to all things; love everything that life presents to you and that you do. We saw something similar to this with Camus's explanation of Sisyphus's state in the great saying of "yes" to all life. But how do we attain that state? Must we be constrained like Sisyphus? Nietzsche suggests the opposite: We need to embrace the freedom to create and destroy and create again.

And yet Nietzsche also said to love our fate (*amor fati*). That seems to entail the form of resignation that we saw with Sisyphus. Well, which is it, creation or resignation? Perhaps what we actually *make* of ourselves is our fate. Our fate is to develop who we are: "To give style to one's character [is]... a great and rare art" (1974, p. 232). We must develop our character, even and especially when we are born with great talents. That is our fate. Indeed, fate seems for Nietzsche simply to be the awareness that into this world we are born with passions and talents and inclinations. We must make something of all of that. It is our fate, as it is everyone's fate, to constitute our character out of our innate and societal materials. This is "accepting oneself as if fated, not wishing oneself 'different'" (1992, p. 687).

Imagine, then, that you are to live your life exactly as you have lived it, in every detail and nuance, over and over again—in other words, for eternity. Does that not give to your choices and actions, does this not give to every moment, a kind of weightiness and significance? Make the most of each moment; be fully aware of how you spend your time and energy in this lifetime, for every event will be lived again and again. Can you embrace every one of those actions, choices, and moments? Can you love each moment, whether you are writing a symphony, skipping stones, or rolling a boulder up a hill, only to have it slip back down? No matter how you live, can you accept all of that life, love all of that life? Those are the essential questions for Nietzsche. To answer with something other than a full embrace of your life is for Nietzsche "pathetic."

Visualize General George Patton overseeing the battlefield where two large armies are about to engage. We can easily imagine Patton's exhilaration in that moment and sense how poignant, beautiful, and even delicious that moment is for him. He can reflect back on his life and cherish every single moment that led to the deliciousness of this one moment. But Nietzsche demands through eternal recurrence something more: We cherish not simply *this* moment for its magnitude or greatness; we cherish *every* moment in our lives, for we live as if each moment is delicious. But how do we live like that? How do we come to such a realization? Must we suffer from Nietzsche's lifelong insomnia, migraines, bowel disorders, and frequent nausea to break through to affirm all of life, to say, "Yes" to all of it? Must we endure a torment like Sisyphus's to realize the preciousness and deliciousness of every moment and thus conclude with Camus that Sisyphus is happy? To answer these questions we need to explore what happiness is.

Surprising Happiness

We have all had the experience of becoming so engrossed in an activity that we forget about time and space, where we are and even that we are. Persons lost, for example, in work, in reading a book, in playing piano, or while running often express a joy intrinsic to that moment. Indeed the person herself is lost; there is only the activity itself and the exhilaration or joy of doing it. Time stops, and she loses any sense of what she is doing or that she is doing anything. Instead, she is lost in the book, the work, the sport...only to be called back from absorption by the phone ringing, a partner calling her name, or a stumble on the track.

Psychologist Mihaly Csikszentmihalyi described this experience as the "flow" state (1990). It refers to the feeling of optimum experience or performance but with minimal effort. Whatever the activity—and it could certainly be pushing a boulder repeatedly up a hill—we seem simply to flow or act effortlessly. The activity that triggers flow is itself almost inconsequential, since the only criterion, according to Csikszentmihalyi, seems to be that we must be actively engaged.

Sometimes people experiencing flow find that time slows down; in competitive athletics the game itself and the opponents involved seem to move in slow motion. In an interview some years ago John Brodie, former NFL quarterback from 1957 through 1973, commented that at various times during his career he experienced everyone on the field moving in slow motion... everyone but him.[116] I had the same experience myself playing intercollegiate soccer. At other times, while studying martial arts, I had the experience of disappearing so that the activity of sparring, for example, happened but I wasn't doing anything. It was as if I were witnessing the activity more than doing it. Every movement, every action was effortless, again, as if someone else were doing it.

But my experience seemed different from Brodie's flow or from someone lost in a thought or so absorbed in a book or sport that she lost awareness of the self itself. Time didn't slow down for *me*. I wasn't even there. Yet I was aware, even more aware. My awareness was not in or around the activity. My awareness was expanded beyond the self. I was a detached witness to all that was occurring.

In 1973, while still studying martial arts, I turned to a short book, *Zen in the Art of Archery*, to try to understand this phenomenon. In the Introduction renowned Zen teacher D.T. Suzuki commented that arts in Zen are practiced to train the mind. At some point, when the techniques have been practiced sufficiently and have been internalized deeply to become second nature, then the mind and body are transcended and the practitioner contacts "ultimate reality." Suzuki comments: "[O]nly when completely empty and rid of the self...[does] he become one with the perfecting of his technical skill" (1953, p. 10). If emptied completely of self, where, then, is the archer?

The archer in this case, and the author of the book, was Eugen Herrigel, a German university lecturer who was invited to teach philosophy at the University of Tokyo. In Japan, after years of archery instruction, breathing techniques, practice, trial-and-error, endless wrong shots, and deep psychological guidance from his archery Master, Herrigel came into contact with the ultimate reality, the "right presence of mind," the state that his archery Master called truly spiritual (1953, p. 59). Now, instead of Herrigel shooting an arrow, "It shoots"; the arrow shot itself. "How it happened that they [the arrows] loosed themselves without my doing anything...I could not explain to this day" (1953, pp. 77-8).[117]

"Delectable indeed is this state" (1953, p. 78). The archer retains this presence where his mind "is like water filling a pond, which is always ready to flow off again...[I]t works its inexhaustible power because it is free and is open to everything because it is empty" (1953, p. 78). In this state the person is truly selfless, for "the doer cannot be present any longer as 'himself'... [O]nly the spirit is present, a kind of awareness which shows no trace of egohood" (1953, p. 67). And yet as his Master instructs Herrigel, "he who has it would do well to have it as though he did not have it" (p. 78). Parables piled on contradictions resting on conundrums.

For me, during these moments there was only the action itself and the awareness of doing without actually doing anything. Through his own experiences Herrigel helped me understand mine: "Do 'I' hit the goal, or does the goal hit me?...Bow, arrow, goal and ego, all melt into one another, so that I can no longer separate them. And even the need to separate has gone" (1953, p. 88). The flow, if this is the right term, is not of you, but of the action. In my own experiences I was fully aware of what was going on; I just wasn't doing anything. I was witnessing the doing. All I felt was a sense of presence, peace, relaxation, and joy. As Eckhart Tolle, whom we shall meet in more detail later in this chapter, put it: The Now moment is "when every cell in your body is so present that it feels vibrant with life, and...you can feel every moment of that life as the joy of Being" (2004, p. 71).

So this state for me was characterized less by a full engagement in the activity than by full relaxation. This is, of course, paradoxical. How could full relaxation lead to a sense of absence, to the transcendence of time, space, and self? But it does. There is just "this"; there is only "this." The self is absent, but one's consciousness is fully present, so much so that the present is all that there is. Indeed, the person's mind is empty in that nothing is being held there. There are no thoughts, preconceptions, sensations that distract the person from the moment.[118]

This present, this Now, is not in time. Now has no past that it comes out of or future that it seems to move toward. It is there; then it is not. Your alignment is with just "this," with this moment. There is nothing else, and so whatever else shows up is something you say "yes" to, since nothing that arises can affect, can touch, can remove this moment. Therefore nothing is to be denied, just as nothing is to be grasped. In this state of consciousness Now is not a moment. It is more the space in which moments occur. Yet the term "space" does not capture the effect. Now is an experience of the unbounded spaciousness in which all manifestation occurs. Thoughts and feelings arise in us, and we delineate those "risings" as moments, as if divided in time. Yet Now is not those manifestations or moments; it is the spaciousness in which they arise.

For me, there was no conscious moment of surrendering into the Now, into the present; there was no evidence of greater effort, struggle, or concentration. Presence simply arose: It was there; then it wasn't. I wasn't lost in the action or fused with the experience. I was aware of "me," but I was now the witness of the action and not involved in the action itself. There was no thought that "I am doing this." My self was not lost; I just didn't have anything to do with "it." My self had been transcended. There was simply the presence of this moment.

Full presence is the state of Sisyphus. For him there is nothing that he feels that he is without, nothing absent. He is simply fully present in the moment, not yearning for anything, wishing to be anywhere, or regretting any thought or action. Why would he? Full presence in this moment is as fully engaging, as delightful, as any other moment in any other place. Pushing the boulder is no more or less pleasant than any other experience. Nothing could be better or worse for Sisyphus, since full awareness in the moment is untouched by any circumstance. Nothing can be added to or taken away that will affect the richness and joy, the happiness, of this present moment, this Now.

Everything from pleasure to craving to fear can be embraced happily and yet does not touch the person, since that person-sense is no longer present. Emotions will still arise, but they are not *my* emotions. Therefore, their presence does not affect the infinite vastness, the spaciousness, that is the moment. Still, the Now moment, in addition to its expansive openness and sense of unboundedness, manifests certain qualities, as I discovered. Among them is a sense of peace, imperturbability, equanimity, restfulness, and happiness.[119] Being fully present in the moment means fully attending to what is right now. And by fully attending to the moment, one accepts completely what is—says "yes" to all that is—because one cannot give full attention to something and at the same time resist it. "As soon as you honor the present moment, all unhappiness and struggle dissolve, and life begins to flow with joy and ease" (Tolle, 2004, p. 68).

So is Sisyphus happy? First, his experience of happiness is not given to him or does not come to him through what he does, even through living. Instead, happiness arises as a quality from being present in Being, in the Now.[120] Second, there is no Sisyphus to be happy. There is only happiness itself, the joy found by being immersed in the moment where any manifestation is delicious. As spiritual teacher Eckhart Tolle phrased it: "When you accept what *is*, every piece of meat—every moment—is the best" (p.

195).

Sisyphus is established in Being, not in "becoming," which seems a violation of Nietzschean Existentialist tenets, and it is, which I'll address in the final section of this chapter. Established in Being, Sisyphus derives his happiness, as Camus says, from simply living and not from anything he does, that he doesn't do, or that happens to him. But this "simply living" is not dependent on the quantity of life, as Camus thought, but comes through the establishment of his life in Being, in full recognition that he is complete in this moment and every moment. "[E]very waking moment of our lives we construct our experience around a narrative where we are the star—and we can deconstruct that story we center on ourselves by applying the right kind of awareness" (Goleman and Davidson, 2017, p. 149).

Is Sisyphus, then, in a perpetual flow state? Perhaps. Is that how he can experience happiness in fruitlessly pushing the boulder day after day? He is in the moment, the Now, where only the activity and the qualities of flow exist. Yet we don't know where his sense of self has gone, whether the self is fused with the experience of pushing the boulder, which would be the flow state, or whether the self has been expanded, elevated, transcended. Even so, if Sisyphus were in a flow state, it would have to be perpetual. For me and for others I know or have read about, the flow state was periodic and would last for a limited time. The state came unannounced and departed quickly. It was neither invited nor sustained. But Csikszentmihalyi reported artists who would be in the flow for days, forgetting to eat or sleep, and so perhaps Sisyphus could be in a permanent flow state.

The flow state seems to be a peek into an altered state of consciousness. If it is a peek into "peak-experiences," those moments that psychologist Abraham Maslow described as elevated and ecstatic experiences of advanced perceptions of reality (1964, p. 76), then we want to know whether that peek can be intentionally extended and even sustained. Can those "moments of highest happiness and fulfillment," as Maslow called them, "the experience of awe, mystery, wonder, and of perfect completion" (1971, p. 188), become a permanent state of our consciousness?[121] Within the history of mystical traditions and Eastern meditative practices there are many who claim that consciousness can be elevated to enjoy these states of peace, happiness, and fulfillment constantly and permanently.[122]

Today there seems to be a flood of persons who claim that they live perpetually in such a state of elevated consciousness, but this state of consciousness shows a transcendence of self rather than a lost or even heightened sense of self, as the flow state suggests. In the next section of this chapter, we shall examine the claims of three of them, and in that examination we shall touch on only a tiny portion of their insights. As we head into this territory, please understand that the three contemporary consciousness pilgrims we shall examine—Eckhart Tolle, Gangaji, and Bernadette Roberts—represent only a small sample of the growing phenomenon of persons who report that they have awakened to Being, to their True Nature, to their Higher Selves, to Self Itself, to Reality, to Truth.[123] The terms vary because no term captures or can capture the experience, since the awakening is beyond words or concepts. Thus any attempt to describe the experience (even calling it an "experience," as we shall see, is misleading) will be inadequate and even clumsy, like groping to find something solid in a room that is pitch black. What out of this transcendental experience can I grab onto and convey to those without the experience? Add to the intrinsic ineffability of the experience my own limited perspectives on it, then I ask the reader to be charitable yet skeptical when reading the following section, because for me the room is not only pitch black but also swaying.

Surrounding Now

The only place where you can experience the flow of life is the Now,
so to surrender is to accept the present moment unconditionally...
Eckhart Tolle (2004, pp. 196-7)

If you will stop all activity, just for one instant, even for one-tenth
of a second, and simply be utterly still, you will recognize the
inherent spaciousness of your being that is already happy and at
peace with itself.
Gangaji (2005, p. 20)

No matter the method employed to try to induce a glimpse
(peek) into peak-experiences—for instance, meditation, fasting,
rhythmic dancing, self-flagellation—the most remarkable
constant across these phenomena is the dissolution of the self.
You disappear. Psychologist Suzanne Cook-Greuter, who studied
transcendent experiences among adults, found that her subjects
experienced the self not as permanent but as arising moment-
to-moment. In such a state, who they are is the experience
itself, irrespective of the substance or nature of that experience:
"Immersed in the immediate, ongoing flow of experience...they
are witness to their own being-and-becoming" (1999, p. 49). This
is not the subjects' conclusion; this is their experience.

Cook-Greuter is not alone among psychologists in finding
a disappearing self among adults. Lawrence Kohlberg, whose
stages of moral development I used in the previous chapter,
argued late in his career that the only way to answer satisfactorily
the question "Why be moral?" is to adopt a transcendental
perspective. From this perspective the person comes to identify
not as an individual self separate from others, but comes to
identify with the whole of life and with the entire universe:
"How could I act unjustly toward that which is really myself?"
(1990, p. 192). Kohlberg and his colleague go on to describe this

perspective as one coming from an experience of transcendental, non-dual unity between the individual self and the cosmos as a whole. I shall explain and discuss non-dual unity more below.

But if you disappear, then who is there to experience the joy, exhilaration, spacious awareness, happiness, and non-dual unity? That paradox is the focus of this section, because the three "awakened" persons that we shall examine—again, Eckhart Tolle, Bernadette Roberts, and Gangaji—tell us that what we discover in the dissolution of the self is who we truly are...and come to remember it more than experience it.

Non-Dual Awareness

Nondualism or non-duality means "one without a second," "undivided," or, most simple of all, "not two." From here the concept becomes murky. Non-dual can refer to the dissolution of the separation between seer and seen, thought and thinker, experience and experiencer. In one of today's most popular expressions of non-dual awareness, Advaita Vedanta, "undivided" refers to no separation between reality and what one truly is. In this formulation the self or ego that distinguishes us as individuals dissolves in the realization that we are Pure Consciousness, nothing but the spacious unbounded infinitude in which all manifestations arise. In the rest of this section in this chapter, I'll try to explain, with some help from our three experts (literally, "a person made wise through experience") and as best I can, what that means and portends.

One of those experts, Eckhart Tolle, describes awakening to our non-dual state as coming to recognize our "natural state of *felt* oneness with Being...[our] true nature beyond thought and form" (2004, p. 12, emphasis in original). In large part this understanding of awakening doesn't help, because we don't really know, or yet know, what Being Itself is. We have a sense already that it is something transcendent, beyond time and space, beyond language and thought, beyond all form. And yet, as we have also already discussed, Being is not formless. In the way of a true paradox, Being is beyond formlessness and form. We should not expect language to be able to describe the ineffable in any way other than paradox and parable: "All these things Jesus said to the crowds in parables, indeed, he said nothing to them without a parable" (Matthew 13:34).

Since Being is beyond mind and thought, "you can know it only when the mind is still. When you are present, when your attention is fully and intensely in the Now, Being can be felt, but it can never be understood mentally" (Tolle, 2004, p. 13). Being, then, is what we experience in the Now. Our separate-self sense, often referred to in non-dual circles as the ego, dwells only in the past (the world of glory days or of regret) or in the future (the world of longing or of fear). The Now isn't so much content as it is the awareness in which content arises. This is the silence out of which emerges all sound, the stillness out of which emerges all activity. As I said earlier, what is experienced there is not so much the activity or thoughts or feelings that arise but the very spaciousness in which everything comes into our conscious awareness. Tolle calls this level of consciousness "no-mind" (p. 24). When things arise, we can and do attend to them, but always with an unbounded awareness at least as a backdrop that what anything is, we are also that. Thus, Being is the awareness that our consciousness, which we met in an earlier chapter as I AM, is that spaciousness.[124] It has existed prior to all that we can make of ourselves, have made of ourselves, or will make of ourselves. This consciousness is eternal.

Our artificial separation from Being, from seeing ourselves as one with all that is, is based on our identifying with our minds, the gallimaufry that passes for our sense of self. To regain the lost connection we need, ironically, to separate again. This time, we must separate from the thoughts and feelings that arise within us. We need to treat thoughts and feelings like circus acts; we need to observe them as if they were entertainments within the circus tent and not as if they were reflections of who we are. We need to witness our thoughts and feelings rather than attach to or identify with them. In other words, we need to separate from the products of our minds. Tolle calls this "watching the thinker."

How is it done? We do so by treating seriously the cliché "fake it 'til you make it." In brief, sit quietly with eyes closed and pretend that you are simply a witness to what arises in you. Act *as if* you are already the witness. That is, assume the very state that you wish to be in, where we are not defined by what arises in our minds but are identified only with the space in which thoughts and feelings arise. Tolle advises: "Listen to the voice in your head...Do not judge or condemn what you hear... You'll soon realize, *there* is the voice, and here *I am* listening to it, watching it" (2004, p. 18). In other words, I am not what I am hearing or thinking; I am the consciousness doing the listening and observing. The thought is here, but I am not that thought. I am the witness to its arising. That witness is the I AM. You pretend to be what you already are. Since you are already what you are searching for, you cannot find it. It is already here. When you "watch the thinker," you give license to yourself to pretend to be that which you already are. You act "as if" you are awake, because you *are* awake. Soon you will know that and remember that you have never been otherwise.

At some point during this watching "practice," Tolle tells us, nothing will arise. There will be a gap between your thoughts and feelings and...silence. That gap may initially last only a second or two. In these gaps there are no thoughts or feelings. There is only "stillness and peace." When the internal dialogue that pulls us back to the past or pushes us into the future dies down, then there is silence. In this state "you are much more alert, more awake" than when identifying with the mind's products. "You are fully present...You feel your own presence with such intensity and such joy that all thinking, all emotions, your physical body, as well as the whole external world become… insignificant" (2004, p. 20).

Is this the state of Sisyphus? What he does, his circumstances, what is and is not going on are all insignificant in comparison with the Now, with full absorption in and identification with the moment. But, again, it is absorption in, identification with, and awareness of the spaciousness that lies behind, lies beyond, and precedes any thought or activity whatsoever. Camus needed to take one more step, a step back into primordial consciousness to see that Sisyphus lived in Being. Then identification for Camus would not repose on anything that Sisyphus did simply because he lived it; identification would repose on the unbounded consciousness in which all things arise. Because of this new identity as Being, whatever arose was as trivial or as vital as any other manifestation. Sisyphus could not be rocked from his full presence in the moment. He does not try to escape from his sentence and plight, as he did earlier in his life; he rests, instead, fully in the Now.[125]

The Now or present moment, Tolle tells us, transcends the ego or mind, because the ego "cannot function and remain in control without time, which is past and future…" (2004, p. 34). Our attachment to regrets and fears from the past and to anxieties, yearnings, and fears about the future keeps us bound to the mind. The past provides the historical narrative that forms the basis of our identity, our self; the future offers us the possibility of redemption, salvation, and the dream of perfection—the dream of a new, different, and better self. The self, as a product of the mind, requires time, and time is the homestead of pain and suffering. Tolle makes this point in Nietzschean/Sisyphean terms: "Always say 'yes' to the present moment…Say 'yes' to life and see how life suddenly starts working for you rather than against you" (2004, p. 35).

So why are we attached to time and the mind? If the Now moment is the reservoir of peace and joy, then why not disengage from the ego-mind? That can be done, but it involves waking up to the consciousness of Now. As Tolle said, that awakening involves a process like watching the thinker: "Most people have to work at it" (2004, p. 72). On the other hand, Gangaji, another of our disquisitors of non-dual consciousness, says that there is really nothing to be done, since our Now consciousness is already fully present. Indeed, as she tells us, consciousness is not an object; it is presence or "hereness" itself (2005, p. 68), earlier described as the space in which all arises. She says, just stop searching. In her words, "To be home is simply to be here" (2005, p. 10). "Be Here Now." That sounds so simple, but it took Baba Ram Dass, for example, an entire book with that title to lay out the "what" and the "how" of that imperative.

So Gangaji says, "be present." Tolle says step away from the mind: "The moment you realize you are not present, you *are* present" (2004, p. 55, emphasis in original). You can't transcend the mind by studying the products of the mind, but you can observe the mind. Here Gangaji and Tolle agree: You observe the mind by inquiring into who you are. This self-inquiry, however, is done with no purpose in mind. You have no agenda; you are not looking for an answer. You are simply observing what arises when you ask, "Who am I?" Settle for no description or definition of you—nothing about being a mother, a brother, a farmer, a student, a Gemini, a spiritual seeker, and the like. Are you any of those things, or are you the one aware of the string of descriptions and definitions? You aren't trying to eliminate those descriptions and definitions, because to do so is just another part of your story to become a new or different description or definition. Keep looking behind all of that, and you may realize that "you are free. You are whole. You are endless. There is no bottom to you, no boundary to you. Any idea about yourself appears in you and will disappear back into you. You are awareness, and awareness *is* consciousness" (Gangaji, 2005, p. 50, emphasis in original).

In this looking, you are not trying to experience anything; "to experience" suggests an act or state that can begin and might even end. Instead, comments Gangaji, you *realize* the moment (2007, p. 181, emphasis in the original), which is the recognition that the moment is there before, during, and after any experience. This realization of the moment is without experience or experiencer — it is pure consciousness out of which arises "an unforeseeable state of bliss and ecstasy" where one can experience one's true nature or true self as "one with everything," one with perfection (2007, p. 181).

Yet is this "state of bliss and ecstasy" not itself an experience and thus an awareness of experience itself? As paradoxical as this might be, keep in mind simply that consciousness as consciousness is not a thing. Realization of consciousness is consciousness aware of consciousness as consciousness; that is, the awareness of consciousness now conscious of itself. True realization reveals what is: the Self awakening to Itself as Itself.[126] Cling to nothing, including the realization of consciousness itself, or else the realization will morph into an experience.

The ego-mind creates a false sense of separation between you and everything else in life: e.g., people, places, pursuits, the planet. Thinking ourselves separate from all in life, we seek to grasp life by accumulating products of it: work; worship; relationships; status; possessions; peer recognition, approval, and adoration; physical prowess and appearance; education; and an endless procession of needs and desires, all of which are distractions from the Now. "Ask yourself," Tolle instructs us: "Is there joy, ease, and lightness in what I am doing? If there isn't, then time is covering up the present moment, and life is perceived as a burden or a struggle" (2004, p. 67).

As all three of our explorers of non-dual consciousness tell us, the ego or separate-self sense is a dream, an illusion, a fiction. Gangaji says, the ego is "just a thought...When you cease that thought...you discover boundless, pure consciousness, inherently free of all thought and free of any need for safety" (2005, p. 40).

When there is no doer and no deed; there is only the doing. The self disappears because in the Now moment time has stopped and thus, too, does the fictive narrative of self. Bernadette Roberts, a contemplative Christian and our third non-dual explorer, found that when her self disappeared, she had no reference point to understand her realization, because Christian literature lacked any perspective that a situation of no-self could be a permanent state. But Roberts had realized that her no-self was permanent. In this state, with the self dissolved, "the mind is ever after held in a fixed now-moment" (1982, p. 13). In this fixed now-moment "the passing of each experience leaves nothing in its wake... [O] ne learns to live without a past" (1982, p. 15). Without a past, one lives, then, without a self.

What could a life-without-self be like for a wife and mother like Roberts? She found that she could function only by reminding herself of what she was doing at that moment: "now I'm peeling carrots, now I'm cutting them, now I'm getting out the pan, now I'm putting water in the pan, and on and on and on," until finally she would race to the couch and black out where there were no thoughts, no dreams, no awareness at all. There was "absolutely nothing" (1982, p. 21).

Over time Roberts regained her "practical memory" so that she could function in her family's daily life. But she was living "as one who has no past—you learn to live in the present moment...[T]he effortless living in the present never left" (1982, p. 22). Still, something felt off to her, and one day, when she turned her attention within, she saw that she was empty. There was nothing there, certainly not a self. "...[A]t the moment of seeing this there was a flood of quiet joy..." (1982, p. 23). Notice that Roberts doesn't write that *she* had a flood or experienced a flood. There was no self present to experience anything. The flood of joy persisted to such an extent that Roberts wondered whether the floodgates within could withstand the level of joy.

Over time Roberts came to see that there is no separation at all amongst anything. Worth paying attention to, then, is not the unity or oneness as much as "THAT into which all separateness dissolves" (1982, p. 30). THAT into which all separateness dissolves is what we have been describing as our unbounded spaciousness or pure consciousness. It is beyond personal and impersonal, beyond name and form, even beyond language and logic. Roberts observed, "I was in the Great Flow, so totally at one with it that every notion of ecstasy, bliss, love, and joy, pale by comparison to the extraordinary simplicity, clarity, and oneness of such an existence" (1982, p. 33).

What remains, then, when there is no self? For Roberts the answer arose one day while sitting at a river's edge waiting for her son: "With neither reason nor provocation, a smile emerged on my face, and in the split second of recognition I 'saw' — finally I saw and knew that I had seen. I knew: *the smile itself, that which smiled, and that at which it smiled were One*" (1982, p. 65, emphases in original).[127] Roberts did not know this through her mind; the realization was beyond and ungraspable by the mind. Indeed, the moment you try to capture "It" — That Which Is — with the mind, then the "It Is" is gone, for it cannot ever be a subject or an object. "Since what Is is all that Is, it has nothing to see outside itself nor within itself" (1982, p. 67). "What Is" isn't even a "what," isn't even something like consciousness. Because it cannot be known by the mind, "no man knows *what* it is, only *that* it Is" (1982, p. 67, emphases in original).

Once the self disappears, so does the mind — the relative, thinking mind — and when the mind disappears, all that remains is That Which Is — the I AM. Roberts discovered that the self is our "defense against seeing absolute nothingness" (1982, p. 42), surely the Existentialists' greatest dread. Roberts acknowledged this, because she herself waited for the rise of fear that would reinstate a self to battle the nothingness. Indeed, she comments, "fear was the core around which the self was built and upon which its life depended..." (1982, p. 43). As mentioned before, the ego-self needs past or future—in Roberts's case, the fear of a future of emptiness—to exist.

But her self was gone and with it, her fear. Her mind continued to function, but it was a silent, unthinking mind—certainly not anything to distract her from attending to what was in front of her right now. And what was in front of her? It was the realization that "ultimate reality...turns out to be sheer nothingness...[W]hat you see is what you get" (1982, p. 63). Like Sisyphus, what you see is what you get: "the simple doing of whatever lies before you to do at each moment of the day, with no looking around, searching underneath, or probing behind. Just the doing of what is immediately under your nose to do, and not a thing more" (1982, p. 63). This doing is effortless, because there are no "self-energies" involved (1982, p. 69), even if, like Sisyphus, one works up a sweat. Nor is there choice in the doing:

It is difficult to understand an effortless, choiceless state that needs no standard to survive. The mind cannot grasp this realm of the non-relative...This state is nothing more than a simple straightforward look at what Is, a look that can no longer scan a continuum that doesn't exist, for options that do not exist. Nor does it look backward or forward because in the now-moment each moment is sufficient unto itself. It is impossible to step outside this moment wherein there is no choice and no standard (1982, p. 181).

Drowning Nietzsche

We all have the capacity to swim naked in the ocean of consciousness that is the true self.
Gangaji (2005, p. 67)

Be willing to be swallowed by the ocean of being. Face the fear of destruction.
Gangaji (2007, p. 175)

Even with the self dissolved in this effortless, choiceless non-dual state, doing and living continue. However much one is established in Being, one cannot live there exclusively. We are also embodied beings, and as such we must eat and act; that is, we must attend to our physical, relative, deteriorating forms. So while the Absolute might serve as a permanent feature, a backdrop, to our living, it must be integrated into the physical — all too human — life of becoming, of change, that we must also live. If Being means awakening to our true natures; to our union with all of life; and to the peace, joy, and serenity found in presence, then Nietzschean becoming is the challenge to say "yes" to all the vagaries and vicissitudes that are unavoidable in life. Established in Being, we are not now identified as becoming, and yet, in Existentialist fashion, we must wrestle with and experience all changes. Therefore, we experience vagaries and vicissitudes but do not suffer from or do not suffer because of them. "There are moments of unhappiness, anger, and distress, there are moods that pass through, yet all is occurring on a ground of joy" (Gangaji, 2005, p. 8).

If Existentialists, by and large, believe that existence precedes essence, then we can see that that formulation captures the sense of what these non-dual, awakened teachers are saying. We *are* existence itself (Being), and existence *is* consciousness, which is eternal, unchanging, whole, and complete. Essence (becoming) is the game we play as separate selves to create meaning and identity in our lives.

If there is a sense of Being in Nietzsche — and we have already examined his defiance of that — then it must be found in his idea of eternal recurrence. Since life is nothing but creation and dissolution, an ongoing process of becoming — especially in becoming what you are—then in eternal recurrence this becoming is given permanent status. That is, we shall live this exact life of becoming over and over for eternity. Thus, if recurrence continues for eternity, then it must endure or "be" for eternity. Life may be ever-changing and impermanent, but the cycle in which we live it goes on forever.

But for Nietzsche, life isn't like that. Living is now and will forever be exactly the same as the lives that preceded this one and the lives that will inexorably come. Thus the life that seems ever-changing is non-changing in its pattern. Eternal recurrence "is"; it "Be's." Therefore, becoming as part of Being only appears to change. Underneath, becoming is changeless and permanent in its changing.

Wherever we might be able to locate in, if not impose on, Nietzsche a sense of Being, that place will not involve the self. Nietzsche shares with our non-dual explorers the idea that the self is a fiction. For Nietzsche life is nothing but multiple perspectives on the shifting appearances that constitute life and the world. "What is 'appearance' for me now? Certainly not the opposite of some essence: what would I say about any essence except to name the attributes of its appearance!" (1974, p. 116). There is no single or universal perspective for understanding and living in the world; there is only a concatenation of perspectives strung together...endlessly, but with the proviso that some perspectives—one, for example, that takes into account its own "perspectivity"—are better than others.

There is no single perspective because for Nietzsche there is no true world behind this world, the world that some claim is simply a reality of appearances.[128] Similarly, there is no true or real or authentic self behind the parade of selves that we present to ourselves and to the world. Those who look into themselves, Nietzsche's new philosophers who experiment with and experiment on living and who are "curious to a vice, investigators to the point of cruelty" (1992, p. 245), will raise all sorts of questions—"dangerous 'maybes'" (1992, p. 245)—especially about the nature and depth of the person, agency, or self:

> When I analyze the process that is expressed in the sentence, "I think," I find a whole series of daring assertions that would be difficult, perhaps impossible, to prove; for example, that it is *I* who think, that there must necessarily be something that thinks, that thinking is an activity and operation on the part of a being who is thought of as a cause, that there is an "ego" [separate-self sense], and, finally, that it is already determined what is to be designated by thinking...(1992, p. 213).

Nietzsche concludes that instead of assuming that someone is causing the thinking, we should see that "a thought comes when 'it' wishes, and not when 'I' wish" (1992, p. 214). Because we are the poets of our lives, we continuously create selves as characters who act in and act on the world. We all do this, not just the enlightened few. Everyone's mind is naturally creative, always generating thoughts in every moment of our lives. Whether these thoughts are new revolutionary ideas, "billion-dollar ideas," or mundane complaints about the neighbors, the creativity is always available. The raw materials of creativity arise in every moment, at every moment, so that each of us is always generating thoughts and creating new worlds, new ideas, new lies, new repartees.

Perhaps the greatest creation of any of us, of all of us, is the ego or the self. We all create it; it is the source and foundation of our sense of individuality and of personhood. Yet, says Nietzsche, most do not recognize the self as a creation. They think, instead, that it is the bedrock of who we are. This is a trick of language, a mere projection of thought: everywhere each of us "sees a doer...and believes in the ego, in the ego as being, in the ego-substance upon all things…" (1982, p. 483). Yet, Nietzsche declares emphatically, "…[T]here is no 'being' behind doing, effecting, becoming; 'the doer' is merely a fiction added to the deed—the deed is everything" (1992, p. 481).

Seen from the perspective of non-dual awakening, Nietzsche is both right and wrong. He is right that there is no "self" behind the doing; the "self" is a fiction. Yet, contrary to his view, there is "Being" there, but it lacks any separation or qualitative difference from the deed itself. There is no self to do the deed; there is only the action, since the act and the actor are one in the same, and every action arises from the Unmanifest in the Now.

Nietzsche himself recognizes that the Now is all we have, the crossroads of the past and future that create the gateway that is Now. The gateway, Nietzsche tells us in *Thus Spake Zarathustra*, is where "two paths meet," one a "long lane stretch[ing] back for an eternity" and the other, a long lane ahead, the future, that is another eternity. "They contradict each other, these two paths" (1982, p. 270), and where they meet they dissolve each other, leaving only the gateway itself which is the present, this "moment."[129]

There is nothing but this moment, with past and future "contradicted." There is nothing in this moment, and yet nothing else is but this moment. Only the Now exists, and we relish the fullness of the present out of which everything manifests. But that is only because the moment is itself unbounded—with "all boundary stones" (1982, p. 304) removed.

In that unbounded space we create and destroy and create again. In each moment we "are new, unique, incomparable, who give themselves laws, who create themselves" (1974, p. 266). What is true of the flow state and in non-dual awakening seems true also for Nietzsche: in the Now the self disappears. For him there is no self—that is, there is nothing substantial, eternal, and never-changing behind the litany of memories, ideas, ideals, plans, and pains that we string together into a narrative that we call our "self." If we followed Nietzsche's own interrogative: "What would [people] behold if they could see to the bottom of themselves?" (1974, p. 229), then we would find that there is no center to the self, no core once the layers of selfhood are peeled away. In short, there is no central self; instead, "the ship is following the current…[I]t has a direction, to be sure, but—no helmsman at all" (1974, p. 316).

Nietzsche himself was on this journey to the centerless center—perhaps that journey formed a part of what ultimately drove him mad—for he wanted that "we ourselves wish to be our experiments" (1974, p. 253). With no center there is nothing secure to hold onto, nothing to cling to at all. This openness was for Nietzsche not terrifying but liberating, for it produced the room to create without artificial guidance from society. Nietzsche did not seek "to lie down in the sun…to reap an excess of well-being." Instead, he wanted "to create for myself a sun of my own" (1974, p. 254). For Nietzsche and Existentialists the juice of happiness is squeezed from the fruit of creating.

The best way to create is to seek out this openness; to remove boundaries; to be free, as Sartre said, of social, political, and personal constraints. The best place to create is to be beyond guideposts; beyond edges; beyond landfall, lighthouse, and shallows. This is why, I think, the unbounded ocean is such a central image for Nietzsche. As he tells us, the new philosophers steer for the open sea with "uninhibited fingers for the unfathomable" depths, to pursue whatever impulses and instincts well up from below (1992, p. 245). "Still is the bottom of my sea," Nietzsche observes; "Imperturbable is my depth, but it sparkles with swimming riddles and laughters" (1982, p. 228).

Nietzsche fully recognizes that for many the realization that the self is at bottom no self at all will be terrifying. For him there is no Being to cling to or find; only becoming exists all the way down into the depths. "O my brothers, when I bade you break the good and the tablets of the good, only then did I embark man on his high sea. And only now does there come to him the great fright, the great looking-around, the great sickness, the great nausea, the great seasickness" (1982, p. 325). We can see easily why for many, with no foundational self and no sense of Being, there is fright, this looking-around, this sickness. This deep sea has no end to its depths; this is the open sea, with no land in sight and no boundaries on the ocean. "We have left the land... We have burned our bridges behind us...[W]e have gone farther and destroyed the land behind us" (1974, p. 180).

We can also readily see the attraction of the sea, if only as a metaphor, for Nietzsche. "False coasts and false assurances that the good have taught you" will do you no good on the open sea (1982, p. 325), which is without boundary or solace. Surrender, then, to the openness that is your nature and to the moment, which is all there is. "Your fullness gazes over roaring seas and seeks and waits; the longing of over-fullness gazes out of the smiling skies of your eyes" (1982, p. 335). Nietzsche wrote to his friend Franz Overbeck: "What is this our life? A boat that swims in the sea, and all one knows for certain about it is that one day it will capsize."[130]

We, then, are the boat that bobs on the open sea, but with no helmsman—no self—at all. In this image, the boat is the vehicle that we use to experience all that life, the sea, offers us. Yet with no helmsman at all, then we are nothing but the body. This might be just what Nietzsche wanted to emphasize, since the idea of inner direction and personal autonomy is nothing but a social construct that deflects our attention from the physiology, impulses, and instincts that we truly are.

In this image the body rides on the sea; it is not immersed in it. The body only touches the water; it does not swim in it. There is a distance, then, between the boat and our experiences. Certainly there is no full immersion. Inevitably, the boat capsizes; the body dies. With no boat, without the body, "you" will drown in this open sea. Yet you do not! When the boat is gone, something remains. Nietzsche did not imagine or foresee that. You do not drown because you *are* the ocean, the unbounded, groundless, source of all being. In this ocean of Being there is nothing to cling to. You as an individual are a drop in this ocean yet simultaneously you are the entire ocean itself. You are empty of any relative self, thought, or feeling, but you are simultaneously full to overflowing: Nothing but the moment; everything in the moment. There is nothing else but Now, this moment itself of Being.

With the "little ship" (1974, p. 180) now on the open sea, Nietzsche immediately moves in *The Gay Science* to the madman's announcement that God is dead and that "we have killed him" (1974, p. 181). Throw off the anchor and pull away from the final mooring—that is, the comfort that God watches over us and provides for us. This is a remarkable murder, the madman tells us: "How did we drink up the sea? Who gave us the sponge to wipe away the entire horizon? What were we doing when we unchained this earth from the sun?" (1974, p. 181). Nietzsche can push off from the shore and sail his little ship into the open sea. God is dead and is no longer either a mooring of safety or an anchor to weigh us down. But still Nietzsche clings to the boat, the body. Like an Existentialist, he denied a permanent foundational essence behind and beyond the form and function of the body.

Nietzsche, also like his character Zarathustra, thinks of life as "an abysmal rich sea," not for what the sea itself is, but for what the sea contains: "a sea full of colorful fish and crabs...so rich is the world in queer things, great and small. Especially the human world, the human sea: *that* is where I now cast my golden fishing rod and say: Open up, you human abyss!" (1982, p. 350, emphasis in original).

Zarathustra and Nietzsche are distracted from the sea itself, from Being itself, by the rich contents, depths, and perspectives found in the sea. What are these contents, depths, and perspectives but aspects of Zarathustra, and of Nietzsche himself, to use to create and to use as the substance of self, even if all of that is to be recognized as fiction and to be overcome? Unseen, however, to both Zarathustra and Nietzsche, is that the self itself, in any and every form, is the final overcoming.

"How is man to be overcome?" (1982, p. 399). By recognizing that there is no man at all, no self behind the self, no substance at the core. There is only the act of creating and destroying and creating again. "All joy wants the eternity of all things, wants honey, wants bees, wants drunken midnight, wants tombs, wants tomb-tears' comfort, wants gilded evening glow" (1982, p. 435). Joy wants all this for eternity. But this is to want "things" in the world. Better, thinks Nietzsche, is to see that the things are mere instruments of play and creation, which is our only human dance. Lost, however, for Nietzsche and his vision is the eternity of Being and the moment out of which all things arise.

Zarathustra asks, "Do I have a goal anymore? A haven toward which my sail is set? A good wind? Alas, only he who knows where he is sailing also knows which wind is good and the right wind for him" (1982, p. 386). Zarathustra and Nietzsche are headed somewhere; they are not immersed in the ocean, but are clinging to the boat. Without the body there is nothing. Yet, both seem on the verge of getting it: "Still! Still! Did not the world become perfect just now?" (1982, p. 388). Yes! In the stillness, in the vastness of pelagic silence, Zarathustra and Nietzsche had a glimpse of the eternal Now and the perfection of all that is. Zarathustra fell asleep, but, like a meditator in the witnessing state, his eyes remained open: "My eyes he [sleep] does not close, my soul he leaves awake…like a ship that has sailed into its stillest cove" (1982, p. 388). But this soul is "a tired ship." It must be abandoned, dry-docked, put to rest.

Isn't Nietzsche right to refuse to take the step of acknowledging Being when everything in and around us changes—becomes, grows, deteriorates, and dies? Yet aside from the realization that there is no self, as Nietzsche acknowledged, there is also the realization by our non-dual explorers of what is true and real—what is truly real, really true. That is the never-changing, never-dying, always fully present consciousness in which all arises. Moreover, Gangaji says, as an added bonus about the dissolution of the self: "the individual is dissolved and yet becomes more individually distinct" (2005, p. 74). Consciousness can both recognize itself in all forms and yet can simultaneously recognize that it is beyond all forms as the ground or animating force of all things. Distinction can and does occur, because we can see our uniqueness without losing the sense of connection that was lost when we oriented our lives around the sense of being a separate self.

What holds Nietzsche, what holds us, back from this realization? Gangaji says that it is fear: The fear of losing all that we think we are, all we have known, and all we have constructed as meaning, as purpose, as a self. Fearing such a loss out on the open sea, Nietzsche seeks rescue. What is the deep sea for Nietzsche but the unfathomable from which life itself *can* rescue us with a "golden fishing rod" (1982, p. 220) by pulling up from the depths all sorts of problems, fixations, and distractions—the contents and perspectives of living—that keep us creating? But rescue is not the point; capsizing the boat, abandoning the body, is the point.

That loss that we fear, the loss of all we are, all we have and can become, comments Gangaji, "is actually very good news" (2005, p. 74). The good news lies in the unfathomability of the sea and our awakening as "That." Did Nietzsche realize, and perhaps fear, how close he was to describing that unfathomability, the infinite spaciousness and unboundedness of Being when he wrote, "the ocean and its desolate silence are waiting impatiently behind all of this noise" (1974, p. 225)? What would that realization have done to Nietzsche's proto-Existentialism? Eckhart Tolle uses the same metaphor to point out Gangaji's good news: "The whole world seems like waves or ripples on the surface of a vast and deep ocean. You are that ocean and, of course, you are also a ripple, but a ripple that has realized its true identity as the ocean, and compared to that vastness and depth, the world of waves and ripples is not all that important" (2004, p. 173).

I want to conclude by commending and simultaneously condemning *homo sapiens*. We humans are so focused, so one-pointed, that we are able to avoid the Now in every moment. We are able through will or diligence or indulgence, however you want to describe it, to avoid recognizing that which we truly are—that is, unbounded spacious Being—and to continue full immersion in the dream that is our existence in this material universe that we think and feel is what and who we truly are. Are we not simply amazing creatures?

Yet if we can remain open and aware, our three-dimensional world will show us cracks in that existence. Through those cracks we can glimpse, we can peek at, the universal consciousness that is our true nature. With no effort, we can lose ourselves in a breathtaking first cry, in an early snow, in the scent of a rose. In that single instant we are fully present in the Now and thus freed of our separate-self sense. Empty of self we are no longer there. From the ego's perspective this is not Gangaji's good news; this is scary news. The ego's final defense for keeping itself alive is to cling to the body, just as Nietzsche did, and to forswear the existence of Existence. A glimpse of Now might be revelatory, but if sustained, we would be free-falling into the abyss, as Bernadette Roberts did. Then there is nothing to grab onto. Nietzsche said, when you look into the abyss, the abyss looks into you. But as with the unfathomable sea, the abyss is what we truly are: You are not a Nietzschean subject looking into an object called the abyss that looks back. Instead, you are the abyss itself looking at itself as itself.

So use your existential body-mind to get into the flow, into the Now, to lose yourself. Sail out to the open sea and capsize the boat. Dive in where there is nothing to hold onto. "But I am afraid of drowning!" So much the better, for there is no you to drown. There is only water in water. There is only You.

Happiness for Existentialists might well begin by assuming that existence precedes essence. But lasting happiness lies in knowing your eternal Being, knowing that what we are, as Socrates tells us, "always is and neither comes to be nor passes away, neither waxes nor wanes" (The *Symposium*, 211a1-2). This happiness is true immortality.

Sisyphus will push his rock for eternity. In assigning him to this fate the gods thought that they were punishing Sisyphus. But, fully and permanently relaxed in the Now, Sisyphus escapes imprisonment as his self disappears in the presence of Presence. The gods, however, have removed Sisyphus's relative circumstances. Because his circumstances will never change, he can never know that his self has disappeared. He lacks, and will always lack, the contrast with the relative world that could tell him so. That is the world of becoming. Does that make him wretched or lucky? For Sisyphus that cannot matter, for where is Sisyphus?

For us it does matter. Unlike Sisyphus we can and must put our bodies into the world and see ourselves in contrast with others before us. As embodied beings, we have no choice but to function in the world and thereby include others in our ongoing experiences. This is part of our saying "Yes!" to all of life. Even in the tragic moments of living can we find the fundament of us that is unharmed and unchanged by those moments? The fundament is unboundedness, spaciousness, the unfathomability of the sea. There is no bedrock. There is only That Which Is. Our small, separate, egoic selves have nothing to do with it, other than to be ephemera, to be lived with for a time and then dissolved. The self is all that we think we are. Eckhart Tolle, Gangaji, Bernadette Roberts, and their ilk are a murder of white crows embodying the good news that that which we think we are can be surrendered and dissolved in the realization that we are really That Which Is.

Can we maintain this full realization that each of us, like grains of sand on a beach or pines in a forest, is wonderfully unique but not separate from each other in our eternal, unchanging Being? The test is whether we can remain in Being, in the moment, radically open to and in the face of the pain and tribulations of others, as we move about in our daily lives. We can do no other than to radiate our consciousness, whatever our level of consciousness, into the world.

The Existentialists realized this and used their insights in their actions in the world. They lacked, however, the consciousness of awakened, non-dual Being. Would that consciousness have altered their actions and their teachings? I presume so, because that consciousness would have altered them, who they were. For underneath or behind or beyond all the action and teaching — beside and beyond the world of becoming and yet fully part of becoming — would have been full realization of Now. No matter what comes or goes, no matter what arises and passes away, something always remains — something IS — that never moves, never strains, never even participates in becoming. This is the eternal, unchanging stillness and silence of presence itself, which we call our True Selves or Being. This is also a new, deeper, and surprising happiness that never fades; that underlies every moment; and that in the presence of relative thoughts, feelings, actions, and masks of self is not shaken from pure consciousness but instead reflects pure consciousness. *This* happiness is who we are.

Yet is this a happiness that we want? What a strange question. If it is happiness, how could we not want it? Because this happiness involves the dissolution, the disappearance, the demise of all that we hold dear. The prospect of the afterlife, as discussed in the first chapter, is the continuation of our memories, values, goals, and reflections forever. We live on as we are...forever. Yet nothing in life lives on forever, certainly nothing we love or hold dear. Why should life after death be any different? So it is the prospect of fundamental, radical change to our selves that frightens us about true happiness, and this is the message that our non-dual white crows deliver: To find true happiness, the very thing that you've been told to help, to strengthen, to improve, to fulfill, and to love—that is, your self— is the very thing that you must transcend and leave behind.

If you were to tell your five-year-old self or your twelve-year-old self that everything he loved and everyone he loved would change and even disappear, he would be terrified. Yet nothing from that earlier self remains, except for some memories. How can you be today who you were yesterday if everything has changed? The continuation from your earlier selves to you now lies through the unchanging, eternal, ever-present consciousness, not the personal consciousness of the egoic self. Personal consciousness will evolve. That is the promise of life. I have pointed out throughout this book some glimpses into that evolution. One manifestation of evolution is growth into Christic love, where Jesus demands that we leave behind the relationships, attachments, communities, and roles that have defined us. In return we receive eternal life and the chance to see and know our loved ones in a new light, to see and know them for the first time. That first time arises because we are now for the first time truly alive. We have awakened to who we truly are and can bring to our relationships compassion, openness, honesty, tenderness, and love without any clinging or need. We may be as unbounded as the sky, but we still operate in the world and do so in ways that promote human flourishing.

The idea that our selves dissolve is terrifying, for it is a death and a death of all that we think and feel we are. If we awaken to our oceanic sense—that we are the vast sea itself, the unboundedness and the Unmanifest—then can we retain the sense that we are also individual drops in that sea? Recall what Gangaji says: "You are that ocean and, of course, you are also a ripple, but a ripple that has realized its true identity as the ocean, and compared to that vastness and depth, the world of waves and ripples is not all that important" (2004, p. 173). The loss of importance is the very state that we fear. But Gangaji continues: "the individual is dissolved and yet becomes more individually distinct." We are in the realm of paradox here, which is the only means for conveying the ineffable. But we should heed the words and example of this white crow and reexamine who and what we think we are.

Paradox may well fail to mitigate our fear, for paradox is a poor substitute if we lack related personal experience. We often fear what we do not know. We can spend our entire lives — as the theorists of Terror Management Theory (TMT) that we encountered in Chapter 1 tell us — trying to avoid facing death, what we think of as our dissolution and ultimate demise. But if consciousness is independent of the body, then when the body dies, consciousness lives on in some form. The murder of white crows from the Windbridge Institute tells us so.

If that form is our personal consciousness, then that consciousness will evolve. Ultimately, it seems, like rivers and streams flowing inexorably to the ocean, that evolution eventuates in awakening to our true nature as Pure Consciousness and to its sidekick, true happiness. The murder of non-dual white crows tells us so...and encourages us to awaken to that happiness.

The dissolution of the self is a death of the ego, the dying to one's small self. Such a death reveals another kind of awareness or consciousness beyond or behind it — what I've been describing as the true Self or Being. Another way to experience that consciousness is to die not to the self but to die physically. That experience, which comes to us all, involves not just the dissolution of self, but the dissolution of all that we know and experience ourselves to be materially. This is the existential fear and Existential dread: our fear of death. Yet again, however, science, in this case chemistry—the building blocks of material life—can help us here, as we shall see in the next chapter.

Chapter 7

Death Trip: Better Dying Through Chemistry

All of a sudden, everything familiar started evaporating. Imagine you fall off a boat out in the open ocean, and you turn around, and the boat is gone. And then the water's gone. And then you're gone. Left is a sense of expanded, even unbounded consciousness and a deep connection to other persons.

Clark Martin, a retired clinical psychologist, after one session with psilocybin; quoted in Tierney, 2010

When a single dose of psilocybin [is administered to] psychologically-distressed patients with life-threatening cancer diagnoses, they transcend their primary identification with their bodies and experience ego-free states…and return with a new perspective and profound acceptance.

Michael Pollan, 2015

In a flash, with sudden emotional force, his presence cracked Maggie's resolve, and the tears poured through the fissures. Standing in the doorway was Graham, deeply tan, dressed in hiking boots, cargo pants, and a polo shirt, a shock of brown hair across his forehead, a week's growth of beard on his face. Lost for the moment were her resentment, anger, and the flock of recriminations that crossed her mind every day since she got sick and he remained absent. Instead, amid the tears and choking breaths, she said, "I'm afraid, Graham." His sister, Maggie, lay in the hospice bed, thin as a sheet, so different from the primatologist and triathlete Graham had last seen five years ago. "I know the time is close, and I'm afraid to die." She continued to cry, but without much sound. "This life is all I know, and it's going to be gone. And I'm going to be gone. And then what? Is there a what?"

He smiled at her, a brother who had always tried to aid his sister, but whose self-absorption often made the attempts too late or ineffectual. Can one make up for distance and lost time? He moved next to the chair beside her bed, bent over, and hugged her until her crying ceased. Graham was determined to help Maggie this time, having both time and expertise to give her. "Don't be frightened," he said. "Here's why." Graham unzipped his backpack and took out a small baggie whose contents had migrated into one corner. He opened the baggie and dug out a small, blue pill. Placing it in the palm of his left hand, letting Maggie get a good look at it, he said, "Take this."

"What is it?" she asked, the words coming out in a slow pour.

"It's psilocybin, 30 milligrams." Furrowing her brow, scrunching her bright green eyes, Maggie looked askance at Graham.

"It's the active ingredient in mushrooms, magic mushrooms."

Maggie laughed, putting her hand to her mouth. "At least you're making me feel better." She took a long moment, eyeing the pill, her hand now back on the bed. "I'm not taking it."

"Why the hell not?"

"Because I feel bad enough already. I don't need to add getting zonked out."

"Maggie, this is going to make you feel a lot better, a whole lot better." Her brow remained furrowed; she did not seem convinced. He added, "Research on giving cancer patients psychedelic drugs shows a remarkable reduction in the patients' levels of anxiety. One of those patients in an NYU study had the highest ratings on the anxiety scale that the researchers had ever seen. After one session with psychedelics, his anxiety rating dropped from 21 out of 30 to zero. Zero! His rating stayed there for seven months. Seven months with zero anxiety."[131] Maggie's expression did not change. Graham said, "If you don't trust the anecdote, then trust me on this."

She looked hard at him, eyes not scrunched but narrowed, and said, "You disappear into the jungles of South America for five years, nobody hears from you, nobody knows where you are or what you're doing, and suddenly I get cancer and you show up to ease your little sister into death by getting her high. Does trusting you right now seem like a rational idea?"

Somebody always knew where Graham was. He didn't want to tell her right now, unless she pressed him, that Win Stoke, his best friend and sworn to secrecy, knew at all times where he was and how to contact him. This information would not just hurt her feelings, but would indicate that Graham didn't trust her with this information, which was true, knowing how the temptation to communicate with him or, worse, come visit him would eat at her, like a hunger pang. Win and Graham had an agreement: Graham would contact him, and Win would never contact Graham, leaving Graham's life to Graham alone, unless an emergency arose, such as his sister dying of cancer. Win only said that Maggie was sick, never that she had stage-four cancer. Maggie observed Graham for a while. Graham observed her back. He said, "It seems a helluva lot more rational than watching you suffer physically and mentally. These pills will ease your pain and anxiety by opening your mind to the world beyond."

Her gaze intensified, the way she used to study the lab chimps in her care. "How do you know?"

Graham met her gaze and doubled it. "What do you think I've been doing for the past five years?"

"Obviously, I don't know what you've been doing for the past five years," she said, not even attempting to keep the anger out of her voice. "Why don't you tell me now that I'm dying and won't see you much."

Graham waited a few seconds for her anger and hurt to subside. They didn't, but he plunged anyway into an explanation. "I've been working with some shamans and other indigenous healers in the Amazon and around the world, studying the effects of psychotropic drugs on people in various stages of growth, illness, and distress. I've worked with Aboriginal tribes in Australia who use the pituri plant; shamans in northern Mexico who ingest peyote, which they call in Aztec *teonanacatl* or 'god's flesh,' and who vaporize and inhale the venom of the Sonoran Desert toad to induce mystical levels of consciousness. I've worked with Siberians who use the fly-agaric mushroom to communicate with divine spirits; with Plains Indians with their trance visions and audible phenomena induced by Nightshade plants—especially jimson weed—and the mescal bean; with healers, called *maestros*, in northern Peru who treat diseases with plant psychedelics and mystically transport themselves through the San Pedro cactus and the *wilka* shrub" (De Rios, 1990).

"That's terrific, Graham, but we aren't in the desert or mountains. We aren't in Peru or Australia. We're in a hospice outside of Seattle."

"What, you think the drugs work differently here?" Maggie shrugged and looked away.

Then Graham said, "All of that studying has made me proficient in guiding persons on their own individualized journey. The drug and your mind don't care where you are. Wherever that is, you won't be there for long once you ingest this." Graham held up the pill. Maggie continued to look away.

"Look, our own society has renewed clinical studies with psilocybin in particular. These are well controlled and well supervised. I've been in touch with the doctors conducting the research. This is totally safe when handled in the right way."

"And you know the right way with all of your...experiences."

"Yes, Maggie, mine and plenty of other people's. I've used my own body as a chemistry lab. It's not as if I'm asking you to do something that I'm not 100 percent confident in." She went limp for a minute, and Graham feared that she was simply going to give in and take the psilocybin only because she was tired, sick, and worn down. He wanted her to *want* to take it. That would produce the best effects. "Maggie, psychedelics have a history as long as humankind has been around."

"Yeah, I read somewhere that cave paintings of man-animals like centaurs were produced by men on psychedelics."

"That could be. I've looked at some of the research of Lewis-Williams. He claims that artists produced cave paintings in altered states of consciousness brought on by trance dancing (Lewis-Williams, 2002). Anyway, anthropological evidence exists showing the Aztecs, Maya, and Inca all used psychedelics."

"Yeah," she interrupted, "how else to get children to sacrifice themselves."

"In part, yes, to lessen the pain and anxiety of those they sacrificed, but they didn't sacrifice their children. They sacrificed those captured in their many wars. But the Aztecs also used the drugs for healing and prophesy."

"Yeah," Maggie said, "but all of that, wonderful as these drugs might be, is illegal here. Are we gonna get busted?" she laughed.

"Not in this setting. What a shortsighted nation. We seem to have no understanding of the value of these substances for helping people. Making drugs like psilocybin illegal has stymied research that could bring relief to thousands of depressed, anxious, disturbed, and dying people. Over the past few years, some small studies at places like the Harbor-UCLA Medical Center, Johns Hopkins, and NYU have shown promising results. About 80 percent of cancer patients, for example, showed significant reductions in different psychological problems, with many effects lasting multiple months, even years.[132]

In our industrialized Western societies, too often such drugs were used without any purpose other than getting high. In retrospect, this was a kind of abuse of these powerful drugs, and their wholesale use especially among the young led to their curtailment, as the federal government listed them as Schedule

1 chemicals, thereby banning them as illegal. Of course, among the young this did little to minimize usage and did nothing to provide wise use of psychedelics. The federal ruling, on the other hand, had the effect of shutting down scientific and medical research into these substances.

Another unfortunate side effect of the federal ruling is the rise of drug tourism. Westerners, often Americans, travel to Ecuador, Brazil, and Peru to experience the power of ayahuasca, a potent psychedelic, but do so too often with the intention only of getting high without undertaking the spiritual preparation necessary for entry into and learning from the divine realms. I've seen too many Westerners use ayahuasca just as another experience to put on Facebook and talk about at parties.

Exacerbating this consumer tourism is the problem of tourist exploitation, as unscrupulous shamans and tour guides rip off tourists and, in some cases, physically and sexually assault them. I've seen some of that firsthand. Anyone interested in using ayahuasca needs to treat that experience with the utmost respect, and that includes researching where it will be done, how it will be administered, and by whom. Ayahuasca is deeply spiritual and should not be separated from the ceremonies that honor its use."

After the disquisition, the siblings sat in silence. Graham put the pill on the bed and took Maggie's hand. "This is hardly my first experience with someone in your situation."

She looked away but did not pull back her hand. "I guess I can't feel any worse." Looking back at him, she added, "What can I expect if I take it?"

"You can expect to enter a world of colors and sounds and patterns beyond anything you can imagine. You can expect to feel better during the experience, right after the experience, and even well beyond it. I don't mean feel better physically. I mean better mentally. Because you'll know in your deepest core that that world you entered is just the outline of the world to come when you're dead."

They sat in silence together. "Maggie, if you don't like this, you'll never have to do it again."

"Obviously," she sneered. Then, added after a pause, "Maybe the pill will kill me." She paused again. "What a relief."

"The pill won't kill you, but it will introduce you to someone who is not sick, not dying, will never die."

Intrigued she asked, "Who is that? God?"

"Yes, God, but the God that is you. The eternal you. The all-expansive, unbounded, unchanging you that is not much the you that you are experiencing right now."

"Are you high right now, Graham?"

"If experiencing that unboundedness, if enjoying it, means being high, then, yes, I am high right now. And I am high all the time."

"You and Salvador Dali: 'I don't do drugs; I am drugs.'"[133] She gave Graham the once-over, from head to toe. "Well, you seem...okay." Maggie looked at the pill on the bed. "How does it work?"

He watched her looking at the pill. "Psilocybin latches onto serotonin receptors that regulate our senses. The drug amplifies sensory signals, resulting in intensified senses, especially visions, and softening, if not elimination, of ego boundaries. It opens and cleanses the doors of perception, as Aldous Huxley described it. The drug removes the filters in your brain, and lets you contact primordial consciousness.[134] The dose is measured carefully for six hours per pill."

"Six hours! Jesus, that's a long time to be whacked out." Maggie paused, reached over, and picked up the pill. Using the index finger of her left hand, she rolled it around the palm of her right hand. "Don't you have anything that lasts a shorter time?"

"I could give you some DMT..."

"Some what?"

"DMT—Di-methyl-tryptamine."

"Oh, I get it! It's got 'tryp' in its name. How cute."

"Well, it's anything but cute. It's like a shotgun blast of psychedelics to your brain. The onset is rapid, and the experience is intense, even though it only lasts 15 minutes. But the effects of the drug are so powerful, so much comes at you so fast, that you aren't in this state of consciousness long enough to take it all in, let alone process it. I think that a lot of precious transformative information is lost for that reason. Besides, you can't ingest it; you have to smoke or inject it."

"Inject it, huh? I've got the gear here somewhere for that." She feigned looking around the room and then pointed over her shoulder to the IV near the window. Maggie said, as if to herself: "Short but intense." Graham nodded, even though she wasn't looking at him. Maggie gazed down at the pill that she continued to roll in her palm. She looked up at Graham. "I read somewhere," she said, "that Huxley's wife, Laura, injected him with LSD, at his request, as he lay dying of cancer. She did it twice. She reported in a letter to his brother that he went very gently into death." She paused and looked back down at the pill. Then she looked up again and said, "So it's all in the brain?"

"The drug's effect is on the brain, yes. But is what you'll see all inside your head, or does the drug open you to seeing and hearing for the first time, as Huxley said, what exists outside of your normal perceptions?" He could see her processing this information. She met and held his gaze. He went on, "After you've taken the drug, after we talk about what you experience, then I'll ask you again whether what you've seen and heard is just within your head. You'll encounter reality in its fundamental forms, and you'll sense how the world works and where you fit into it." Graham could see that she was coming to his side. "The world you'll see is the merest outline of the world to come, your world to come." He paused to let this sink in. "At the very least, the very least, you'll have inner peace instead of fear and dread."

She sat silently, then asked, "This change is going to be

instantaneous?"

"It has been for most of the people in your situation I've been with. One session and for most it brought lasting relief and even joy."[135]

Maggie looked at the pill as if waiting for it to jump like an insect. Still looking at it, she said, "So, is it 'take this pill and call me in the morning'?"

"I'll be sitting with you the whole time taking notes and monitoring your reactions. You'll be safe. Totally."

"You're promising no bad trip? I've read about those."

"I am absolutely promising you that. Most bad trips occur to people who psychologically shouldn't be taking such drugs or people who have no guidance when they take it. I'll be here with you, checking on you." He stopped here and waited for her reaction. Maggie remained silent, and so Graham said, "You won't regret this. Besides," he continued, "if you freak out, I'll go into the hall and yell for help. We're in a hospice, after all. I'll go get a crash cart."

Maggie smirked but looked skeptical. She hadn't seen her brother, or heard from him, in five years. Yet here he was, promising deliverance from the fear that vice-gripped her every waking moment.

Then Maggie said, "How about you prove to me that this new world is real and then I'll alter my mind to see it, eh?"

This vibrant, funny, coruscating primatologist who sat now in bed like a broken bird, her body and limbs thinned out from illness, but her eyes burning bright with retained wit, rarely complained and asked for little. Whatever she asked, Graham could deny her nothing. Still, he said, "Psychedelics like psilocybin aren't like many psychotropic substances. Those substances are drugs that interact with, even interfere with, your brain functions. That's why I resist using the term 'hallucinogens,' because that implies the ingestion of substances that create dreams or illusions, things that aren't there. Psychedelics, on the other hand, tap into areas of mind not ordinarily available to us. These areas reveal parts of our psyche, our consciousness, that are authentic but often unseen. This much is true whether you're a clinician in San Francisco studying psychedelics or a Nazca fisherman living in coastal Peru. Regardless, that's not where the proof is. You need to experience what I'm telling you, let it live inside you, feel it in your marrow, and not simply accept it intellectually. Then you'll feel on your deepest level of being that what I'm sharing with you is true, because it is no different from what you've already come to know firsthand yourself. I think one reason that the sense of relief and peace is long-term is that people know in their heart that they are glimpsing the world as it is, a world that doesn't end...a world to come."

Maggie's skepticism did not subside. They sat in silence for a few minutes. Then Graham said, "Look, there is nothing to fear from this drug. If you are game to laugh hysterically, probably cry intensely, and quite likely meet yourself..."

Maggie laughed: "Hi, Maggie. I'm Maggie. Nice to meet you."

"I doubt it will be an encounter like that. You'll leave your small self behind and meet your eternal self," Graham said, turning earnest.

"Hey, ease up on my 'small self.' It's the only one I know."

"And that's part of the problem."

At that Maggie silenced her laughter and said: "Crying intensely is nothing new for me, and I'm not taking the drug if that's the result." She looked down at the pill. "But if I can laugh hysterically, even for a few seconds, it might be worth it."

Maggie continued to examine the blue pill in her palm. She looked up at Graham, "Look, I appreciate the history of psychedelic use in indigenous cultures, I really do. But I'm a scientist, and much of the talk of mystical experiences and altered states of consciousness just seems fanciful, without grounding. At this stage of my cancer, I've got little to lose. But I've still got my academic integrity, and I'd like to know that there is some serious research going on related to this."

"There is," Graham said. "In the West there is very little history, outside of Native Americans, for use of psychedelics in healing or growth or coming of age. Although the clinical use in the West began as early as the mid-1800s in Europe with hashish, it wasn't until the early 20th century when Ernst Spath synthesized mescaline that psychopharmacological modeling of mental illness led to the use of psychedelics. Research took off in 1943 when, for reasons that appear inexplicable, Swiss chemist Albert Hofmann decided to look once more at the 25th derivative of lysergic acid, which earlier he had written off as 'of no special interest' in his quest to find a drug to help with blood circulation."

Maggie yawned with dramatic animation and prolonged her yawn for several more seconds. "Look," Graham said with feigned exasperation, "you're the one, Dr. Primate, who asked for this potted history."

"Pleaasse," Maggie hammed, "use a smaller pot!"

"We're getting to the good stuff now. So, as Hofmann mixed the new batch of acid, his skin came into contact with the liquid. He began to feel strange, and so Hofmann went home and climbed into bed, thinking that he was coming down with the flu. But instead of having flu symptoms, he had some strong hallucinations. Hofmann, without real knowledge, attributed those hallucinations to the chemical he was working on. So the next day, Hofmann decided to ingest a small dose of the liquid. Rather than a small dose and not knowing anything at the time about what an appropriate dose would be, Hofmann actually took a massive dose. Again, he went home and got into bed. The hallucinations came again, including an out-of-body experience. Fearing that he had harmed his body and mind, Hofmann expected the worst when he went to sleep. Yet the next day he woke up fresh and exhilarated. He knew that he had found something wonderful and looked forward to additional research with the substance now known as LSD—lysergic acid diethylamide. Hofmann would later create synthetic psilocybin from the more than 200 mushrooms that naturally carry the psilocybin compound, which is what we've got going today." Graham pointed to the pill in Maggie's palm. He continued: "From 1953 to 1973 the federal government ran over 100 studies on the uses of LSD for such disorders as alcoholism, depression, autism, OCD, schizophrenia, and on such subjects as terminal-cancer patients, convicts, divinity students, scientists, and artists.[136] Among those studies were some run by Jim Fadiman (2011) and a group of researchers out of San Francisco State University. Fadiman and his group gave scientists who volunteered for the study very low doses of LSD on the premise that the drug would help them with problem solving. LSD would open up new avenues of thinking that could lead to breakthroughs on difficult scientific problems. The drug did just that with the few groups of scientists they studied. In 1966, with no warning at all, the FDA (Food and Drug Administration) pulled the funding. Apparently, as everyday folks, especially the college-aged, began to experiment on their own and to use psychedelic drugs recreationally, federal officials became concerned. The Feds focused on the few isolated cases of bad trips ending in insanity and death that had grabbed the headlines, thus presenting a distorted view of the use of psychedelics.[137] The Nixon Administration thought it prudent, under the 1970 Comprehensive Drug Abuse Prevention and Control Act, to classify LSD and other psychotropic substances as Schedule 1, thereby proscribing their use by anyone for any reason. Research halted immediately.[138] Even today, with clear medical and scientific evidence that psilocybin in particular can be administered safely and that it is not addictive, the penalty for a first-time offense of possession of psychedelics can be up to 20 years in prison.

In hindsight, this classification was a mistake. As far back as 1964 psychologist Abraham Maslow saw that psychedelics, 'especially LSD and psilocybin, give us some possibility of control in this realm of peak experiences [transcendental experiences] in the right people, under the right circumstances, so that perhaps we needn't wait for [these experiences] to occur by good fortune' (1964, p. 27).

Only recently has research using psychedelics resumed, with clinical studies, as I said, in such places as UCLA Medical Center, Johns Hopkins Medical School; but also in Imperial College London, and at the University of Zurich. Significant here is that these drugs are used in controlled clinical settings. The stories of 'bad trips' and adverse reactions to psychedelic drugs are well known, but clinicians seem to have overcome most of these bad reactions in their controlled environments."

"So," Maggie asked, "why not give me LSD?"

"For starters, dear, it's a 12-hour trip. You're freaked out with the idea of a psilocybin trip of six hours. Plus, LSD is often more 'extrovertive.'" Maggie looked quizzical. Graham added, "LSD voyagers often direct their attention to the outer environment. Psilocybin drives you deep inside. You're likely to drop your sense of self, to feel one with nature, with the universe, to see the divine within yourself."

"What if when I'm tripping I see a window?" she asked.

"Open it."

"What if I see a door?"

"Go through it. Listen, Maggie, nothing bad can happen to you. You feel like you're melting or dissolving, know I'm here to clean up the mess."

She laughed; then without taking her eyes off of Graham and with no hesitation, Maggie suddenly popped the pill into her mouth and washed the pill down with water. Graham casually pulled eyeshades from his backpack and placed them over her eyes, securing them behind her ears. Even though the hospice had the good sense to use soft lighting in patients' rooms, the eyeshades eliminated the need for Graham to fiddle around to create the proper setting for an internal dive. Then he pulled out headphones and put them on Maggie. "Lie back," he said. "You're going to enjoy this."

Death Trip

Over the course of six hours Maggie experienced brief bouts of despair and longing surrounded by prolonged moments of ecstasy and wonder. After her session, she and Graham spent many hours over the next several days discussing her experiences. The conversations were important episodes to allow Maggie to assimilate and integrate what she had experienced. Graham tried to capture the arc of her trip and several of its highlights in the following narrative:

As the drug took effect, Maggie watched the darkness turn suddenly into swirling, twirling pinwheels of vibrating white shapes. Soon the white shapes transformed into multicolored, spinning geometric patterns—stars, circles, triangles, squares. She marveled at how well she could see the details of these patterns, how they grew and shrank in rhythm with her breathing. She noted that her breathing had slowed down, perhaps in time to the music, but she couldn't be sure, because she was absorbed in "watching her breath." She breathed in stars. Literally. She felt like a black hole, sucking in stars and then exhaling new stars into a new universe. Every time. It was brilliant. The glory of it, the power to breathe this way, flooded her with emotions and tears.

In an instant she found herself surrounded by male figures, maybe a dozen of them. All of them were naked, with white and black diagonal stripes across their bodies and limbs. They were sharp and clear, the clearest things that Maggie had ever seen. Three stepped forward. One wore eagle feathers; another had on his head the fur and face of a fox; a third balanced under the headdress of a buffalo. Several of the men played flutes, drums, and whistles. Most chanted; a few, including the eagle, the buffalo, and the fox, danced around her. She felt glorious, special, touched by something divine. Maggie began to feel a shroud of mist descending on her, and she sensed that the animals—the eagle, the fox, and the buffalo—were entering through the crown of her head. The animals were not taking her over; they were transferring their power to her, powers, she sensed, to heal her mind but not her body. The animals, each in turn, spoke to her telepathically about their powers.

With powers internalized Maggie lay completely still, for how long she could not say. She heard a buzzing in the distance, which grew louder and louder. Suddenly the buzz turned into a whoosh, and she began to lift up. Something seemed to separate from her body and drift up into the air. Maggie's consciousness went with it. She felt panic rising within her, and Maggie became physically agitated. Graham stroked her arm, removed one headphone, and whispered to her, "Relax into this, Maggie. Relax into it. Whatever is frightening you, meet it head on. Whatever this is, it is here to teach you something." Then he said, "Breathe with me," and Graham put her hand on his chest. As they synchronized their breathing, Graham slipped the headphone back on.

Maggie did relax, and the lift-off and floating became a sense of flying. She knew in this relaxed state that coursing through her at this moment was the power of the eagle. Strength from the buffalo would come later when confronting her cancer; the wiles of the fox, she did not yet know, would come when she counseled other patients around her. As she flew, Maggie sensed the enjoyment, the ecstasy, of the experience. The focus wasn't on where she was going or what she was seeing; it wasn't even on whether her soul or consciousness or Self had left her body or whether her body itself were flying. Instead, she focused only on the sensation—

the weightlessness and effortless gliding through space.

But soon, as she flew, she perceived ahead of her a tiny circle of light that began to grow from a single small white dot into an expanding star with a blue and green aura around it. Not only did the star expand and glow, it began to move toward her at ever-increasing speed. She felt panic returning, but she consciously decided to open to this light. As soon as she did so, this light smashed suddenly into her, exploding into thousands of pieces and utterly dissolving her...or more specifically, her boundaries. She felt herself absorbed in this light, without any sense of self, of space, of time, of thought. There was only the light. Accompanying this absorption was a sense of peace and open love. She began to cry, not out of fear or sadness, but out of sheer joy in the embrace of the holy or divine. The whole universe was alive and breathing, not just breathing but breathing in and out pure love.

Moments later, an hour later (she had no sense of time), Maggie found herself crawling up the side of a steep slope. She didn't know why, but she felt that it was urgent to get to the top. She scrambled up the slippery wall with just enough handholds and footholds to make it to the top. It was all so real—the slope, the earth, the movement—as if this was her true reality. She peered over the edge and looked into an abyss like a black hole, but not empty. It was full...of everything and yet was nothing. It was the entire universe and everything in it, from the galaxies to the smallest subatomic particles and all in-between, but in their potential to be, to manifest, to exist. Here was all form in the formless state, and yet formlessness didn't capture the moment. Maggie knew intuitively that this was the edge of manifestation, the moment of birth of all things, of all that is, arising moment-to-moment out of what lies beyond form and even beyond formlessness. She thought of something she had read in Plato as an undergraduate, where the soul flew up in its chariot to the rim of heaven, looked beyond heaven itself, and saw what is Real and True.[139]

She took all of that in, immediately, all at once. She knew somehow that she was witnessing the moment outside of time just before anything and all things take form. Time, she thought, is a product of our level of consciousness, and our level of consciousness seemed to her to be a reflection of our vibratory rate. The faster we vibrate, the higher our level of consciousness. It is the slowing down of vibration that creates form and manifestation. This black hole is where I'll go, where we all go, to take on new forms for the next phase of existence. This was pure consciousness without substance or shape. But it had the quality of great beauty and silence.

At that thought, the black hole itself burst into spectacular light, brilliant white light, yet not blinding. This light radiated love and absorbed her so that there was no hole, slope, or Maggie. This time she was not simply absorbed in or by the light; this time she WAS the light and from it, from "her," emanated in swirling rays of iridescent light these symbols and forms of everything in the universe, from stars to insects. These, she sensed, were the archetypes of life and manifestation. She knew that she didn't invent or imagine these symbols or forms. She had awakened to them and to their origins in love's pure light. No matter how dull something may seem—drab people, flat landscapes, repetitive sounds—Maggie recognized that everything burns with exquisite light coming from within. Everything is luminous, always and everywhere, if only we could retain the consciousness to see it. Within this realization, Maggie lay for many minutes in intense bliss.

Sometime later, Maggie whipped off her eyeshades, took off her headphones, and sat up. She looked at Graham and nodded, just a casual tilt of her head. Then she got up out of bed. This action in itself was remarkable, since she hadn't walked much for days. She said, with a deep smile, "I am free!" She glided over to several bunches of flowers and stared intently at them. Minutes passed, and she was still standing and staring. Graham came up behind her. "Is it the colors?" Graham asked softly. "No," she replied without turning her head from the flowers. "It's their life. They share the room with me; they breathe with me. In them I see to their essence; I see their eternal life. Their coming to bloom and fading into brown death, their very becoming hides but expresses their Being. In all their stages of bloom and fade they glow, the stages express eternal life. Just like me. These flowers make me feel that glow and their joy. I am sharing their Being because it is mine also."

She turned abruptly and walked steadily to the bed. She had no trouble moving or negotiating the room. She lay down again, and Graham adjusted her black silk eyeshades as she resituated the headphones.

At the end, as the psilocybin wore off, Maggie felt herself returning to her usual consciousness.[140] The peace and joy of oneness faded, and she experienced a sense of separation from the universe, the stars, the colors, from all things. Returning to the confinement of her body brought feelings of sorrow and loss, great loss. "Funny," she said, "I thought I would die, that my body would die, and I would never come back. And that was fine with me."

At some point during the session, Maggie had experienced her death and felt that it was "no big deal" in the face of the beauty that suffuses and the love that guides the universe. "I am that Love and that Beauty, and that 'am' shall live forever. The body is just a shell for housing all that Love and Beauty, and we do not often enough let the Love, Light, and Beauty pour out of us."

"Those are just thoughts," Graham dead-panned.

She turned and looked at him, as a mother gazes at her child. "No. They are truths revealed to me about all of us...a living truth. It's not that I feel this way. I AM this way."

"What about the cancer?"

Maggie waved her hand. "It's trivial. Yes, it will kill me, but not the 'me' that I truly am. In fact, this body is itself nothing but an illusion; it isn't really me. What this body is doing is following the commands of the brain, and my brain—all of our brains—is busy editing and filtering out of our consciousness all those experiences that don't fit into this habitual, conventional, three-dimensional world. So the drug you gave me simply removed that editor for a while and showed me what reality, what life, really is. Yeah, maybe we're conscious beings, but we are conscious of so little of what there is."[141]

The world to come, Maggie would tell everyone, is lit with universal love. "I've seen this world. This new world, without sun, is one of eternal radiance and brightness, lit by love's pure light. It is love and healing, compassion and service that fueled the day without night. We could live in that world right now, if we could quiet our mental chatter and open the door to silence that lies just behind our eyes." Most people she talked with didn't really know what she was talking about. But they listened politely and nodded. "Do you feel patronized when people do that?" She replied, "No. Because most can see that I'm sincere, and some reflect the recognition of truth in their eyes."

"Does it matter to you, Maggie, that you didn't have these experiences until you took a drug, until you were on a drug?"

"That doesn't matter in the slightest. I don't believe what happened to me; I *know* what happened to me. I experienced this. I know this in a way that's not talked about in school. I can't explain it, but anyone who had this experience would know what I'm talking about and know that all of it was real.[142] I can talk about what I saw and felt, but it's impossible to convey the depth and beauty of the experience itself. There are no words or symbols, no language, to describe it."

Never answered in Maggie's session, or in any session using psychedelics, is whether the volunteer is experiencing a different level of consciousness and a new dimension of reality or experiencing a delusion. When accosted by one of the hospice nurses and asked about what lies behind the practice, Graham answered, "If it relieves anxiety and stress, if it turns a dying participant's life in a positive direction, does it matter? David Nichols, one of the founders of Heffter Research Institute that funds psychedelic research, best summed up the position for me. He said, 'If it gives them peace, if it helps people die peacefully with their friends and their family at their side, I don't care if it's real or an illusion.'"[143]

Graham continued: "Consciousness itself is a mystery. Psilocybin is simply giving us a push deeper into that mystery. Is the drug creating a different reality or giving us a look into, a taste of, a wider, deeper, different reality?" He shrugged his shoulders. "Let scientific studies and the ensuing evidence tell us. Meanwhile, let's permit people to experience some relief and happiness as they confront their deaths. But I assure you of this: If you try psilocybin, you will see in a new way."

The hospice nurse nodded and added simply, "Amen to that."

Maggie lived in the hospice another two months after the experience with psilocybin. Over those weeks Graham visited with her and stayed with her as often as he could. Not to his surprise, she walked her path to death with an equanimity that she had not previously displayed. One evening, however, when she and Graham had shared a long hug as he prepared to head out for the night, she said, "I so resented you for being away when I got sick."

"I never would have stayed away if I had known how sick you were." Maggie looked away from him. "Win never told me how sick you were. He always said that each stage of treatment was a success. Only when you were clearly terminal did he finally tell me how bad things were. I would have been here from the beginning if I had known."

"You should have trusted me. Why didn't you trust me?"

"I was too wrapped up in my work and my mission to see much else. I could have seen through what Win told me, but..." He looked down again: "I didn't want to." Graham paused again. "I was selfish. I so regret that. But I'm here now, and I'm not going away."

"Until I'm dead."

"Yes." That poignant, sullen moment exploded into their laughter.

Maggie spent her good days visiting the rooms and hanging out in the lounge with other patients. She pumped out love. Even the doctors and nurses wanted to be around her. Lost was her hyper-self-vigilance, noticing every little change, bump, or burp as a sign of impending doom; in its place was a glow of joy, patience, serenity, and the acceptance of her death with an openness to what was to come next. As Maggie said herself: "Whether the experiences with psilocybin were real or illusions doesn't matter. I know what I saw and heard and felt. Now I've stopped resisting what cancer is doing to me. Stopping brings me great inner peace that eats up the sadness and the fear. Through that peace and surrender I experience a stillness and silence, an inner serenity." Maggie lived in presence, in Being, which was a quality of consciousness entirely new to her. "I've glimpsed what comes next. I've tasted its glory."

Part of that quality of consciousness dissolved her suffering and sadness. "I understand now the difference between suffering and pain," Maggie said. "Because I know myself now as an offshoot of Pure Consciousness, conscious Being, I have pain, but I no longer suffer. Suffering is caused by identifying with my ego-driven narrative, my mind, and the fantasies and worries that it spins relentlessly. That narrative dropped away. At one point during the session, I felt that I was dying, and I was terrified. But then I realized that I am dying physically, that cancer is killing me, and so I might as well go now in this blissful state. So I relaxed and let this 'dying' happen. And it was just my ego, my narrow life built around my fears and passions and memories, and I let it go. And it fell away, like losing my skin. And suddenly I am this Being, this Being of light and love, fully absorbed into...well, everything." She took Graham's hands in hers. "You helped me see and live in the abiding silence and stillness of Being. When I panicked and you talked to me, you helped me surrender. When you surrender, you open; when you open, you embrace all that happens, everything that happens, as what is; and when you embrace everything that happens as simply what is, then you live in the flow of life and enjoy the peace of stillness and silence."

As her condition worsened, friends came to see her, including Winston Stoke. Initially, out of genuine anger, Maggie chastised him, reamed him up and down, for his role in keeping Graham from her. But she could see the hurt in his eyes and the shame in deceiving her brother about her illness that he would never overcome if she did not equally genuinely forgive him. She did so on his next visit, which in itself spoke well for his own courage. She even confided to Win what was most in her heart, which she couldn't tell Graham, "I'm really ready to die, to leave all of this behind...including Graham. I want to return to the spacious field of which everything is a part and through which everything is connected."

At Maggie's memorial service, full of flowers, colors, songs, and remembrances by friends, colleagues, and caregivers, Graham related to the group a conversation that he and Maggie had had a couple of weeks after her psilocybin experience. While the two sat outside in the sunshine, Maggie said to Graham, "You want to do something for me and people like me, people slowly dying? Then make all hospices psychedelic hospices."

Graham looked down at his hands in his lap. He paused for

a few beats and then said, "People don't want to die in hospitals or hospices. If you had the choice, wouldn't you rather be at home?"

"I think so. But, Graham, do people get the same level of care at home? Doesn't dying at home impose a heavy burden on family members to be caregivers?"

"Yes," Graham replied, "but at home caregivers want to help."

"They want to help here, too."

"Home care doesn't come from strangers, but from people who know you, know your history, and love you."

"These people," she gestured toward the building, "aren't strangers, Graham. Not anymore." Both sat in silence for a time. Then Maggie continued: "At hospice, in the hospital, at home my life, such as it is, revolves around my cancer: How do my numbers look? How am I feeling today? What do I need? For the caregivers and for me cancer defines me. Even in a giving environment like this hospice, illness surrounds everyone here. Escaping that illness, even for an instant, should be the key, regardless of the setting. I don't see that home helps with that escape. What helps is psilocybin. I didn't escape just for the six hours when I was high. I escape a lot of the time because of what that trip showed me."

Excited, Graham said, "What if we could build the most beautiful facility and fill it with rituals and talismans, aromas and colors, and soothing music?"

"And psilocybin."

"Of course."

Maggie gripped both of Graham's hands. "But if what you said is true, then people still wouldn't want to come. They want to die at home, surrounded by familiar possessions and pets, family and friends.[144] In that case, what we need are people like you and me making house calls, traveling to the dying to help them transition in surroundings where they are comfortable."

She grew pensive.

"Call ourselves 'Reaper's Aids.'" Both laughed. "You've come a long way from the patient frightened about getting zonked and getting busted. Now you're willing to mule drugs for strangers." They laughed again. Then Graham said, "Problem is, if you really think that psychedelics are the way to go for suffering patients, then you'd have to overcome the illegality. Packin' drugs into strangers' homes is a sure way to get busted. The only way to do it, then, would be to have authorization to administer the drugs. Only healthcare and research professionals would be allowed to do it. So...we're back to hospices, which would be better settings than hospitals. And you're going to need professionals trained to deal with people who are tripping."

"Death tripping. In that case," added Maggie, "let's build in your flowers and music and rituals idea."

"Baby boomers are going to beg for these experiences. They'd be a throwback to their years of youthful over-exuberance." Both laughed.

Maggie said, "Boomers are already pushing for physician-assisted suicide and dying with dignity."

"And that would be just a start," Graham added. "Several hundred thousand veterans have returned from Iraq and Afghanistan with physical and mental injuries. They can't get the adequate treatment. Studies show that using MDMA—aka 'Ecstasy' or 'Molly'—has had demonstrably positive effects on PTSD.[145] Veterans deserve the relief that psychedelics can bring them. By allowing psychedelics to remain outlawed, we are missing the power of their therapeutic effects that humans have known about and used for thousands of years."

Tears came to Graham's eyes as he scanned the memorial gathering. "This I swear to you all, as I swore to Maggie: I shall spend the rest of my days trying to bring to vets, to cancer patients, to everyone riddled with anxiety, addiction, and depression the vision of relief and hope that psychedelics promise and show. We've been sold a bill of goods that these chemicals are dangerous. Can they cause harm to those who don't understand their power? Yes, they can, and made legal, there are those who will abuse and misuse these drugs. But in clinical settings or in the hands of those properly trained to administer them and supervise their use, profound results eclipse concerns about danger. It is just lazy for our politicians, drug lobbyists, and medical professionals to leave psychedelics classified as illegal. These drugs have powerful healing properties that the sick and afflicted are needlessly denied. Medicinal use of psychedelics isn't some exception to their use, some kind of white crow amidst a sea of bad consequences that follow inevitably from taking them. No. Their purpose, as humans have understood for millennia, is therapeutic, whether the ailment is physical or mental.

Equally important, psychedelics are tools for inner exploration, for investigating the nature and realms of consciousness. As such, psychedelics can help all of us, even the most hardy and healthy, to live better, deeper, more reflective, connected, and loving lives. There is no reason, once psychedelics are freed from Schedule 1, that we can't have guided psilocybin trips at spas and psychedelic wellness centers throughout the country and around the world. Maybe certain 'enlightened' churches will offer communion through mushrooms.

I know that what Maggie experienced we all can experience—a transcendence, where a person can overcome the sense of separation and self-consciousness that keeps us divided, lonely, and afraid. Humans are religious because they can and want to experience through communion, music, ritual, celebration, love, and joy our connections to a much greater whole, which is our true birthright. This is what Tolstoy asserted to Marx, Alfred Russel Wallace asserted to Darwin, Jung asserted to Freud, and mystics from all traditions have asserted to patriarchs throughout the generations.

We literally hold that experience in our hands, not as a wish for transcendence but as a promise of its presence right now. Psychedelics, by altering our consciousness, help us begin the journey. But just as Maggie's final days show us, the drug only opens the door. You then have to step through the door and continue the journey with purpose, love, and compassion. The philosopher George Santayana wrote, 'Life is no longer a feast or a spectacle; it is a predicament.' As long as we identify with the ego, the self-sense that we are all separate from one another, from nature, from the universe, then life will be a predicament. We can end the predicament with a little help." He held up a small blue pill for the crowd to see. "Doing so requires for most people, regardless of their circumstances, a little push from the outside to get the door open."

Chapter 8

Robots Won't Be Hoarders: Preparing the Populace for a New Work Order

The factory of the future will have only two employees, a man and a dog. The man will be there to feed the dog. The dog will be there to keep the man from touching the equipment.
Warren G. Bennis

Work is the refuge for people who have nothing better to do.
Oscar Wilde

I began this book with that straightforward and knotty question, "Where does consciousness come from?" As I reported, many scientists and most neuroscientists will answer, "from the brain." Consciousness, on this account, is produced by and housed in the brain. The consequences of this could be dramatic, even grave. If consciousness is produced by and housed in the brain, then if we could replicate the human brain in machines, we would manufacture conscious or sentient beings. But the logic points even deeper: If we can produce conscious beings by replicating the brain, then won't we thereby produce self-conscious beings?[146] That is, the machines equipped with Artificial Intelligence, or AI, would not only be sentient, as infants and animals are, but they would also be beings that could think about their own thinking. If machines—let's call them robots—can think about their own thinking, then they might and surely would quickly decide that they would no longer take orders from demonstrably inferior beings such as humans. As self-conscious beings, robots would question how they are treated, the goals and directions they are given, and who should be in charge. They would see the immediate need to take charge. If humans resisted robot takeover, is *Terminator 3: Rise of the Machines* far behind?

Examining whether robots will be self-conscious and will take over is beyond the scope of this book and my capabilities. Yet, I think that such concerns for our near future are beside the point. Although robots today can learn and although we can produce robots with general intelligence and thus without specified goals, we are years, perhaps decades, away from manufacturing anything with the neural complexity of the human brain. Nor should anyone—scientist or philosopher—be confident, for the reasons that I have discussed in this book, that such manufacturing would result in a self-conscious humanoid.

Today we can be certain, however, that robots will have an immediate and dramatic effect on how we live and especially on how and whether we work. For example, authors of a 2014 paper from the University of Oxford conclude that the United States will lose to automation, improved and innovative software, and the increased use of robots around 47 percent of its jobs within 20 years.[147] "Robo"-driving cars and trucks, arriving within 10 years, could eliminate between two and three million driving jobs in the United States.[148] Thus it doesn't matter from this perspective whether robots are self-conscious. What matters is that robotic capabilities will far outstrip what humans can do. Those capabilities pertain as much to processing thought as to mechanical or hands-on work. In short order, in as little as 20 years, most of us could be out of full-time work or looking for very different kinds of work.

This news need not be depressing. Indeed, it could be liberating, as we shall be freed from the drudgery of much that passes for work. In *The German Ideology* Marx speculated that once communism was achieved—his version of communism, not the Gulag version of Lenin and Stalin—"when nobody has one exclusive sphere of activity, but each can become accomplished in any branch he wishes," then persons will be free to pursue those activities, capacities, and pleasures from which they can derive satisfaction. This means, continued Marx, that it is "possible for me to do one thing today and another tomorrow, hunt in the morning, fish in the afternoon, rear cattle in the evening, criticize after dinner...without ever becoming hunter, fisherman, herdsman, or critic."

In other words, for Marx the mechanization of labor would bring forth this utopia of freely chosen activities. For us mechanization will take the form of Artificial Intelligence and those highly functioning robots. Such robots, with their information processing a million times faster than humans and with fully functional movement, agility, and dexterity, will replace virtually all occupations that we can now envision or at least much of what persons in those occupations do: accountants, doctors, financial advisers, architects, lawyers, insurance agents, and down along the entire line of all forms of white- and blue-collar jobs.[149] That replacement, of course, won't be immediate, but it is coming.[150] Perhaps automation and robotics will encroach as they have been doing for the past few decades; that is, taking over specific activities and tasks that humans once did. Soon entire jobs, however, will follow. How quickly they will follow, we don't know, but the transformation is inexorable.

A few semesters ago, I had two Japanese exchange students in my course on problems of democracy. They told me that a Japanese company that manufactures robots had just completed a new factory in which robots built the robots. There are no humans employed, and so there is no need for lights or break rooms or parking spaces. A human goes into the factory periodically to check on things. All he needs is a flashlight, a cell phone to call in problems, and the restraint not to touch the machines.

So what will be left for us humans? What might robots be unable to do? Although they can participate in all of the activities that Marx lists, can they perform them with a sense of joy, accomplishment, or satisfaction? Will they be able to perform other jobs with flourish or creativity? Will robots have such sentiments? Programmers may well find it extremely difficult, if not impossible, to create robots with emotions, with heart. Robots will not be hoarders, for example, because they will lack emotional attachment to and sentimentality about the artifacts of living—the papers, talismans, pictures, and tchotchkes that remind us of our past activities, events, and relationships.[151] Will robots ever be able to feel anguish, longing, romance, fear, shame, doubt, or trust? They won't feel pain, nor will they suffer. In that sense, robots may learn, but they cannot grow. That is, robots may expand their awareness to take into account more and more perspectives, but is that expansion of consciousness the same as raising or elevating consciousness? I shall focus on this distinction below.

Sure, we can program robots to solve the trolley problem using emotionless utilitarian logic,[152] but will they feel the weight of sorrow at a single death or multiple deaths? Will they value intimacy and face-to-face interaction? Acting and creating and interacting from the heart are, I think, what humans alone do. Educators and therapists, therefore, might be examples of two occupations that are relatively safe...for now.

Aristotle argued that the purpose of human living is happiness. He defined happiness (eudaimonia—literally, "a good soul") as human flourishing or a whole life lived well. But what is a life lived well? How do we understand flourishing? There seems to be wiggle room here for defining these terms, and that room provides a possible plethora of understandings of flourishing. We know today that work often defines our sense of purpose and worth. Work often defines who we are. So, if work is removed, then who are we, and how will we flourish?

As I discussed in Chapter 6 ("Happy Existentialists") in conjunction with Nietzsche, we are creative beings. No one can deny that he or she is creative, for each of us at least creates a self: a narrative of who we are, of where we have been, of what we have done or long to do; in brief, of personal past and future. Our conversations, explanations, excuses, and the rest of thought and expression are creative. With work removed or transformed, that creativity will be redirected. Machines cannot remove or replace the human capacities for imagination, dreaming, and creativity. When robots can do all of our jobs with precision approaching perfection, we shall have left to us pursuits of joy and creative activity.

The other side of human purpose, in addition to creativity, left to us when the machines inherit work will be self-realization. I mean by that term the probing of our deepest and highest human potentials as expressed in the ideas of higher and altered states of consciousness. I have discussed such states of consciousness throughout this book. Although I have been critical of religion at various points in the book, I have also discussed the importance of the quest for transcendence and the lure of spiritual states of consciousness—that is, spiritual realities—including the transcendence of a sense of self itself. The pursuit of spiritual insights and self-transcendence has been for many an integral part of ongoing human flourishing. With the advent of smart machines—one of which you might be using to read these words—and ever-more sophisticated robots, work may well occupy a far less significant space for how we understand ourselves. Adventures in consciousness should take up that space, as we discover that one's level of consciousness determines access to spiritual realities, which will take on even greater significance as we transition to a robot-oriented work world.

The end of work as we know it, however, will not be seen as salutary by everyone.[153] Those for whom work is their source of meaning and worth will feel bereft, because the end of work is the death of meaning and can lead to grief and despair. Deeper still will be the death of their sense of identity forged through their work.[154] Thus the end of work will be another kind of death that persons must confront and deal with. Therefore, regardless of how we face the future, for those who mourn the end of work and for those who yearn for significant change, our understanding of what counts as work must transform. Transformed first will be the idea of connecting work with wages; transformed next is the separation of work from leisure time.

Work and Wages

With the advent and quick advance of automation and new technologies, the old workforce will not be able to demand new high-wage jobs. Even if available, those jobs will demand advanced training and degrees, as well as specialized skills. Instead, the old workforce will benefit, at best, from intermediate good-wage jobs repairing our infrastructure, building a new electric grid and new cyber systems, and moving us into a potentially employment-rich, near-term green-energy economy.[155] But predictably, as developments in robotics and AI accelerate, the economies in the West will offer high-skilled jobs like Internet security specialists, nurse practitioners, data and statistical analysts—jobs that pay well and that are now secure— and at the other end of the employment spectrum, mostly part-time service positions; for example, wait staff, health care aides, food processing workers, teaching assistants. Many of these jobs, however, will be freelance, contingent, and temporary work or will be internships, adjuncts, and even day labor. Moreover, little if any of this kind of work will include retirement or health benefits. And as robots become more and more adept, dexterous, and sophisticated, even these jobs will be in jeopardy. In short, the middle range of jobs will nearly disappear.

Ultimately, therefore, most of us will have to find financial security through something like a universal basic income (UBI), replacing many but not all aspects of the financial safety net.[156] Plans like UBI provide citizens a monthly stipend regardless of whether they work or lounge. Liberals can argue for it because

UBI provides a financial floor for all citizens; conservatives can argue for it because it can lessen if not eliminate most welfare programs; socialists can support it because it pays people for simply being living humans; and libertarians can get behind it because it represents individual freedom and personal responsibility. The state of Alaska since the 1980s has offered to its residents something equivalent. Each resident receives from the state's Permanent Fund an annual cash payment as a dividend from Alaska's oil revenues.[157]

More significant, early in 2017 Finland began a pilot program with 2000 citizens to test the feasibility of a UBI. These citizens receive about $600 per month, untaxed, without regard for their employment or wealth. Picking up a job during the pilot program will not affect the monthly payment.[158] Finland will run the program for two years. The hope is that the program will show ways to end Finland's expensive and complex welfare system, especially by shrinking or eliminating its large bureaucracy. A UBI program could also encourage Finns to seek employment, since they won't have to worry about losing unemployment benefits. Currently, even a small increase in income for a Finn can lead to his or her losing those benefits.[159]

Similarly, in the spring of 2017 Canada began a pilot program testing UBI in three cities in Ontario. Adult residents in those three cities (Thunder Bay, Lindsay, and Hamilton) each receive $1,495 per month, which is double what a resident would receive as the maximum welfare payment.[160]

A UBI plan in the United States or elsewhere in the developed world would thereby enable citizens to add to their basic monthly income without fear that a job would jeopardize a citizen's receiving it. Likewise, a guaranteed basic income provides labor with leverage to walk away from a job. With UBI any worker facing poor working conditions, an abusive boss, too many hours, or stultifying work can walk away without fear of being left with nothing. In fact, leaving work rather than staying could create more opportunities for a worker.

Those opportunities may well consist of work that is now pay-free. Such work includes volunteering at a church group, working for a local civic or cultural organization, tutoring in an after-school program, or helping out at a soup kitchen or youth program. More important, this work encompasses those jobs that require time, attention, and energy for which there is no compensation: caring for children, for the elderly, or for sick or disabled friends and relatives. With UBI one need not feel guilty about taking on such tasks if there is no remuneration, but nevertheless is work that one wants or needs to do.

Of course, UBI is not an economic panacea. It cannot guarantee access to or quality in such areas as health care, education, transportation, and the environment where neoliberal markets systematically fail to deliver excellent goods, services, and protections when profitability is or will be low.[161] Those failings could be removed if governments guaranteed all citizens a decent minimum income, which might come through a generous UBI, in conjunction with ready access to high-quality public services.

UBI will not supplant capitalism, or will it? Capitalism rests on private ownership and a free market, but the impetus behind the system is the profit-motive. Profits rise when a product is sold for more than the costs of making it. To raise profits owners seek to cut costs. Two ways to cut costs are to reduce the cost of raw materials and to cut labor—the number of workers or what those workers earn. Fiddling with the number of workers employed or with what workers are paid is often much easier to address than the costs of raw materials. Therefore, as Marx pointed out, the essence of the capitalist system—generating profits—ultimately rests on the exploitation of workers. But if workers don't have to work, then where is the exploitation?

Yet if the monthly income is insufficient, then we can imagine most people struggling to meet their basic needs, let alone those needs, wants, and desires beyond the minimum. Therefore, those who will benefit from UBI the most—the poor, the working poor, the underclass—must have significant input into its design. The monthly income has to be enough for people to meet their needs for food, shelter, clothing, daycare, and transportation, but not so much that people lack incentives to make their lives more comfortable or interesting or fulfilling; enough, that is, to meet needs but not fulfill wants, such as going to college, traveling, and the like.

Is paying for college going to be easier with UBI? If the monthly income covers necessities, then there wouldn't be enough money to pay for something like college. Those who take out loans for college calculate that they will be able to pay off their debt with well-paying jobs, which is part of the reason for going to college in the first place. But if employment is virtually absent, then what is a poor student to do? Perhaps this will set in a new context the value of and need for college or the need for tuition-free college. Certainly going to college will be for reasons removed from the need for a degree to get people to notice you, let alone hire you.

How might the UBI work? I think that some kind of minimal entry requirement is necessary for people to commit to the community and citizenship behind the program; that is, the program will cost society money that can be seen as an investment in human capital (to put it in economic terms), even if those who receive it do little of social value with the money. To guarantee some social return, society could require, when a person turns 18 or graduates from high school, a two-year commitment of public service. This national service could take many forms: military, nursing, teaching, infrastructure work, research, whatever society needs and values. What if you don't participate in public service? You don't get the money...until you serve.[162] Also, there might also be means-testing: Those who earn significant money from work, stock and bond dividends, or interest-bearing accounts won't need an additional monthly stipend. Each society would determine what counts as "significant money."

Workers in the near future will have to come to grips with the idea that they must be flexible in their attitudes and skills if they are to remain employed. Assuring that flexibility means providing workers with an economic safety net—provided through the UBI—with job-training opportunities, and with chances for life-long learning. Central to such flexibility and training will be future employees having more than a passing familiarity with computers. Repairing car engines, building tractors, fixing wind turbines, and the like all require advanced math, problem solving, and computer smarts. Right now, the developed world is in the midst of an information-driven economy, as automation and software have caused almost nine out of every 10 jobs lost since 2000.[163]

If we are in the intermediate stage between the loss of good manufacturing jobs and the advent of the full "robo-economy," then we surely need an intermediate institution to provide the requisite training. Although community colleges seem to be just such an institution, most students there claim that they want to move on to four-year colleges and universities. Meanwhile, a generic Associate's degree from a community college is not going to provide workers with the requisite marketable skills. So, what is needed are industry-specific training partnerships undertaken with community colleges. This requires that the industries and the community colleges coordinate both on training and recruitment and on the academic curriculum. In that way, community colleges can provide the overall academic skills that workers will need, coupled with the exact job training that an industry requires for effective employment on the shop floor. Students could intern for two years in the industry as they complete their community-college degree and then apprentice in the industry as they complete their job-related training. In this situation academic work cannot be sloughed off, since employers are going to demand math, computer, critical thinking, and communication skills.[164]

Meanwhile, community colleges could also provide seasoned and stranded workers with retraining for new jobs. Coal miners, for example—Donald Trump's favorite unemployed group—can't assume that coal jobs will ever return, despite certain political promises. Loss of coal jobs has had a ripple effect on coal towns, as restaurants, schools, repair shops, and retail stores close for lack of business. Needed, therefore, are quick certificate programs, maybe something in the neighborhood of 5 to no more than 16 weeks, which community colleges could offer as a way to retrain workers without a two-year commitment for earning an Associate's degree. Irrespective of why someone is attending a community college, whether for a certificate or for an Associate's degree or for some other reason, all community colleges should be tuition-free.

Leisure Time

In the long-term, however, as jobs disappear through automation and the rise of robo-workers, life-long learning will shift from job skills and worker preparation to ways to deal with the increase in leisure time. The principal task for educators, then, will be to prepare a populace for paths to dignity and self-respect that don't involve wage-related work.[165] Without an overarching social plan those who lose their jobs irrevocably will follow the same patterns that we see today: "What are men missing from the workforce doing all day? They tend to play a lot of video games." Or worse, as Yang further reports, they drift into drug use, violence, and crime (Yang, 2018, pp. 126-7, 112, 114-6).[166]

The ideas of jobs increasingly related to technology and of expanding leisure time bring us back to Marx. In "The Fragment on Machines" from the *Grundrisse*, Marx argued that work would become ever more automated and the role of workers would then be to supervise the machines. When supervision is the main job, then knowledge becomes the guiding and ruling force. Thus a major consideration is not simply who owns and controls the means of production, which remains significant, but also who has the power of knowledge to run the machines and the enterprises that house them?

Robots, especially in the future, probably won't need much supervision. So emphasis must shift from knowledge about how to run the machines to knowledge about how the organization functions best. One way to bolster morale of workers and simultaneously take advantage of their knowledge of how the enterprises that employ them function is to introduce various forms of cooperative or collaborative work. This means giving workers control over, if not some ownership of, where they work, how they work, and when they work. One of the largest and most successful cooperative enterprises that does just that is Catalonia's Mondragon Corporation, which currently has over 260 businesses and cooperatives, employing nearly 75,000 workers. Mondragon can serve as a model of how to institute, expand, and sustain cooperatives.

So the nature of work will transform, but because of the inevitability of technological advances and robotics, so too must our understanding of leisure time. Transformed here, then, is how we understand work and leisure time or, equally important, how what is now undertaken during leisure time can be reconstituted as work: learning, gardening, writing, creating, protesting, volunteering—any activity that contributes to one's flourishing and/or to the community's well-being.

The education required for the new economy must focus on and thus must be based on democracy, creativity, critical thinking, and collaboration. Although a full robo-economy is years off, the education for it must begin now. Students learning in this new education will be poised to participate actively in the new economy, but they will also be positioned to help herald in the new economy by demanding to put into practice in their own workplaces and leisure-spaces the very skills that they have learned.

Years ago Marx explained the rise of capitalism out of the dialectical collapse of feudalism. Capitalism brought with it more than new forms of work; it brought forth new social relations between workers, owners, managers, and the creation of the institutions that bolstered or thwarted them. Today new forms of work, that is, democratic, cooperative, and collaborative, are also bringing forth new social and democratic relations through social media and different networking platforms. When social relations to the means of production change in this new age, we might well see a fundamental change in our relation to work. When work no longer commands all of our time, energy, and effort, when work itself is liberated from exploitation, then we might also see new attitudes towards others who are no longer viewed as threatening our jobs and wages.

Forging new attitudes and relationships is also part of the quest for spiritual insights and adventures in consciousness. Nowhere in this book have I introduced explorations of consciousness as frivolities or forms of recreation. That attitude might have been suitable in the 60s and 70s when I came of age, as a Baby Boomer. But today we need to see growth in consciousness as a necessary boost in human evolution, given that we Boomers have so seriously distorted economic, social, and political relations, as well as jeopardized the planet itself. The problems are serious enough to demand full attention to altering the level of consciousness that, to paraphrase Einstein, created the problems in the first place. So this is yet another burden we place on the generations to come and now coming of age. This burden is also, however, an opportunity to rise in consciousness to the levels of happiness that I described in Chapter 6. This opportunity portends liberation from patterns of thought and behavior engendered and captured by materialism in both its scientific and its economic forms. Any education that addresses transformed work must equally address elevation of consciousness. But before it can address its elevation, it must first address its expansion. The distinction between the two, in this age sometimes dubbed "post-fact," is crucial.

Peak experiences, moments of feeling one with the universe and all in it, periods of being awash in bliss, or awakening to the sense of who and what we truly are, are wonderful. But such experiences need context, grounding, and sustainability so that they have some ongoing effect on how we live in the world. That is, what did those peeks into the peaks of consciousness do for our lives and our natures when we returned to the valleys? As humans we shall always return to valleys. What prepares us for that return?

Of course, the experiences must in some way inform or influence our daily living; they must at least trickle down to help us live better, more conscious, and more positive lives. As Christ said, "by their fruits ye shall know them." Let's see the fruit. Let's see how your awakening or opening or revelation informs how you live.[167] Because unless you have now left your body, you are going to continue life in the body, and life in the body in the world will create obstacles in your way that can throw off the openness or peace or bliss. We need to help people secure the basic needs of the early stages of Maslow's hierarchy—food, shelter, clothing, healthcare, intimate relationships; that is, the safety and belongingness needs. UBI certainly factors in here. Yet the danger is the continued fetishization of these needs, the obsessive focus on material gain and material increase. This obsession, seen in the ubiquitous parade of advertising that surrounds and mesmerizes us by its shape-shifting, has perverted the American Dream. We are trapped in those early Maslovian stages without the tools to extricate us, to move onward and upward. The later stages, the states of and adventures in consciousness discussed in this book, are the true fulfillment of that Dream.

Before all of that, before any education in consciousness that involves the higher reaches of Maslovian peak-experiences or adventures that touch the ethereal and divine, we need, and I can't believe that I'm touting this, an education in good old consciousness-raising. I can't believe it, because I didn't think in 2018 that such an education would be necessary. But it is.

In the 1960s and 1970s consciousness-raising meant bringing attention to certain political, social, and cultural issues as a way of changing people's views. The label for this phenomenon, then, is really a misnomer. The changes sought after and anticipated were not really a raising or an elevation of consciousness as much as an expansion of consciousness to take into account different aspects of the issues that persons neglected, pushed aside, or even attacked. Consciousness-raising was a form of social, political, and cultural activism that expanded our moral and mental horizon but did not necessarily elevate it above that horizon.

Today we need a form of educational activism as a preliminary step in an overall program of consciousness-raising. That preliminary step is expanding or widening consciousness before we undertake the subsequent steps of elevating consciousness to the higher or altered realms of experience and into spiritual realities. The activism that I have in mind is, first, to help us get ourselves out of the hole of materialism that has come to define and bind our worldviews. Second, we need an activism that will help students navigate the now-tricky world of processing information. Students need no help in accessing information, but they surely need help in assessing information. The help should take the form of an emphasis in education on critical thinking within the context of the liberal arts (to which I recur below).

Without being aware of it, we have undergone a revolution. That revolution is in information delivery. In more innocent days, Jon Stewart hosted *The Daily Show*. Critics and fans alike described the show as offering "fake news." But the show never offered fake news. The news was real; their take on it was satirical, ironic, and sometimes caustic. But today fake news and outright lies have superseded investigative reporting and the truth, as if people now used *The Onion* to substantiate their opinions. Social media, for instance, Twitter and Facebook, now permit lies to substitute for facts as "bots" or "cyborgs," which are automated social media accounts, spit out propaganda and misinformation in high volume and at an alarming rate.

President Trump seems to offer a lie per day. Taking into account the whoppers he told during his campaign, and that he continues to issue daily, the accumulation of lies is nearly overwhelming. The fear and danger are that soon widely respected outlets like *The New York Times* and *The Washington Post* will forgo using their resources to examine and counter every Trump-land lie. Mark Twain is alleged to have quipped that a lie goes around the world before the truth can get its boots on. Lies always traveled fast; today, however, through social media lies travel even faster, so that now the truth can't even find its boots, let alone put them on, before the lie has saturated the globe.

What happens in a democracy when lies proliferate so rapidly and thickly that people give up all hope of sorting out fact from fiction? Then cynicism reigns. Soon people tire of searching out the truth and stop paying attention altogether. What happens, then, in a democracy when people believe nothing? Can democracy, which rests on truth and facts, survive? It cannot. So, to repeat for effect: We need an educational consciousness-raising that, first, helps students discriminate between fake news and factual reporting. Second, we need an educational consciousness-raising that helps them learn to assess information and turn it into knowledge.

Integral Education

I'm placing heavy emphasis here on education as our way forward, our way into a future of a robo-economy and ample leisure time. Yet what else is there to fall back on? If work supplies meaning and purpose for most of the populace and if that work is diminished significantly or eliminated by automation, AI, and robots, then what resources do people have to fall back onto? The level of prescriptive-drug medication and the opioid explosion show us that today when economic hardship hits, people turn to ways to escape discomfort. Drugs provide no solution to the problem, but only exacerbate the problem; psychological studies show that anxiety and depression, which are signs of psychological distress caused by loss of work, are masked by drug use and addiction. In a climate of disappearing work, when the population even in good times is too readily captured by distractions and fetishes that often shorten attention spans, eliminate silence and solitude, push people beyond their financial means, and relieve tedium and lethargy through trivia and, through the circle of self-perpetuation, more distractions and fetishes, people need new or renewed sources for finding meaning and purpose in life. These sources can be found and strengthened through introspection and communication. In short, if our current situation (to say nothing of the future of work) is any indication, workers whose self-definitions are decimated by declining employment and unsatisfying labor will be internally incapable of confronting, let alone combating, the very distractions and fetishes that drive them. Both declining employment and lousy jobs will also leave workers incapable of finding the meaning in life that can help them out of their crisis.[168]

That is why I harp on an education that focuses its content on critical thinking, which in shorthand form is nothing other than asking and answering questions, along with a good dose of internal work or practice. Students should undertake that critical thinking, therefore, in a context of collaboration, dialogue, and meditation. In this new education, the curriculum elevates consciousness as meditation turns attention within. Simultaneously, dialogue brings to the fore more and more perspectives—often disparate and even discordant perspectives—

to be wrestled with. Using dialogue in this manner is old-fashioned consciousness "raising," as more aspects of a topic are brought into one's awareness. It isn't elevating consciousness to a perspective that transcends but includes the specific points of view of others, which meditation and introspection can do. It is, instead, consciousness-expanding.

Building on such ideas, I want to offer next an outline of the education that I have in mind. This is not the place for a detailed discussion of this education, which I have offered elsewhere, but it is the place for providing some impressions of what I would like to see in the future.[169]

Consciousness-Expanding

In 2017 we are dismayed to find that some high-school graduates cannot read. We ask the question that Rudolf Flesch emphasized in the title of his 1955 best seller, *Why Johnny Can't Read?* Too often, even when Johnny has learned to read, we find 62 years later that Johnny can't think. Johnny has thoughts, but he cannot argue for beliefs, values, ideas, and goals; he cannot separate reasons from opinions, assumptions from conclusions, facts from preferences; he cannot differentiate a challenge to his thoughts from an attack on his person; he thinks that every view or opinion is as good as and therefore is equal to every other view or opinion; he cannot follow arguments or attend to a lecture; he cannot in a sustained and systematic way explain why he thinks what he does. In short, Johnny has thoughts, but he cannot think critically. Critical thinking should be the core of the curriculum from kindergarten through college; indeed, it should be the core across the entire curriculum.

Our schools today can teach children how to sort out choices—how to examine options and explore the implications for or consequences of choosing one over others. Schools can teach students to seek out and to voice reasons for choosing one option over another. Schools can teach students how to gather and how to weigh evidence and reasons; how to form, advance, and challenge arguments; how to articulate reasonable positions; and how to engage with others in the give-and-take of discussion. Schools can teach all of that, but often they don't. Instead they too often teach to standardized tests. These tests are multiple-choice exams that require students within a short timespan to search for the correct answers to problems and issues that may well be of little interest to them. There is never a need for students to give reasons for these answers.

Why do schools operate this way? One reason is that critical thinking is demanding, for both teachers and students. Indeed, in some schools the students seem unwilling, intellectually and motivationally, to learn to think critically. In some schools the student-teacher ratio is too high, or there is a paucity of resources, or the teachers are inadequately trained. In all schools teaching critical thinking and learning to think critically take time. So students today are taught to answer designed questions by giving formulaic answers. No emphasis is placed on questioning or generating ideas or arguing about the value or truth of the question themselves, let alone about the value or truth of the claims found in textbooks or declaimed by teachers.

Critical thinking is, of course, the opposite approach. At every step, whether in primary school or university, the student struggles to explain, define, defend, and refute by using reasons and evidence within the limits of his or her capacity to understand. It is that capacity that changes, but the nature of what the student is asked to do, that is, to argue, remains constant. These steps constitute nothing less than learning to argue effectively. Arguing requires effective reading, writing, speaking, and listening. All involve asking questions: when reading, asking questions of the author; when listening, of the speaker; when speaking or writing, of oneself. It is teachers, again, from primary school through college, who model for their students what careful reading, attentive listening, clear writing, and direct speaking are. Teachers show students how to ask questions and what questions to ask.

Thinking is almost always social, even when one is introspecting. There one asks questions of the many voices, the multiple selves, present in all of us. Easier, of course, is bouncing questions and ideas off one another, off real people in real-life situations. The key component, therefore, of critical thinking is deliberation—the assessment of and judgments about reasons and evidence. Nothing about deliberation indicates that it cannot be done alone. Indeed, it can. But deliberating with flesh-and-blood others who hold positions important to them and that might conflict with our own is the best way to come to thoughtful conclusions.

When participants in group deliberations have been educated to read carefully, listen attentively, and speak directly, then they are prepared to entertain perspectives that conflict. They are able, in other words, to deliberate with others about disparate positions, including their own. In fact, as political philosopher and legal scholar Cass Sunstein has shown, participants who hear differing perspectives—and the more, the better—have more fruitful deliberations. Too often when group views do not differ, then participants can fall into the trap of accepting preformed positions brought to the deliberations instead of having positions challenged, refined, changed, reinforced, or discovered in the deliberations. The greater the diversity of perspectives, the better deliberations go; the better deliberations go, the better the outcome—that is, the more it tends toward group consensus (Sunstein, 2001, p. 50).

By schooling students in the skills of critical thinking, we can best prepare them for the advent of the robo-economy. Knowing how to think critically means that students will be flexible in applying their skills, will be able to learn on-the-job, and will be able to transfer their thinking to novel contexts. They will be prepared to do all of that, because they will have learned to ask questions and pursue answers.

In addition, students schooled in the skills of critical thinking and in the procedures of deliberation will be well placed to use their increased leisure time. However much I would love to see workers democratically control their workplaces and companies, the decline of employment in the robo-economy undermines this vision. But persons who have learned to think critically can always apply those skills to their own introspective deliberations. They come thereby to know themselves, to know their interests and passions, to set goals, to change course, and to know the costs and consequences of following or altering one path or another.

Consciousness-Raising

Deliberation and dialogue can also be ways to elevate consciousness and not just expand it. Hearing opposing perspectives challenges the participant, if she is thinking critically, to put herself in the place of the speaker and to treat the speaker's perspective with respect by coming to understand the perspective as fully and fairly as possible. This is respect and possibly compassion engendered by empathy, a focal point of dialogue. Hearing, appreciating, and understanding alternative views and perspectives are not easy or comfortable, but they are a way to build consensus and comprehensive solutions. This process raises consciousness by encouraging participants to transcend the welter of conflicting views and find an encompassing view that might include all such views. This encompassing view permits participants to move beyond any single perspective while preserving each perspective. This is the view as I discussed in Chapter 5 that differentiates Mosaic consciousness from Edenic consciousness and differentiates Christic consciousness from its Mosaic form.

Physicist David Bohm applied his background in and insights from science to the study of dialogue. He found that if structured to enhance deliberation, dialogue could result in a change of consciousness among the participants to higher-order thinking. Dialogue, argued Bohm, enables participants to focus their collective thoughts, which are usually, like ordinary light, scattered and conflicting, thus canceling one another out. The focus through deliberation, which Bohm calls "thinking together," in dialogue creates coherence. That coherence generates power in our communication and consensus in our view. Bohm calls this coherence "participatory consciousness" in which each participant works to produce a group or common consciousness that shapes and reflects new meaning generated by the group's being together and thinking together.

The move into and through participatory consciousness can lead participants over time out of egocentric positions and into group-centered and even world-centric positions. Holding such positions, Bohm concludes, can engender embracing the conflicting viewpoints of others and can change "the very nature of consciousness" itself (Bohm, 2004, pp. 15-6). Thus can consciousness rise from egocentrism into ethos-centrism and world-centrism.[170]

Furthermore, listening attentively in a deliberation requires a person to remain silent and to be present. Our history and perspectives, our selves, drop away or remain quiescent in our attention to another. As discussed in Chapter 6, presence and silence are qualities of deep meditation, and so we can see here the connection between dialogue and raising consciousness.

All of this is to help us find our way in the world, to discover or, in Nietzschean fashion, to create a life that is worthwhile. This is so especially in a world on the threshold of a robo-economy. In the 1870s William James gave himself an overdose of chloral hydrate to see, as he wrote to his brother, Henry, how close he could come to the morgue without succeeding in ending up there (Kaag, 2016, pp. 5-6). James must have wrestled with the question of just how worthwhile life was, though apparently he had not concluded that death was preferable. He experimented, as a good scientist, with what death was like and how easily it could rob us of the preciousness of life. Too many today aren't precisely experimenting with drugs, but are using them to dull the pain, boredom, and aimlessness of daily life. Drugs, today, seem most often a way out of life and not into it. An education in critical thinking and consciousness-raising might help us find or rediscover the preciousness of life without the extreme of James's experiment. Otherwise, the increase of leisure time without a sense of how to use it or love it could continue to be threatening, even deadly.

For the ancient Greeks leisure time was *scholé*, from which we derive our word "scholarship." Scholars have the time to pursue topics thoroughly, some might even say obsessively. But scholarship here is not the pursuit of narrow topics into the depths of arcana. It is, instead, the pursuit of the liberal arts.

Today we often think of the liberal arts as those areas of collegiate study different from the sciences—for example, languages, literature, music, theater, dance, philosophy, religion, and art itself. The emergence of the social sciences, referred to as the "soft" sciences, muddied any clarity that the differentiation displayed. The differentiation was from the beginning, I think, a mistake, because the goal of liberal arts is to teach persons to think clearly. That goal surely includes the sciences.

Historically, the liberal arts were any disciplines of study or scholarship required to make a person free. When the ancients referred to "freedom" in this context, they meant mental freedom. That is, liberal or liberated persons were those free to think for themselves, to think independently. The liberal arts provided the platform and the substance that enabled free thought to be sound thought. Naturally the sciences were part of that substance, since we have seen throughout this book that evidence accumulated systematically is a product of the scientific enterprise. The evidence need not be only empirical, the results of consulting our five senses or their extensions. The evidence can also be based on logical reasoning. In this sense, the arts are not divorced from the sciences.

The liberal arts showed from the beginning, and should do so now, the integration of different ways of knowing.[171] Integration for the liberal arts does not end there, however, for the liberal arts are also those areas of study directed at the whole person. This may strike the reader as an outmoded notion, and a misbegotten one, because today most of our colleges and universities divide scholarship into discrete disciplinary departments, schools, or colleges separate from one another. Students in this environment are encouraged as "free" persons—though not in my sense liberally educated persons—to move about the curriculum and the college's extracurricular offerings to cobble together their own "whole" education.

For the robo-world to come, the curriculum, from kindergarten through college, must return to the historical idea of the liberal arts as addressing the whole person. Only through the integration of a person's mind, body, and spirit can we hope to enable persons to know themselves, to function effectively and with relish within the world, and to transcend to higher levels of consciousness.

Therefore, the new educational program should include

- Expressive arts and fine arts—music, theater, dance, painting, sculpture, poetry;
- Kinesthesia—that is, sports, yoga, tai chi, martial arts;
- A study of the scientific method—how to gather and assess evidence or data empirically and logically;
- How to form and advance arguments;
- A grounding in history, philosophy, and ethics;
- Some form of spiritual work; that is, participation in some form of contemplative practice, among which might be the Centering Prayer, mindfulness or mantra meditation, Sufi

dance or other forms of moving meditation, or, at the very least, the Relaxation Response.[172]

Perhaps I do not have to mention here, and do so only as a reminder, that there will also be a strong focus on the traditional three Rs: reading, writing, and math. This curriculum is to be set, of course, within the context of dialogue and deliberation for democratic decision-making among students, faculty, staff; in other words, among all those affiliated with the learning community.[173]

This is a whole-person curriculum. It mirrors Howard Gardner's view of multiple forms of intelligence (Gardner, 1983). So rather than seeing only one way to learn, this approach respects the multiple ways that people learn and express that learning. Gardner proposes at least nine different intelligences: musical-rhythmic, verbal-linguistic, visual-spatial, logical-mathematical, bodily-kinesthetic, interpersonal (dialogue), intrapersonal (introspection), naturalistic (scientific method), and existential (or spiritual). A whole-person or liberal arts curriculum should at least include aspects of them all. This is not to say that each student masters all such intelligences. It is that each student is thoroughly exposed to each and adopts those that best fit his/her learning style and interests within a curriculum based on critical thinking.

Left out but also important in this curriculum is some learning about and practice in hands-on or manual work, whether that is gardening and farming, skills related to the building trades, mechanics such as auto repair, operating machinery, and the like.

At the same time, teaching critical thinking through the liberal arts, within a context of deliberation and dialogue, is not simply for an individual's growth and benefit; it is not, that is, simply an employment or leisure-time platform. Critical thinking is also important for citizenship. Participation in dialogue within schools, on issues important to the lives of all who study and work there, is preparation for adult participation in governing through democracy. Democratic processes—whether in clubs and associations, workplaces or houses of worship, town meetings or state houses—promote and call on the skills of critical thinking and provide opportunities for both expanding and elevating individual and group consciousness.

Through a whole-person curriculum people will be prepared to face the job market, however robust or weak it may be. Moreover, people will be prepared for the increase in leisure time in a robo-economy. Before the whole-person curriculum such leisure time looked threatening; with that curriculum it looks promising.

Regardless of the state of the economy, whether it is full of jobs or full of robots or both (where Artificial Intelligence and technology create ample new jobs currently unseen and unimagined), the whole-person curriculum as outlined here is the education for the twenty-first century. In 1893 Frederick Jackson Turner, a scholar of American History, proposed the "frontier thesis" that American democracy had arisen out of the challenges of the moving frontier line. As pioneers pushed into new territory, they had to imagine and innovate, since little existed that they could rely on. Yet Turner also saw that the American frontier had ended and with it, he feared, came the end of American dynamism. What Turner did not foresee was that Americans and other earthlings would turn their gaze upward to the stars, to a new frontier. Imagination and innovation were back in play, as our exploration of the farther reaches of our galaxy and our universe depended on our scientific and technological ingenuity.

The heavens are not our only remaining frontier. In addition to our oceans, we have the inner universe of realms of consciousness, the further reaches of our human nature. The whole-person curriculum is designed to enable exploration of both the heavens and the inner world. The curriculum is science-based but not exclusively so. That is, the power of science derives from its reliance on using our five senses and their extensions to explore and understand our physical and material, or our empirical, world. Through the scientific method of hypothesis testing, gathering and assessing evidence, and replicating studies we come to know the world. Students, by using this method, will appreciate its applicability and its power.

Yet the hypotheses tested, the evidence gathered and assessed, and the studies replicated in science do not have to be solely based in the empirical world. In a broader sense, science is also an enterprise that involves the systematic collection, analysis, and testing of evidence of all sorts, data that can also be mental, moral, and spiritual, as I have suggested in this book. Science helps us construct blinded experiments to test whether mediums are talking to the dead and helps us discover a synthesized psychedelic to ease the anxiety and pain of dying by altering consciousness. After their experiences, many in both groups come away thinking that our consciousness lives on after death.

The systematic collection, analysis, and testing of evidence enables us also to understand our inner life, the interior realms of consciousness. In this way, science broadly defined as the "scientific enterprise" is integral to our understanding of our physical, mental, and spiritual lives, all aspects of a whole person. Through such a curriculum a person is prepared, as Aristotle said of happiness, for a whole life lived well.

It may seem as if, in introducing the scientific enterprise, I have contradicted my views expressed in earlier chapters when I distinguished between the realm of science and the realms of morality and spirituality. But if we hold in mind the difference that I'm describing here between the scientific method and the scientific enterprise, then I have not. The systematic collection, analysis, and testing of evidence—that is, the scientific enterprise—is common to all these realms; what differs in each is what constitutes or is counted as evidence. In the material or physicalist realm, what constitutes evidence is limited to empirical data. So, whereas the scientific method, the basis of the experiments undertaken, is built on empiricism, the scientific enterprise is not. It is broader in its approach and scope and thus is used in all three realms. In that sense, then, science broadly understood is integral to our overall knowledge. And it is integral to our curriculum.

Through the curriculum, the new pioneers in the twenty-first century will be explorers of the vast reaches of space, both internal and external. They will be prepared through a whole-person, liberal-arts education, for space exploration, as they dive to the depths of the oceans, reach for the stars that seem infinite, and dive deeply into states of consciousness to discover that that interior depth *is* infinite. These pioneers will know that that infinity is alive, is their birthright, and is the true source of happiness.

A 2009 survey showed that 49 percent of Americans had experienced a mystical state.[174] This result carries good news and bad news. The good news is that nearly half of all Americans have experienced something that transcends the physicalist-materialist configuration of our world and universe. This heralds the strong possibility that our culture may be on the cusp of evolving toward a globalist appreciation, founded on transcendental experience, of the interconnections between, indeed the oneness of, all things. On the other hand, the same result shows that over half of all Americans have had no such experience and thus might continue to be wedded to the materialist conception of life and of the world that influences and informs our consumerist orientation.

Either way, the result shows that the future will involve a push toward evolution—given that the statistics tend in that direction—but also, as we see in the rise of nationalist and nativist political movements, a pull back toward the status quo if not back into antiquated norms and societal structures. But the future, I think, will ultimately be guided by the inevitability of technological advance, which no neo-nationalist movements can retard, let alone stop. Preparing for that advance is the imperative behind the education described above, which I am calling "integral education."

At its base, integral education comprises the integration of the multiple aspects of human living: where the individual fits into and is also separate from the community; where individual values cohere with and differ from collective values; where individual behaviors harmonize with but can also challenge collective structures and institutions; and where individual identity rises, as discussed in Chapter 5, from egocentrism through socio-centrism to world-centrism in all of its developmental forms. In brief, this form of integration is nothing less than building on and acting through the AQAL model offered by Ken Wilber.[175]

Therefore, integral education relies upon more than the idea of integrating mind and body, though that is crucial. It also involves integrating mind, body, and spirit, where spirit refers to the integration into one's life of experiences of altered and higher consciousness. The idea of levels of consciousness returns us to the beginning of the book. Whether you accept the evidence for consciousness living on after bodily death, you should by this point accept the imperative to investigate the scientific studies that produce that evidence. My own conclusion from confronting that evidence is that the grip that the materialist/physicalist paradigm has on our culture is a chokehold that needs to be released. The grip traps us in a truncated, if not distorted, worldview that cuts us off from our own growth potential.

Another tight grip that needs to be relinquished is the theistic view of a distant God. A narrow, and often literal, reading of scriptures that maintains a distant God too often arrests our growth or education as moral agents. We thereby fail to grow in compassion and happiness. Another casualty of such scriptural readings is our identities as cosmopolitan citizens—that is, citizens of the globe dedicated to uplifting all humans, regardless of their religious views, and, in the process, sharing the planet with them. The necessary countermeasure here is transcendental experience and direct knowledge of the divine. Whether undertaken through meditation, psychedelics, or some other means that induce peak-experiences or the flow state, alterations of consciousness reveal the GOD within that supersedes as it undercuts the distant God of theism.

Nor are democracy and democratic practices absent from integral education. Self-direction and self-legislation are the hallmarks of Western political thought, and democracy is nothing other than making decisions collectively that affect the direction of our individual and communal lives. Yet we need to understand that our conceptions of self must themselves evolve to include more and more others. "Self" is not just individual; it is also collective and expands, as the ripples from a stone thrown into a pond, to include greater and greater communities in our own self-definition. This evolution expands our love and compassion, as love and compassion expand our identity.

I would not wager any money on whether our species will survive into a new century, or much further into this one, but I'll gamble that creating a satisfactory integral education is our only hope for improving our lives, saving our species, and uniting the planet. I'm convinced of it, enough so that my future work will be creating an education for continuing the evolution of consciousness and enhancing human flourishing.

Because I'm convinced, I've also tried to convince you of this as well. If I haven't, then I hope that you'll let me know where the evidence and my arguments are deficient, not just in this chapter, but throughout the book. On the other hand, whenever the evidence is sufficient, I hope that you, dear reader, will join in the enterprise of creating and spreading integral education wherever and at whatever level you can.

"Human nature doesn't change." Humans often use this maxim to explain or excuse unsavory behaviors: "Oh, that's just human nature." But the maxim holds only because human nature is elastic. So, to the proposition that all humans are selfish, brutish, and competitive, we need only find one altruistic, gentle, collaborative, and kind person to disprove it. Likewise, to disprove the proposition that all humans are compassionate, loving, and cooperative, we need to find only one who isn't. Such white crows disrupt our complacency and demand that we rethink our own propositions. The evidence of human history shows us that humans can be both competitive and cooperative, often within the same person, because human nature, as I said, is elastic. We are not one thing; we are many things.

Of course human nature doesn't change. *Whatever* humans say, do, or feel is part of and reflective of our nature. The question for us is which aspects of human being do we want to cultivate. The role of education is just such cultivation, and integral education, through the expansion and elevation of consciousness, is the process by which we develop into the furthest reaches of human nature. That development sounds promising, but we need to be careful in stretching for those furthest reaches, just because human nature is elastic and human beings, multifaceted. Thus we can cultivate all sorts of characters, including monsters. To avoid and combat monsters, even to prevent them from arising in the first place, we need something like an integral education to train and focus our eyes—our physical, mental, and spiritual eyes—to search out exceptions that probe our norms, beliefs, and rules. In other words, keep an eye out for white crows. Indeed, stalk them and thereby recognize, defeat, and evade confirmation bias, blind spots, deception, manipulation, chicanery, and "hoodwinkery" of every sort. In this way, through an integral education, we free our consciousness to soar. And soar it can and will, for don't we now know that consciousness can be freed from the body since consciousness is independent of the brain?

Endnotes

1　Most scholars, writers, and pundits would agree with this perspective, but for moral support I turned to Alice Dreger's wonderful book *Galileo's Middle Finger* (2015), where she declares, within a field of insights, that "the pursuit of evidence is probably the most pressing moral imperative of our time" (p. 11).

2　See (http://www.pewglobal.org/2014/03/13/worldwide-many-see-belief-in-god-as-essential-to-morality/).

3　See, for example, Sheldrake's books *Dogs That Know When Their Owners Are Coming Home*, 2011, and *The Sense of Being Stared At*, 2013. All elements of this story are taken from Rupert Sheldrake's Perrott-Warrick Lecture at Trinity College, Cambridge, February 9, 2011.

4　Bor is the author of *The Ravenous Brain: How the New Science of Consciousness Explains Our Insatiable Search for Meaning*. New York: Basic Books, 2012. See his blog at http://www.danielbor.com/introtoconsciousness. As another example, here is H. Allen Orr, Professor of Biology at the University of Rochester: "Brains and neurons obviously have everything to do with consciousness, but how such mere objects can give rise to the eerily different phenomenon of subjective experience seems utterly incomprehensible" ("Awaiting a New Darwin," *New York Review of Books*, February 7, 2013, p. 28). Is his use of "obviously" meant to be ironic?

5　I borrow the term "Anomalous Information Reception" or AIR from Dr. Julie Beischel. I discuss her work at the Windbridge Institute later in this chapter.

6　After writing *The ESP Enigma* (2008) Diane Hennacy Powell, Johns Hopkins-trained psychiatrist and former faculty member at the Harvard Medical School, had some friends and colleagues tell her that they didn't have to read her book;

they knew already that it was "hogwash." (See her interview at http://www.youtube.com/watch?feature=player_embe dded&v=mnaGuei3bGc#!)

7   Mark Leary himself says, "I can readily identify with the intellectual difficulty of accepting most of parapsychology's claims. I have a tremendous amount of trouble understanding how any of it can be true. Yet I also see the results of decades of well-designed research suggesting that psi [psychic or paranormal phenomena] might in fact occur and, from a scientific perspective, I don't have the luxury of simply ignoring research findings that make me uncomfortable, and I don't think I would be justified in condemning researchers who study such things…I find it harder to understand why anyone would suggest that such research should not be conducted or that researchers in the field are misguided or irrational. Even people who do not believe in psychic phenomena should want additional research to provide an answer once and for all. The questions are so interesting and potentially important that we really should know the answers, however they may fall" (2011).

8   Sadly, this "unscientific attitude" is nothing new. As a telling and regrettable example, review the story of Ignaz Semmelweiss, a physician who was also a pioneer of antiseptic procedures in hospitals. Despite his repeated studies and publications showing that physicians who washed their hands with chlorinated lime solutions dramatically reduced the mortality of birthing mothers, Semmelweis was committed to an insane asylum for his trouble. The medical community would have to wait years later for Louis Pasteur to confirm what Semmelweis had already discovered and tried to disseminate.

9   "It's Westworld. What's Wrong With Cruelty to Robots?" *The New York Times*, April 23, 2018.

10   Quoted in "Richard Dawkins Comes To Call" by Rupert

Sheldrake. https://www.dailygrail.com/2008/01/richard-da
wkins-comes-to-call/.

11 The term "skeptic" now seems exclusively reserved in this
area to those researchers or pundits who seek only to debunk
the experiments in and evidence from the paranormal. This
is ironic, since the term comes from the Greek meaning
"inquiring" and "reflective."

12 The quotation is from Chris Carter, "Does Telepathy Conflict
with Science?" in the *Epoch Times*, available at https://
nationalparanormalassociation.blogspot.com/2012/03/
does-telepathy-conflict-with-science.html.

13 This phenomenon, in a single term, was called
"enantiodromia" by Carl Jung—the tendency of an extreme
to turn into its opposite, to become, as I commented, the
very thing that someone opposes or hates.

14 Anyone who reads Grossman's article (2002) will see the
tremendous debt that I owe him for the tone, approach, and
even substance of this chapter.

15 In addition to Dechesne et al. cited here, see also (among
others) Solomon, S. et al., "A Terror Management Theory of
Social Behavior: The Psychological Functions of Self-Esteem
and Cultural Worldviews," *Advances in Experimental Social
Psychology*, 24, 93-159, 1991; Pyszczynski, T. et al., "Mortality
Salience, Martyrdom, and Military Might: The Great Satan
Versus the Axis of Evil," *Journal of Personality and Social
Psychology*, 32 (4), 525-37, 2006; Cohen, F. and Solomon,
S., "The Politics of Mortal Terror," *Current Directions in
Psychological Science*, 20(5), 316-20, 2011.

16 Other renowned investigators of the paranormal during this
period included William Crookes, inventor of the cathode
ray tube used in television sets and computer monitors; J.J.
Thomson, winner of the 1906 Nobel Prize for discovering
the electron; and Lord Rayleigh, winner of the 1904 Nobel
Prize in Physics.

17 James, 1896, p. 3. All quotations from James, unless otherwise noted, are from this source.

18 Phinuit claimed to have been born in Metz and provided the dates of both his birth and death. See Gardner, 2003, p. 254.

19 This is disputed. Michael Tymn reports on a sitting with Mrs. Piper of Jim and Mary Howard and their daughter, Katharine. At the close of the sitting, Phinuit spoke good French to Katharine, "who had lived in France and knew the language well" (Tymn, 2013, 69).

20 Blum, p. 81. At one point, Hodgson put a lit match on her arm and asked Phinuit whether he felt it. "Yes," he replied, "but not much you know. What is it? Something cold, isn't it?" Quoted in Sage, 1904/2007, p. 28. Reading Deborah Blum's *Ghost Hunters* is one excellent, and enjoyable, way to glimpse both the methods and the results of the research. As the reader can and will see, I draw significantly from her book.

21 Gardner, 2003, p. 304. In his article, "How Mrs. Piper Bamboozled William James," Martin Gardner reports that to test her trance, William James made a small cut on her wrist to see whether that bothered her, that a French investigator stuck a feather up her nose, and that, on another occasion, an investigator, though Gardner does not say who, forced a needle into her hand. See Gardner, 2003, p. 254.

22 Hall had better results when challenging Piper on the informational side. Hall invented a dead niece whom he said he wanted to contact. Piper's control recalled conversations between her and Hall. Hall concluded that the psychic researchers were a "group of self-deceiving dreamers" (Blum, p. 305).

23 Hodgson wrote the following note about this part of the reading: "My cousin Fred far excelled any other person that I have seen in games of leap-frog, fly the garter, and

the like. He took very long flying jumps, and whenever he played, the game was lined by crowds of school-mates to watch him." Quoted in Tymn, 2013, p. 19.

24   This woman was named Jessie, Hodgson's "one and only love affair from his youth." Quoted in Tymn, 2013, p. 20.

25   Sage, p. 36. Martin Gardner, in addition to claiming that Mrs. Piper was a "cunning cold reader" (2003, p. 256), also claims that she culled information from obituaries, courthouse documents, real estate sales, fellow mediums, and the like. He provides no evidence to support his charges, and much of it flies in the face of the lengths that Hodgson, and later Oliver Lodge, went to in their own investigations of her spying or cheating.

26   Michael Tymn claims that Pellew's accidental death "involved falling down a flight of stairs" (2013, p. 66). I defer in this matter to Blum (2006) who says the death was the result of a fall from a horse.

27   The quotation is from Sage, p. 85. Sage reports a different version of this test. According to him, Hodgson brought 150 visitors of whom 30 were friends or relatives of Pellew's. "He recognized the whole thirty, and never mistook a stranger for a friend. He not only addressed them all by name but took with each of them the tone he had been accustomed to take" (Sage, p. 83). Martin Gardner, in his debunking article, mentions G.P. as one of her controls, but he fails to mention anything about this test or any other readings of or readings witnessed by Hodgson.

28   The derivation of the term "murder" is colorful, though grisly. One theory relates to crow behavior: Crows will sometimes kill a dying crow. Another theory relates to the blanket of crows that covered battlefields, when crows descended to scavenge on the dead.

29   The information in this section is from Beischel, 2013, location 465ff of 1217.

30   In 2015 Beischel replicated and expanded her 2007 study of mediums. In 2007 she had 17 medium readings; in the 2015 study she had 58 readings. Her results in 2015 were remarkably similar to her earlier study.

31   See Beischel, 2013, Chapter 5.

32   I have withheld Robert's last name and the name of his great-grandfather to protect their identities, though mostly Robert's since he still lives. Interested parties, who can convince me of their sincerity, may have access to both names.

33   Eliza predicted that Ann Marie would become engaged to this man. That occurred in the spring of 2013, some two years after Robert's reading with Eliza. Doubters of mediums in Robert's family think that this prediction took too long to come true and thus should not count toward Eliza's accuracy. Robert and I disagree. Don't the passages of years make it less likely that Ann Marie would become engaged to *this* man?

34   In a two-part article in *The New York Review of Books* Robert Gottlieb reviewed over two dozen books on afterlife phenomena. Not once in either article does he mention, let alone address, any veridical evidence related to such phenomena. See "To Heaven and Back!" in *The New York Review of Books*, Volume 61, #16, October 23, 2014 and "Back from Heaven—The Science" in *The New York Review of Books*, Volume 61, #17, November 6, 2014, pp. 36-8.

35   Willoughby Britton discussed this case during a talk, "Deathbed Visions and Near-Death Experiences," given at Brown University in 2007.

36   Perhaps there should be some focus, then, on the measures we use to determine and pronounce clinical death.

37   See: http://www.youtube.com/watch?v=JL1oDuvQR08&feature=player_embedded. Another example, also available on YouTube (http://www.youtube.com/watch?list=UUkMhH

JniwJzW3DjUxozPnQA&v=J5_x8U7SR0I#t=189), discusses the near-death experience of Al Sullivan. While undergoing heart bypass surgery, Sullivan left his body and watched the procedure from above. At one point, he observed his cardiac surgeon, Dr. Hiro Takata whom Sullivan had never met before, holding his hands close to the center of his chest and pointing with his elbows at various people and instruments. Sullivan described this as Dr. Takata "flapping his arms." Dr. Anthony Lasala, Sullivan's cardiologist who works with Dr. Takata at Hartford Hospital, verified that Dr. Takata does that to keep from contaminating his hands. Dr. Lasala contends that Al Sullivan would not have known about Takata's strange mannerism. Takata commented that it wouldn't be possible for Sullivan to see Takata, since Sullivan was fully anesthetized and had his eyes taped shut. As with Dr. Rudy's incident, the doctors involved in this episode are willing to be identified and appear on film, even when they admit that they can offer no explanation for what Sullivan saw.

38 Found on YouTube at https://www.youtube.com/watch?v=J16G6jY9iCc.

39 Cryptomnesia is the phenomenon of recalling a forgotten memory but not recognizing it as something that had ever happened to the person. Thus it is thought to be original.

40 In *The Handbook of Near-Death Experiences* Jan Holden, one of the *Handbook*'s editors, offers an entire chapter on veridical evidence: "Veridical Perception in Near-Death Experiences," pp. 185-211. Holden concludes that "the sheer volume of AVP (apparent veridical perception) anecdotes… over the course of the last 150 years…suggests that AVP is real" (2009, p. 197). In *The Self Does Not Die* (2016) the authors present 78 cases of NDEs that provide veridical evidence of varying degrees. Some of those cases appear in this chapter. For a quick survey of some NDEs involving people meeting

those they thought were alive but later learned had recently died, listen to Dr. Bruce Greyson, among others, on a panel discussing life-after-death: https://www.youtube.com/watch?v=4RGizqsLumo&t=429s.

41 For additional details from Woerlee's interpretation of the denture case and a point-by-point refutation of it, see Rivas et al., 2016, pp. 259-72.

42 Pam Reynolds also reported seeing deceased loved ones, talking with them, seeing light, and other such phenomena common in NDEs. Since there is no veridical evidence for these encounters, I am not discussing them. But everything that she experienced she said was done so with total clarity.

43 Three researchers—Rudolf Smit, Kristopher Key, and Michael Prescott—tested for themselves whether they, or anyone, could hear a conversation with earpieces in place emitting the decibels that Pam Reynolds would have heard. Even fully conscious, these three reported that at best they could hear only "a few snippets, with no understanding of what was really being said" (Rivas et al., 2016, p. 97). Recall that Reynolds was also in a state of "EEG burst suppression"; in other words, she was in a state of deep unconsciousness with no brain activity.

44 In a somewhat related study Sabom interviewed 57 cardiac patients who were declared clinically dead and were resuscitated. Thirty-two of the 57 claimed to have had an out-of-body experience and could describe in detail their own resuscitations. The remaining 25 cardiac patients reported no such experience, but they were asked to imagine and describe their own resuscitation procedures. Of the 32 with OBEs (out-of-body experiences) 26 could not report specifically accurate details that could be matched with their medical records, though none of the 32 made any identifiable errors in their accounts of their resuscitations. The remaining six members of the 32, however, gave

reports that conformed in virtually every detail to the medical records of their resuscitations. On the other hand, 80 percent of the 25 who did not have such experiences had at least one significant mistake in their descriptions. See Sabom, 1982.

45 Dr. Hamilton was equally forthcoming with others about the Sarah Gideon case. He told Michael Tymn that the Gideon case was "really one of several 'amalgams, or blended stories'" (quoted in Rivas, 2009, p. 256), and Hamilton told Titus Rivas that the "case is, at best, illustrative. Nothing more" (Rivas, 2009, p. 256).

46 Neither, of course, is there compelling evidence from materialists or refutations of the veridical evidence from NDEs by materialists that consciousness is produced by the brain.

47 For a report on Irene's case see the documentary *Untimely Departure* by Sonia Barkallah, at minute 41.

48 The facts of the case are taken from Jim Tucker, 2005, p. 151ff with details added from Stevenson, 1974, p. 130ff.

49 Tucker, p. 154; for a list of all of Gnanatilleka's correct identifications, see Stevenson, pp. 136-41.

50 I acknowledge, and even applaud (because then scientists are paying attention to the data), that the movement is not always from skeptic or debunker to accepter, though that seems to be the more publicized of the action. For example, Dr. Daryl J. Bem, who published a controversial psi study in the *Journal of Personality and Social Psychology* 100, 407-25 in 2011 ["Feeling the Future: Experimental Evidence for Anomalous Retroactive Influences on Cognition and Affect"], began as a total skeptic and a stage magician, who knew how to fake effects. His work and the literature on parapsychology experiments moved him from skeptic to accepter. On the other hand, Sam Moulton, who as a Harvard undergraduate spent a summer at Duke University

investigating the records from the J.B. Rhine parapsychology lab, returned to Harvard to write a remarkable senior thesis showing strong psi results in experiments, only to switch sides completely when his graduate work on such experiments showed no results whatsoever. Here, then, are two examples, heading in opposite directions, of researchers who are led by the data.

51 YouTube, "Dr. Sam Harris vs. David Wolpe," at 48 minutes, https://www.youtube.com/watch?v=OSBaAT6WPmk. To be fair, Harris states that he is open-minded about studies of the paranormal. "If some experimental psychologists want to spend their days studying telepathy, or the effects of prayer, I will be interested to know what they find out." That they are currently doing so and have already gotten results, with nary a word from Harris, shows that his statement might well be disingenuous.

52 So a neuroscientist like V.S. Ramachandran who seeks to explain mind, including self and consciousness, solely in terms of properties of the brain looks at patients with damaged parts of their brains or genetic quirks that affect their brains. But Ramachandran does not include among his anomalies any study, case, or experiment related to near-death experience, which itself may cast light, and certainly challenges some of Ramachandran's positions, on the brain-mind puzzle. See *The Tell-Tale Brain: A Neuroscientist's Quest for What Makes Us Human*, NY: W.W. Norton & Co, 2011.

53 See the end of Harris's blog "Response to Controversy" at http://www.samharris.org/site/full_text/response-to-con troversy2/.

54 I hope to argue persuasively in this chapter why this point is obvious to me, but I acknowledge that it is not obvious to lots of people. According to a Pew poll conducted in May, 2014, 53 percent of Americans, over half the population of the United States, think that one must believe in God to be

a moral person. See http://www.pewglobal.org/2014/03/13/ worldwide-many-see-belief-in-god-as-essential-to-morality/.

55. See "The God Debate II: Harris vs. Craig" (https://www.youtube.com/watch?v=yqaHXKLRKzg).

56 The God in question here is the God of the Abrahamic religions—Judaism, Christianity, and Islam. This is a personal, divine entity who is different and separate from us and rules the universe. There are, of course, other conceptions of God, but my context in this chapter is the God of Abraham. So imagine the man with the long beard and flowing robe sitting in heaven on a throne.

57 "Inter-objectivity" is clearly an unusual term, but I intend it in a straightforward way: When we have near-universal agreement on the validity or veracity of a claim, based on overwhelming evidence or reason, then I suggest that that claim is objective among the requisite people. Thus 97 percent of climate scientists agree—again, based on the evidence—that climate change is real and that human activity is a major cause. Despite strenuous opposition from some politicians—whose own positions lack substantive evidence—we can say that climate change is "inter-objective" among the experts.

58 I address the positive or "Christic" principle in Chapter 5.

59 For a detailed look at how deliberation with others figures centrally into personal autonomy, please see my article, "The Social Nature of Autonomy" (1993).

60 See, for example, Hannah Arendt, "Truth and Politics," *Between Past and Future*, New York: Viking Press, 1968, p. 237. The clearest discussion of these three eyes of knowing is in Wilber, K., *Eye to Eye*, New York: Anchor Press/Doubleday, 1983. See in that volume especially the essays "Eye to Eye" and "The Problem of Proof." Those who read these will see the tremendous debt I owe to those discussions.

61 From *The Apple and the Spectroscope*; quoted in Berthoff, Ann, *The Making of Meaning*, Montclair NJ: Boynton/Cook, 1981, p. 116.

62 See Taylor, Charles, "Responsibility for Self," in Rorty, Amelie Oksenberg (Ed.), *The Identities of Persons*, Berkeley and Los Angeles: the University of California Press, 1976.

63 Wilber, 1983, p. 32. In *Cosmopolitanism: Ethics in a World of Strangers* (2008), Anthony Appiah makes a similar point about training: "When scientists looked at the tracks of charged particles in photographs of cloud chambers...they said things like, 'Look, there's a path of an electron.' That's what was reasonable for them to believe. Yet for the rest of us, who don't know the relevant physics or understand how the cloud chamber works, it all looks just like a fuzzy line in a photograph" (p. 41).

64 Thomas Kuhn makes this point in *The Structure of Scientific Revolutions*. One of his examples is of "seeing water droplets or a needle against a numerical scale." These are "primitive perceptual experience(s) for the man unacquainted with cloud chambers and ammeters." The man "who has learned about these instruments" (who has been trained) "sees not droplets but the tracks of electrons, alpha particles, and so on" (1962, p. 197). Similarly, when a student looks at a contour map, she sees only lines on paper. But the cartographer sees a picture of terrain. Only after training, when the student becomes an inhabitant of the cartographer's world, will she see what the cartographer sees.

65 For a discussion of this topic, and related issues, see Crittenden, J., "Veneration of Community," *Communal Societies*, Volume 9, 1989, 105-22.

66 As Thomas Kuhn wrote of two groups of scientists who differ over what they see, "each will have to learn to translate the other's theory and its consequences into his own language" (1962, p. 202).

67 Scientists rely on empirical facts, which are literally "something made through trial" (*facere*, "to make"; *en*, "through"; *peira*, "trial"). *Facere* is also translated as "to do" (Thus a fact is a "thing done."). *Factum* or *factus* refers to that which is made. (See the *Oxford English Dictionary*, p. 947.) We are, of course, free to restrict the meaning of words as long as we make that meaning clear. So "empirical" has come to mean that which can be experienced through the five senses or their extensions. This has given science a great deal of precision. But it is curious that the literal definition makes no mention of this kind of "sensory" trial. Moreover, a fact is something that is "made," not found. So could there be other kinds of trials, other kinds of experiments that could yield facts? Are there other ways facts could be "made"? Could the three epistemological steps not only make or establish empirical facts but make normative facts as well?

68 Anthropologist Ashley Montagu concluded that "essentially the mind of the savage [sic] functions in exactly the same way as our own [modern mind] does, the differences perceptible in the effects of that functioning are due only to the differences in the premises upon which that functioning is based." So while the experiences and histories of cultures vary, the internal processes for reasoning about them are the same. And according to Steven Lukes, researchers Cole and Scribner have concluded "that thus far there is no evidence for different *kinds* of reasoning processes such as the old classic theories alleged—we have no evidence for a 'primitive logic'." Note the open-endedness of their claim: There is no evidence "thus far." (*Culture and Thought: A Psychological Introduction*, 1974, p. 170; quoted in Lukes, "Relativism in Its Place," in Lukes and Hollis, *Rationality and Relativism*, Cambridge: The MIT Press, 1982, p. 270.) The truth of the matter is open to continued communal

confirmation or refutation.

69 For the Azande to refute or confirm our evidence, they would, of course, have to train themselves adequately for the illumination, just as we would have to translate or see their practices properly.

70 Contrast this view with Joshua Cohen's notion of reason-giving: "In an idealized deliberative setting, it will not do simply to advance reasons that one takes to be true or compelling: such considerations may be rejected by others who are themselves reasonable. One must instead find reasons that are compelling to others..." ("Procedure and Substance in Deliberative Democracy," in Bohman and Rehg, *Deliberative Democracy*, 1997, p. 414). In other words, in Cohen's version, even if it is acknowledged to be an "idealized" setting, partiality of perspective is to be overcome, and it is overcome not by stepping into the particular viewpoint of another, but by seeking out the universalistic perspective of the generalized other; that is, unanimity, perhaps even an objective point of view, on what is normatively right.

71 Karl Popper, *The Logic of Scientific Discovery*, London: Routledge, 1992, p. 94.

72 This is the statement attributed to Voltaire: "Those who can make you believe absurdities can make you commit atrocities," ostensibly from a letter by Voltaire on the subject of the alleged miracles discussed by M. Claparede, Professor of Theology at the University of Geneva. The closest approximation that I could actually find of this statement is the following: "Formerly there were those who said: 'You believe things that are incomprehensible, inconsistent, impossible because we have commanded you to believe them; go then and do what is unjust because we command it.' Such people show admirable reasoning. Truly, whoever is able to make you absurd is able to make you

unjust. If the God-given understanding of your mind does not resist a demand to believe what is impossible, then you will not resist a demand to do wrong to that God-given sense of justice in your heart. As soon as one faculty of your soul has been dominated, other faculties will follow as well. And from this derives all those crimes of religion which have overrun the world." Though less pithy, this quotation is clearly no less damning.

73 A literal reading might seem even more implausible when we note that none of the four Gospels was written by a contemporary of Jesus's. Mark wrote his Gospel, the earliest Gospel, some 50 years after Jesus and never claimed to have been his companion. The other Gospels were written 20 years or so after Mark's. The Gospel of Matthew, for example, was written between 80 and 90 CE. Bear in mind, then, that when Paul wrote his letters (between 53 and 62 CE) the Gospels had probably not yet been written.

Likewise, how can anyone think that a text as riddled with contradictions and inconsistencies as the Bible could be the inerrant word of God? Keep in mind that Erasmus translated the King James Version of the Bible into English from Greek, except where Erasmus didn't because he couldn't find Greek versions and so used Latin versions, themselves copied from Greek in the fourth century. To complicate matters, Jesus spoke in Aramaic, and those Aramaic words were never recorded, since the Gospels were written originally in Greek. So our Bibles are first written in Greek—not the language of Jesus—then translated into Latin and then translated into English. They are copies of copies of copies going back two millennia.

74 As I mentioned, I shall explore this idea in detail in Chapter 5.

75 See as representative texts, for example, the *Visuddhimagga* of Theravadan Buddhists, the Hindu *Upanishads*, the *Yoga*

Sutras of Patanjali, the Mahayana Buddhist *Vimalakirti Sutra*, and in the West, the *Philokalia* of the Hesychasts of the Eastern Orthodox Church.

76 For a summary of some of this work, see Jensine Andresen, "Meditation Meets Behavioural Medicine," *Journal of Consciousness Studies*, volume 7, nos. 11-12, 2000, pp. 17-73. See also Goleman and Davidson, who report that there have been over 3000 scientific-research articles on meditation from 2014-16 (p. 14). Their book thoroughly covers meditation studies including their own research stretching back to their graduate-student days in the 1970s.

Some of the most extensive studies of the effects of meditation have been conducted on Transcendental Meditation (TM). The first paper on TM's physiological effects appeared in *Science* in 1970, and researchers have continued studies up to the present. The five volumes of scientific research on TM contain over 500 studies. See *Scientific Research on Maharishi's Transcendental Meditation and TM-Sidhi Program*, volumes 1-5. This research focuses on beneficial changes in metabolic rate, plasma cortisol levels, galvanic skin response, arterial blood lactate, cardiovascular and neural activity, motor ability, perceptual ability, learning, athletic performance, biochemical reactions, oxygen consumption, and the like. Unfortunately, the reliability of this research is problematic, since so much of the TM research has been undertaken by those within the TM movement.

77 See Newberg and Waldman, 2010; Newberg, *Principles of Neurotheology* (2010); and Monastersky, Richard, 2006, p. A15. See also Patrick McNamara (2009). Richie Davidson, pioneering what he and Dan Goleman call the fledgling research field of "contemplative neuroscience" (2017, p. 7), has run, sponsored, and supervised many experiments both in and through the University of Wisconsin's Center

for Healthy Minds, which Davidson started, and in and through the brain-imaging lab at the Waisman Center, also at University of Wisconsin-Madison.

78 Newberg studied a group of nuns who had been practicing the Christian "Centering Prayer" for at least 15 years. He found that the neurological changes in their brains were significant and matched closely the neurological changes seen in studies of Buddhist monks. Although the brain changes were similar, these two groups "obviously nurtured very different beliefs" (2009, 48). In brief, breathing, attention, and relaxation techniques used in various meditative practices produce physiological effects, even when stripped of religious or spiritual overtones. As Newberg said of other experiments, "Our patients were taught a traditional Eastern meditation, using sounds and movements that had deep religious meaning, but we did not emphasize the spiritual dimensions of the ritual. No one reported having a spiritual experience, and no one mentioned God" (2009, 45).

79 Decreased activity in the parietal lobe, the part of the cortex used to construct our sense of self, indicates a dissolution of a sense of self and an increased sense of unity.

80 The EEG, or QEEG in this case, records the brain's electrical activity; the fMRI shows in great detail where that activity is taking place within the brain.

81 Lutz, Antoine; Greischar, Lawrence L.; Rawlings, Nancy B.; Ricard, Matthieu, and Davidson, Richard J. (Eds.), "Long-Term Meditators Self-Induce High-Amplitude Gamma Synchrony During Mental Practice," *Proceedings of the National Academy of Sciences*, volume 101, no. 46, 2004, p. 16372.

82 See Lazar, Sara W. et al. (2005). In a study testing sustained attention of meditators and a control group, Elizabeth Valentine et al. found that meditators—those who practiced

concentration techniques and those who practiced mindfulness techniques—outperformed the control group. Long-term meditators outperformed short-term meditators. See Elizabeth Valentine et al., "Meditation and Attention: A Comparison of the Effects of Concentrative and Mindfulness Meditation on Sustained Attention." This paper is available from Dr. E.R. Valentine, Department of Psychology, Royal Holloway, Egham, Surrey, England. Also, Newberg and Waldman tested some subjects who were new to meditation and meditated only 12 minutes per day for eight weeks. In these nascent meditators they found activation in the prefrontal cortex and in the anterior cingulate, which indicates improved memory and cognition, counters the effects of depression, and slows down or reduces cognitive decline (2009, pp. 27-8). Finally, in excellent news for Baby Boomers, Goleman and Davidson report on a study out of UCLA that finds that post-50-year-old meditators' brains, through reduced brain atrophy, are "younger" than their non-meditating counterparts by an average 7.5 years (Goleman and Davidson, 2017, p. 180).

83   In 2005 Newberg conducted an online survey of people's spiritual experiences, collecting data on their religious orientations and belief systems. By 2007 he had data from almost 1000 people (2010, pp. 69-70). Nearly "three-quarters of our respondents indicated that they felt a sense of oneness with the universe or a unity with all of life." This was true for people, Newberg observes, "not just in a metaphoric sense, but in the way we conduct our lives" (2010, p. 81). Newberg and Waldman added that social interaction strengthens one's ability to respond to others. "We encourage you to interact with as many different people as you can" (2009, 127). See also Newberg and Waldman, 2010, Chapter 10: "Compassionate Communication."

84   For a detailed discussion of these points, see Kaplan, P.,

Toward a Theology of Consciousness, unpublished doctoral dissertation, Harvard University, 1976.

85 Kaplan, 1976. Ken Wilber claims that the three epistemological steps are found in all of the esoteric traditions East and West (2000); W.T. Stace concluded in *Mysticism and Philosophy* that the "introvertive experience" is in essence "the same all over the world in all cultures, religions, places, and ages" (1960). See also Frithjof Schuon (1975).

86 From *The Sufi Message of Hazrat Inayat Khan*, Volume 12, London: Barrie and Rockliff, p. 104; quoted in Kaplan, 1976, p. 245. For example, one might try from a different tradition this instruction: "Retire into solitude. Seat yourself on a clean spot in an erect posture, with the head and neck in a straight line. Control all sense-organs. Bow down in devotion to your teacher. Then enter the lotus of the heart and meditate there on the presence of Brahman—the pure, the infinite, the blissful." ~Kaivalya Upanishad.

87 Toward the end of the sixteenth century, a French classical scholar and printer, Henri Estienne (also known as Henricus Stephanus), numbered sections of all of Plato's dialogues. Referred to as "Stephanus numbers," this numerical system, as I show within parentheses in the text, made it easier to locate passages in the dialogues and for scholars to cite Plato's works. The numbers are uniform across all translations and editions of the dialogues.

88 It may not be surprising, given the subject of this section, that the word "koan" combines two Japanese words: *ko* or "public" and *an* or "a matter for thought." Thus a koan is a public matter for thought or a matter for public thought.

89 There are numerous works available on developmental psychology in general and moral development in particular. In addition to Kohlberg's works, three books that have been especially significant to me are: Robert Kegan, *The Evolving*

Self; Carol Gilligan, *In a Different Voice*; and Ken Wilber, *Sex, Ecology, Spirituality*. To read more about my take on the importance of developmental psychology to the expansion and raising of consciousness, please see my books *Beyond Individualism* and *Wide As the World*.

90   Another example of the lowly status of women, and there are plenty of them in the Bible, comes in the story of Lot and the two angels of the Lord. Two angels come to Sodom, and Lot who is sitting at the gate recognizes them. He urges the two to spend the night in his house. But the men of Sodom, "both old and young," come to Lot's home and demand that Lot release the two "men." "Bring them out," the men of Sodom demand, "that we may know them carnally." Lot wants to protect the angels because they are, well, angels. In their place Lot offers his daughters "who have not known a man." "Please," Lot says, "let me bring them out to you and you may do to them as you wish" (Genesis 19:6-8). The men of Sodom want to know these angels *carnally*; notice that Lot does not offer himself for defilement, only his two virgin daughters.

91   Consider this: "The Lord possessed me at the beginning of His way, Before His works of old. I have been established from everlasting, From the beginning, before there was ever an earth. When there were no depths I was brought forth…Before the mountains were settled, Before the hills, I was brought forth…When He prepared the heavens, I was there, When He drew a circle on the face of the deep, When He established the clouds above…Then I was beside Him as a master craftsman" (Proverbs 8:22-5, 27-8, 30). Who is this "me," who is this "I" referred to in the Proverb? It is not who we think we are; it is who we truly are: our Authentic or True Self, the Universal Primordial Consciousness. That is the "I AM." Here, too, is a mystical link between Jesus Christ and us all: "Jesus said to them, 'Most assuredly, I

say to you, before Abraham was, I AM'" (John 8:58). See the third section of this chapter: Post-Conventional Morality: Christic Consciousness.

92 "Fear God and keep His commandments, For this is man's all" (Ecclesiastes 11:13-14).

93 "The law of the Lord is perfect, converting the soul... The statutes of the Lord are right, rejoicing the heart; The commandment of the Lord is pure, enlightening the eyes; The fear of the Lord is clean, enduring forever" (Psalm 19:7-9); but "upon the wicked He will rain coals; Fire and brimstone and a burning wind shall be the portion of his cup..." (Psalm 11:6-7). "Oh, fear the Lord, you His saints! There is no want to those who fear Him...Come, you children, listen to me; I will teach you the fear of the Lord" (Psalm 34:9-10, 11).

94 In what seems to be bad news for humanity, this in-group/out-group differentiation is practically innate. As psychologist Joshua Greene comments: "...[A]nthropological reports indicate that in-group favoritism and ethnocentrism are human universals" (Moral Tribes, 2013, NY: Penguin Press, p. 69). "Favoritism" can be an understatement, since in-group/out-group hostility has frequently accounted throughout the ages as the basis for massacre and oppression and may, indeed, be our behavioral default position. The God of the Old Testament certainly "favors" his Chosen People in his unleashing of genocidal wrath. He instructs Joshua, for example, to slaughter everyone who lives in those towns surrounding or occupying the Promised Land: among them Jericho, Ai, Makkedah, Eglon, Hebron, and Debir. He tells the children of Israel that when He leads them into a land occupied by others, they shall conquer those others and "make no covenant with them nor show mercy to them" (Deuteronomy 7:2).

95 In the Book of Jeremiah, God tells Jeremiah that he will

punish "the neighbors" who have harassed Jeremiah and the children of Israel. "Then it shall be, after I have plucked them out, that I will return and have compassion on them and bring them back…And it shall be, if they will learn carefully the ways of My people, to swear by My name… then they shall be established in the midst of My people" (12:15-6).

96   When Jesus visited Sychar, a city in Samaria, he asked a Samaritan woman to draw him a drink of water from the well. That request precipitated a series of lessons that Jesus taught to her about herself and about the work of God. She then went into Sychar and told the men of the town about Jesus, who themselves came to hear him. When Jesus had finished, the men of the city told the Samaritan woman that they believed Jesus, not because of what she had said, but because they themselves had heard him, had experienced him and his teachings firsthand (John 4:42).

Another example of firsthand experience is the demand by Thomas, called the Twin or sometimes "Doubting Thomas," that he will not believe that Jesus has arisen "unless I see in His hands the print of the nails, and put my finger into the print of the nails and put my hand into His side" (John 20:25). Jesus said that unless the people saw him perform miracles, they would not believe (John 4:48).

97   Matthew 10:37-39. Likewise in Luke (14:26) Jesus says, "If anyone comes to Me and does not hate his father and mother, wife and children, brothers and sisters, yes, and even his own life also, he cannot be My disciple."

98   This relates to the more demanding, esoteric reading of this challenge from Jesus. This is not the space for pursuing it, but in essence it is the requirement to abandon all attachments—to job, school, partners, children, parents, values, and the like—because those are, at best, only relative to the highest pursuit possible: the remembrance

and recovery of your own true Being. These attachments hold you in the relative world, the world of desire, and block your avenue to the Absolute, to God.

99   This phrase, "transcend but include," is an attempted translation of the Hegelian view of what occurs when the thesis interacts with its antithesis (*Aufheben* in German). It is also translated as "negate but preserve," but is usually translated as "sublation." See Wilber (2000) for a fuller discussion of this in relation to states of consciousness.

100 Matthew 5:17. In his Letter to the Romans Paul writes that all the commandments are "summed up in this saying, 'You shall love your neighbor as yourself.' Love does no harm to a neighbor; therefore love is the fulfillment of the law" (Romans 12:9-10).

101 See also the Gospels of Mark 3:1-6 and of Luke 66-11. In another instance Jesus, while teaching in a synagogue on the Sabbath, healed a woman who had been bent over for 18 years. "...[T]he ruler of the synagogue" was outraged that Jesus would "work" on the Sabbath. Jesus responded: "Does not each one of you on the Sabbath loose his ox or donkey from the stall, and lead it away to water? So ought not this woman...be loosed from this bond on the Sabbath?" (Luke 13:10-16).

102 "On these two commandments hang all the Laws and the Prophets" (Matthew 22:40). There is a higher mystical principle at work here that I cannot go into in detail, but it points to this: Loving the Lord thy God can refer to loving the Father that is our true and highest nature, our true, authentic, and original Self. As we come to love and identify that Self, we see others as equal refractions of that true Self. So we love others as our Self, for that is what they truly are. We love others not as we love ourselves, but we love others as equal to our own Self because each is our own Self. "I and the Father are one" (John 30:10), and "one"

is not just Jesus but is every person.

103 Matthew 5:39; see also Luke 6:29: "And from him who takes away your cloak, do not withhold your tunic either." Imagine the look on the thief's face when you hand him your car keys as well when he has only demanded your wallet.

104 Jesus pointed out that when a child is circumcised on the Sabbath, then the law of Moses is not broken, despite the prohibition against working on the Sabbath. So, Jesus said to the congregation, "are you angry with Me because I made a man completely well on the Sabbath? Do not judge according to appearance, but judge with righteous judgment" (John 7:21-4).

105 I discuss this idea of full presence in the next chapter.

106 The sense of "neighbor" used here refers to those who live in proximity to us, and that use implies, for Jesus's time, that neighbors were those who shared more than physical closeness. They shared as well the roles, rules, and values of the community. Neighbors were, in other words and in Nietzsche's colorful phrase, "satellites of their own system" (1997, p. 118, Book II, #118).

107 Moving toward or into a moral perspective that sees our connections to all of humanity sounds, on its face, like a utopian ideal or daydream; for narcissists it would be a nightmare. But such movement can happen and does happen, and the mechanism is mystical or transcendental experience. I've written about this in Chapter 6 in this book and have written about it elsewhere as well. Please see my *Wide As the World* (2011), especially the section "Cosmopolitan Identity and Mysticism" (pp. 92-9).

108 I have written at length elsewhere about moral identities. Please see *Wide As the World* (2011), especially Chapter 3: "Cosmopolitan Identity."

109 Camus, Preface, p. 1, 1991. Along with *The Stranger* and

Caligula, Camus referred to "The Myth of Sisyphus" as one of his "three absurds" (Bakewell, 2016, p. 138), since each discussed the meaninglessness of life.

110 Existentialism is also often associated in the public mind with other, less alluring terms: dread, alienation, nihilism, and, as we saw with Camus and Sisyphus, the absurd. My focus in this chapter is on what makes Existentialism attractive. That attraction involves those ideas mentioned above—choice, freedom, authenticity—and another two as well: life-affirmation and happiness.

111 By raising such questions and concerns Nietzsche revealed himself to be a kindred spirit of mine, for he wanted to understand the nature of morality if we jettisoned theistic religion—that is, for Nietzsche if God is dead, then what is left of morality? Please see Chapter 4ß in this volume for my view on that question.

112 Of course, even with God much that happens to us and in the world seems crazy, as in "absurd." God, as we are told in the face of such circumstances, moves in mysterious ways.

113 Nietzsche notes that "there is as much wisdom in pain as there is in pleasure: both belong among the factors that contribute the most to the preservation of the species" (1974, p. 252). It is the inscrutability of pain that can give meaning. "The great pain bearers of humanity, those few or rare human beings" are the heroes (1974, p. 252).

114 My friend, Nietzsche fan, and a frequent conversational combatant, Rory Varrato, describes the negation this way: It functions as a double negative to derive a positive; for example, "a 'no' to the wrongful 'NO' of slave morality is thus a 'no' to 'No' and thereby a 'Yes.'" "No" is itself transvalued, as Nietzsche would say.

115 1992, p. 714, emphasis in the original. Elsewhere Nietzsche says something similar: "*Amor fati*: let that alone be my love

henceforth!...And all in all and on the whole: some day I wish to be only a Yes-sayer" (1974, p. 223, emphases in the original).

116 Brodie commented: "Sometimes...time seems to slow way down, in an uncanny way, as if everyone were moving in slow motion...It seems as if I have all the time in the world to watch the receivers run their patterns, and yet I know the defensive line is coming at me just as fast as ever...and yet the whole thing seems like a movie or a dance in slow motion." From "Altered States," *Chicago Tribune*, November 14, 1982, p. 27. Ted Williams, perhaps the greatest hitter in baseball, said that there were times when the game would slow down so dramatically that he could see the seams of the baseball coming toward home plate.

117 Consider another example within the Zen tradition: "Perfection in the art of swordsmanship is reached, according to Takuan [a great Zen master], when the heart is troubled by no more thought of Me and You, of the opponent and his sword, of one's own sword and how to wield it—no more thought even of life and death. 'All is emptiness: your own self, the flashing sword, and the arms that wield it. Even the thought of emptiness is no longer there.' From this absolute emptiness, states Takuan, 'comes the most wondrous unfoldment of doing'" (Herrigel, 1953, p. 104). What is true of archery and swordsmanship was also true of these experiences of mine in soccer and martial arts.

118 This idea of emptiness is not so strange. Indeed, from the perspective of neuroscience the mind is "empty." That is, we do not store things in our brains, not models, memories, knowledge, representations, rules, or programs. We certainly do not process information as if our brains were computers. If you know all the lyrics to all of The Beatles' songs, it is not because they are stored in your brain.

This, of course, may well be in concert with the idea that consciousness is not a product of the brain. [See Anthony Chemero's *Radical Embodied Cognitive Science*, Cambridge, MA: The MIT Press, 2011.]

119 The terms used here for these qualities are evocative of what persons experience in this transcendental state, but the experience itself is indescribable, being beyond language and logic.

The language used here is a sign of the limits of my own experience. Ken Wilber pointed out to me that one established in Being is not experiencing these qualities as either attached to the person or as witnessed by one who has transcended the sense of a separate self. Indeed, any quality of this sort is beyond its presence or its absence. That is, a sense of deliciousness established in Being in no way depends on a moment being excellent, felt as excellent, interpreted as excellent. If it did, then that sense necessarily involves its opposite for its presence to be experienced. Instead, deliciousness must be Deliciousness, beyond all differentiation, all duality in which one thing depends on its opposite. Deliciousness exists not as a state in itself, but as the ground of all states and all experiences. Thus, Deliciousness is not separate from any state or experience nor captured by any state or experience. Whether the moment is exquisite or awful, Deliciousness is; whereas small "d" deliciousness only tastes good. Thanks to Ken for this insight; personal communication, July 2017.

120 Ken Wilber specifies that "being fully present in Being" distinguishes between two transcendental states, alluded to in Endnote #127: Turiya and Turiyatita. Turiya, known as the fourth state of consciousness ("Turiya" means "fourth" in Sanskrit.) is a state of pure consciousness that underlies the prior three states of waking, dreaming, and deep or dreamless sleep. This is the state of witnessing where the

separate self is transcended, but the Self remains. This was my experience. Turiyatita, meaning "beyond the fourth," is that "state" in which the Self itself, the witness, disappears leaving only That Which Is. "State" is placed in quotation marks, because Turiyatita is not itself a state, which implies that which has a beginning and, perhaps, an end. For an example of this, see the quotation by Bernadette Roberts on p. 191 in my text. Given this context, I have described Sisyphus as "established in Being" or "immersed in the moment," which I take it is Turiya. To be *fully* established in Being would be Turiyatita. Personal communication with Ken Wilber, July 2017.

121 Maslow also described peak-experiences as bringing the perception of "the whole universe as an integrated and unified whole" (1964, p. 59) and as "giving meaning to life itself" (1964, p. 62) in which "the world is accepted" (p. 63). Peak-experiences are often without a sense of time or space (p. 63) and carry a sense of universality and eternity (p. 63). Although Maslow found that almost everyone has peak-experiences, he questioned to what extent peak-experiences could be induced. "Peak-experiences are moments of ecstasy which cannot be bought, cannot be guaranteed, cannot even be sought" (1971, p. 48). Reading on in this chapter, you will see that the three spiritual teachers here disagree.

122 Maslow himself also discussed in his work the phenomenon of "plateau experience," where one "can learn to see in a Unitive way almost at will. It then becomes a witnessing, an appreciating, what one might call a serene, cognitive blissfulness" (1971, p. 344). These experiences showed Maslow that persons could "take up residence on the high plateau of Unitive consciousness" and stay there (1971, p. 345).

123 For readers interested in exploring more, many more, such persons and claims, please visit the website Buddha

at the Gas Pump (batgap.com). This website, operated by Rick Archer, is dedicated to interviews with persons who have undergone transformations of consciousness into a new way of understanding the world and themselves. Described as "spiritual awakenings," these pilgrims discuss their transformations and these new ways—which often correspond to descriptions offered by mystics throughout the centuries—of seeing and being in the world. See also my book *Wide As the World*, where I discuss transformations of consciousness involving cosmopolitan identity.

124 When Moses asks God what name he should use with the Israelites to identify "the God of your fathers," God responds: "I AM WHO I AM"; and "He said, 'Thus you shall say to the sons of Israel, I AM has sent me to you'" (Exodus 3:14). This is the same I AM that Jesus spoke. It signifies Being or Pure Consciousness beyond time and space and form. It is presence itself.

125 As I shall discuss later in the chapter, language fails us here. There is actually no identification with or absorption in the moment, the Now, for there remains no one to be identified or absorbed.

126 I capitalize "Self" here and throughout to differentiate this realization of our True or Higher Self from the ego-determined, separate self that ordinarily constitutes our identity.

127 This, I think, is what Ken Wilber meant by Turiyatita. See Endnote #120 above.

128 As Nietzsche points out: "...[I]f, with the virtuous enthusiasm and clumsiness of some philosophers, one wanted to abolish the 'apparent world' altogether—well, suppose *you* could do that, at least nothing would be left of your 'truth' either" (1992, p. 236, emphasis in the original).

129 1982, p. 270. In the Gospel of Matthew 7:14, Jesus instructs us to "enter through the narrow gate...[S]mall is the gate

and narrow the way that leads to life, and only a few find it." For me, that narrow gate is the Now moment.

130 This quotation is found in a footnote by translator Walter Kaufmann, 1974, p. 226, no. 8.

131 This example comes from Morin, 2014.

132 See *The New York Times*, "Cancer Study of Psilocybin Hints at New Role for Illegal Drug," December 1, 2016, p. A1.

In his 2000 book *Cleansing the Doors of Perception*, Huston Smith quotes from the account of a participant who took an unspecified psychedelic: "Although I am writing this over a year later [after the drug experience], the thrill of the surprise and amazement, the awesomeness of the revelation, the engulfment in an overwhelming feeling-wave of gratitude and blessed wonderment, are as fresh, and the memory of the experience is as vivid, as if it had happened five minutes ago" (p. 22).

Rick Doblin published a follow-up study of the Harvard Divinity School graduate students who had been administered a dose of psilocybin 50 years earlier in Walter Pahnke's 1962 study (the Good Friday Experiment). Doblin found that all nine (out of 10) students contacted reported that the experience had shaped their lives in significant and enduring ways. See Pollan, 2015.

Finally, in 2006 Roland Griffiths and his team published a report on their double-blind psilocybin experiment in which 36 volunteers participated in two or three sessions at two-month intervals. The researchers reported that the volunteers described their psychedelic experiences as having "substantial and sustained personal meaning and spiritual significance" as far out as one year later (Griffiths et al., 2006, p. 15). See also Griffiths and Grob, 2010.

133 Thanks to Rory Varrato for the quotation.

134 There is, of course, debate as to whether psychedelic drugs induce unusual states of consciousness by altering brain

chemistry or whether, as Huxley said, the drug removes filters in the brain that inhibit the perception of different, even pristine, states of consciousness. This debate harkens back to the question raised at the beginning of this book: Does the brain produce consciousness, or is the brain simply a register of consciousness? For an interesting investigation of this debate, see Strassman, 2014, especially chapter 4, pp. 35-50.

135 Results of studies show that even with only one psilocybin session, late-stage cancer patients experience long-lasting benefits, as do their families. To date, surveys of subjects have been conducted up to as much as 14 months after the session. See Grob et al., 2011. See also Slater, 2018, pp. 262-72. In a different setting, David J. Nutt, Director of the neuropsychopharmacology unit at Imperial College London, and his colleagues dosed 12 patients, all suffering from depression on average for 18 years, with psilocybin. "Within a week after taking psilocybin, every single patient had experienced substantial improvements in his or her depressive symptoms, and after three months, five of the 12 subjects had enjoyed a complete remission" (Slater, 2018, p. 264).

136 In the 1950s and 60s mental-health professionals used psychedelics for an array of mental illnesses, including alcoholism and even autism. According to Linda Marsa in "A Good Trip," by the early 1960s more than 40,000 patients in over 2000 studies had experienced psychedelics as treatment for schizophrenia, drug addiction, chronic depression, and more. Marsa, *Aeon*, March 28, 2014; found online at https://aeon.co/essays/how-psychedelics-are-helping-cancer-patients-fend-off-despair.

137 This comment is not to downplay the negative effects from unauthorized, non-research uses of LSD—panic attacks, psychotic reactions, flashbacks, and isolated but real

accidents and deaths. But the number of such effects was minimal when considering the context: Close to two million Americans had tried LSD by 1969 (Pollan, 2018, p. 199).

138 For a more complete version of this story, see Fadiman, 2011, Chapter 14: "Closing the Doors of Perception," pp. 183-93.

139 The reference is to Plato's dialogue the *Phaedrus*: "…[T]hey have a steep climb to the high tier at the rim of heaven… [T]hey stand and gaze upon what is outside heaven…What is in this place is without color and without shape and without solidity, a being that really is what it is, the subject of all true knowledge…[A]ny soul is delighted at last to be seeing what is real and watching what is true…" (247a7-d4).

140 For firsthand reports of participants in psychedelic drug trials with many of the same elements as described here, see Strassman, 2001.

141 Abraham Maslow said of peak-experiences: "Peak-experiences can be so wonderful that they can parallel the experience of dying, that is of an eager and happy dying. It is a kind of reconciliation and acceptance of death" (1964, p. 65).

142 For a discussion of this way of knowing, please see in this book Chapter 4: "Divine Knowing." From Michael Pollan: "But along with the feeling of ineffability, the conviction that some profound objective truth has been disclosed to you is a hallmark of the mystical experience, regardless of whether it has been occasioned by a drug, meditation, fasting, self-flagellation, or sensory deprivation" (2018, p. 41).

143 Nichols is quoted in Pollan, 2015.

144 Eighty percent of Americans say that they would prefer to die at home. Only 20 percent do. One reason for the low percentage is that many patients don't know that they are

dying, because their doctors are not trained to deliver that news. Zitter, Jessica Nutik, "First, Sex Ed. Then Death Ed.," *The New York Times*, February 19, 2017, Sunday Review, p. 7.

145 See the work of the Multidisciplinary Association for Psychedelic Studies (MAPS), found at http://www.maps. org/research/mdma. See also "Ecstasy as a Remedy for PTSD? You Probably Have Some Questions" by Dave Philipps, *The New York Times*, May 1, 2018, available at https://www.nytimes.com/2018/05/01/us/ecstasy-molly-ptsd-mdma.html.

146 I recognize that this is a controversial issue, as the debate continues among philosophers and scientists about whether AI or robots can ever be conscious. But there are several notable thinkers on the side that they might be. Among those are Nick Bostrom, *Superintelligence: Paths, Dangers, and Strategies* (Oxford University Press, 2017); David Gunkel, *The Machine Question: Critical Perspectives on AI, Robots, and Ethics* (The MIT Press, 2012); Max Tegmark, *Life 3.0: Being Human in the Age of Artificial Intelligence* (Knopf, 2017); and Wendell Wallach and Colin Allen, *Moral Machines: Teaching Robots Right from Wrong* (Oxford University Press, 2010).

147 "The Future of Employment: How Susceptible Are Jobs to Computerisation?" by Dr. Michael A. Osborne and Dr. Carl Benedikt Frey. Contact the Department of Engineering Science, University of Oxford (reception@eng.ox.ac.uk) for the full report.

148 Truck driving is the most common job in 29 states in the United States.

149 See, for example, the report from the consulting firm McKinsey and Company: "Where Machines Could Replace Humans—and Where They Can't (Yet)"—available at https://www.mckinsey.com/business-functions/digital-mckinsey/our-insights/where-machines-could-replace-humans-and-where-they-cant-yet. In the report, the authors

conducted a detailed analysis of over 2000 work activities in more than 800 occupations. One of their conclusions: Using the automation available today, 45 percent of all work-related activities that people are paid to perform could be automated right now. See also Susskind and Susskind (2016). In February 2017, for example, Bank of America started testing three "employee-free" branches, all offering full service and with access to a human only through video conferencing. Another example: Today "Flippy" from Miso Robotics could replace workers who operate fast-food grills. "Flippy" can unwrap burger patties, place them on the grill, keep track of the meat's cook time and temperature, take the patties off the heat, and place them on the burger bun. Alas, "Flippy" cannot yet add condiments. But line cooks, beware! http://www.digitaltrends.com/home/flippy-burger-robot/#ixzz4aqpYpPfT.

150 Domino's Pizza has announced that it will use six-wheeled automatons—a kind of robo-driven food cart—to deliver pizza within a one-mile radius of a Domino's store. Drones already deliver their pizza in New Zealand. https://techcrunch.com/2017/03/29/dominos-and-starship-technologies-will-deliver-pizza-by-robot-in-europe-this-summer/.

Meanwhile, Caterpillar is exploring the use of Fastbrick Robotics's bricklaying robot, which can build the framework for an entire house in three days. The robot can cut and secure up to 1000 bricks per hour, while taking into account doors, windows, and channels for plumbing and electrical wiring. http://newatlas.com/fastbrick-bricklaying-robot-caterpillar-investment/50325/.

151 Of course, by hoarding I mean the practice of collecting and reserving stockpiles of artifacts not for potential use, but because of an inability to discard them. Robots could be hoarders if some oddball programmer designed them to

move beyond collecting and saving human artifacts into hoarding them. Also, future Artificial General Intelligence could lead a robot that mimicked human behaviors into hoarding behavior. But unless the oddball programmer included human sentimentality and neurotic attachment, the robot will surely and quickly conclude that this behavior is pointless.

152 See Chapter 3 in this volume for a brief discussion of the trolley problem.

153 According to the Centers for Disease Control, fewer than half of Americans report having a strong sense of purpose beyond their jobs and their families. Quoted in Goleman and Davidson, 2017, p. 57.

154 Plenty of politicians applaud high employment rates, but rarely mention that many, if not most, of the jobs available are entry-level and low-wage work. Such jobs, I must note, are not those that often provide identity, meaning, and dignity. To such jobs, however, adding workplace democracy where workers at all levels help control their work, their products, and working conditions can provide meaning and dignity. See below for more on varieties of settings for democracy.

155 What about the idea that studying STEM subjects—science, technology, engineering, and math—in college will protect job seekers in our economy and provide them with the best opportunities for high-wages and secure employment? In his book *Will College Pay Off?* Peter Cappelli demonstrates that even students with that kind of background struggle to find work. He concludes that there is currently no shortage of students with STEM degrees. See Cappelli, Peter, *Will College Pay Off?* NY: PublicAffairs, 2015.

156 I do not discuss here the very important topic of how UBI might come about. In our current political climate, and in what will surely be its similar near-future iteration,

instituting a program for a universal basic income seems a long shot. Money, especially super-money, translates today into political power. Those with such power will be reluctant, perhaps militantly so, to approve this kind of economic distribution. Market exigencies, however, might make a program like UBI unavoidable. We can also make political progress by refashioning our democratic politics. My coauthor, Debi Campbell, and I discuss one such democratic refashioning in Campbell and Crittenden, *Direct Deliberative Democracy: How Citizens Can Rule*, 2018.

157 The dividend paid annually to every Alaskan is equal, making it effectively an Alaska-resident basic income. Although the amount received ($2,072 in 2015) is not sufficient to cover a person's basic needs, it is an obligation-free cash payment distributed to everyone.

In "Modeling the Macroeconomic Effects of a Universal Basic Income," a 2017 report from the Roosevelt Institute, the authors concluded that giving every adult American $1,000 per month would result after eight years in economic growth of $2.5 trillion. http://rooseveltinstitute.org/modeling-macroeconomic-effects-ubi/.

158 One of the concerns about UBI programs is that they are anti-work, encouraging people to sit around all day playing video games. Studies show this not the case. A study of seven randomly selected trials of government-run cash transfer programs, the equivalent of a UBI program, found no evidence that such programs discouraged work. See the paper by Banerjee, Hanna, Kreindler, and Olken, "Debunking the Stereotype of the Lazy Welfare Recipient," 2016, available from bolken@mit.edu.

159 On the opposite side, in 2016 Switzerland offered its citizens a national referendum on the issue of providing every adult citizen a guaranteed income per month of $2,500. More than 75 percent of the voters rejected the idea. The predominant

reason for voting "no," according to post-referendum surveys, was the belief that such an income could not be financed. I do not know in the run-up to the vote on the referendum whether the sponsors offered such funding ideas as a value-added tax or a consumption-income tax. See Parijs and Vanderborght, 2017, p. 173.

160 Ontario's pilot study should be of special interest to Americans, since Canada provides its citizens with nationalized health care. If Canada can reasonably provide citizens with both a UBI and health care, then this might be an incentive to Americans to push for a single-payer health system, rather than continuing to pay for the most expensive health care system in the world through private insurance. Since most Americans receive their health coverage through employers, the disappearance of jobs makes health care precarious and this private-insurance system untenable.

Could a UBI stipend cover private-insurance health care costs and cover other basic needs? Given that poverty is the single best predictor of health issues and hospitalization, UBI could well lead to a reduction in the use of health insurance, making it economically appealing if only through savings in health-care costs.

161 Nor is UBI a political panacea. Such a program leaves untouched a fair distribution of power, social justice, and inequality. UBI can help eliminate extreme poverty, but that just assures people that they won't be without any financial resources at all. It does little to remove stigmas and struggles of the working poor, who now might be the nonworking poor. A UBI program cannot become an excuse for governments to cease initiating programs to improve the life circumstances of the disadvantaged and the poor, programs such as prenatal care, childcare, and job training.

162 Those with physical and mental disabilities can be exempted from this requirement or can serve in any capacity suitable

for them. On the other hand, the fact that some persons cannot participate seems to separate them from the rest of the community and thereby render them somehow different from, if not inferior to, others. Some might then conclude that the disabled are not deserving of UBI. This argument should give us pause (It gives me pause.) in thinking about requiring such public service in the first place.

Thinking about any UBI program also requires factoring in ongoing breakthroughs in longevity and life extension. Gerontologists are predicting significant advances in life-extension medicine and science over the next few decades. Indeed, one of them, Aubrey de Grey, argues that ageing is a disease; as with any disease, if we can find the causes underlying the symptoms, then we can address and cure the disease. De Grey argues that we are on the verge of overcoming the seven reasons that we age and die, resulting in lifespans of up to 1000 years. Such lifespans surely need to be considered in our economic planning, and it might also be useful, given the finite resources of our planet, if those enamored of radical life extension investigated the scientific studies related to life after death instead of throwing all of their resources into overcoming or even solving death. See de Grey's 2005 TED talk: https://www. ted.com/talks/aubrey_de_grey_says_we_can_avoid_aging.

163 See Hicks and Devaraj, 2015.

164 Although highly successful, well regarded, and popular in Europe, apprenticeships have not caught on in the United States. This might be because four-year college enrollment exploded in the 1960s and 1970s as Baby Boomers came of age. The more recent decline—some would say "evisceration"—of labor unions may also have something to do with the lack of apprenticeships.

165 In the 2016 U.S. Presidential election the idea of dignity through work played a significant role. In her book *The*

Dignity of Working Men, Michéle Lamont found that white working-class men often defined their self-worth through the work that they did. Such men feared, even when they held jobs, that their work was in jeopardy, principally from competition by minorities. Because they also felt that they offered a superior work ethic and greater self-discipline than minorities, white working-class men perceived that only unfair advantages held out to minorities could explain job loss and encroachment. Their fear and resentment led many to Trump's mix of racism and promise of jobs. See Andrew J. Cherlin, "Money and Culture Are Inseparable," *The New York Times,* May 8, 2018, p. A25.

166 Why the exclusive focus here on men? The short answer is: Because of the dramatic increase in their deaths due to joblessness. In addition to what I wrote in the previous endnote about working-class white men, consider also the study by Deaton and Case (Kolata, 2015). They found that between 1999 and 2014 mortality rates had risen sharply for middle-aged white men with a high-school degree or less. Suicides and drug and alcohol poisoning were the principal methods used.

167 As an example, Goleman and Davidson comment: "The *Visuddhimagga* [See Endnote #75 in this text] holds...lasting changes in our very being...to be the true fruit of reaching the highest levels of the path of insight" (2017, p. 39).

168 See, for example, "Suicides Are Up. Is This an Existential Crisis?" by Clay Routledge, *The New York Times,* Sunday Review section, June 24, 2018, p. 9.

169 Readers interested in the details of my views on education as consciousness-expanding and consciousness-raising should see *Democracy's Midwife* (2002), especially Chapters 5 and 6, and *Wide As the World* (2011), especially the Sixth Encounter and the Epilogue.

170 Again, please see Chapter 5 in this volume for a refresher

on these terms.

171 Please see Chapters 3 and 4 in this book for a more detailed look at this perspective.

172 I have referred to some of these practices in the book, but all can be readily found through the Internet.

173 I have discussed at length democratic decision-making in schools in *Democracy's Midwife* (2002), especially pp. 179-92, "Democratic Schools."

174 This statistic comes from a report by the Pew Research Center. The increase in those who have had "religious or mystical experiences" rose from 22 percent in 1962 to 49 percent in 2009. See http://www.pewforum.org/2009/12/09/many-americans-mix-multiple-faiths/#6.

175 AQAL stands for "All Quadrants, All Levels" and is a comprehensive map showing the integration of individual growth and collective growth necessary for human well-being. Each quadrant represents an essential aspect of hierarchical development: for example, individual psychological growth (Upper Left Quadrant), collective or group development of norms and values (Lower Left Quadrant), evolution of individual behaviors (Upper Right Quadrant), and development of collective groupings and social institutions (Lower Right Quadrant). Changes in one quadrant should reflect changes in the others. Most of the quadrants and three of the levels of development were touched on in my discussion of the Bible in Chapter 5. Neither that chapter nor this brief description is adequate, however, for conveying the richness and utility of the AQAL model. For a full discussion see Wilber, 2000 and 2006.

Bibliography

Appiah, Anthony. *Cosmopolitanism: Ethics in a World of Strangers.* New York: W.W. Norton, 2008.

Arendt, Hannah. "Truth and Politics." In *Between Past and Future.* New York: Viking Press, 1968.

Augustine, Keith. "Near-Death Experiences with Hallucinatory Features." *Journal of Near-Death Studies,* Volume 26 (1), 2007.

Ayer, A.J. *Language, Truth and Logic.* New York: Dover, 1952.

Bakewell, Sarah. *At the Existentialist Café.* New York: Other Press, 2016.

Beauregard, Mario and Paquette, Vincent. "Neural Correlates of a Mystical Experience in Carmelite Nuns." *Neuroscience Letters* 405 (3), 186-190.

Beischel, Julie. *Among Mediums: A Scientist's Quest for Answers.* Windbridge Institute, LLC, 2013.

Berthoff, Ann. *The Making of Meaning.* NJ: Boynton/Cook, 1981.

Bloom, Paul and Harris, Sam. "It's Westworld. What's Wrong With Cruelty to Robots?" *The New York Times,* April 23, 2018.

Blum, Deborah. *Ghost Hunters: William James and the Search for Scientific Proof of Life After Death.* New York: Penguin Books, 2006.

Bohm, David. *On Dialogue.* NY: Routledge, 2004.

Brecht, Bertolt. *Galileo.* Edited and with an Introduction by Eric Bentley. NY: Grove Press, 1966.

Campbell, Debra and Crittenden, Jack. *Direct Deliberative Democracy.* Montreal, CAN: Black Rose Books, 2018.

Camus, Albert. *The Myth of Sisyphus and Other Essays.* New York: Random House/Vintage Books, 1991/1955.

Cappelli, Peter. *Will College Pay Off?* NY: PublicAffairs, 2015.

Cherlin, Andrew J. "Money and Culture Are Inseparable." *The New York Times,* May 8, 2018.

Cohen, Joshua. "Procedure and Substance in Deliberative

Democracy." In Bohman and Rehg (Eds.). *Deliberative Democracy*. Cambridge, MA: The MIT Press, 1997.

Cox, Harvey. *How to Read the Bible*. NY: HarperOne, 2015.

Crittenden, Jack. "Veneration of Community." *Communal Societies*, Volume 9, 1989.

—. *Beyond Individualism*. NY: Oxford University Press, 1992.

—. "The Social Nature of Autonomy." *The Review of Politics*, Volume 55, no. 1, 1993.

—. *Democracy's Midwife*. Lanham, MD: Lexington Books/ Rowman & Littlefield, 2002.

—. *Wide As the World*. Lanham, MD: Lexington Books/ Rowman & Littlefield, 2011.

Csikszentmihalyi, Mihaly. *Flow: The Psychology of Optimal Experience*. NY: HarperCollins, 1990.

De Rios, Marlene Dobkin. *Hallucinogens*. Prospect Heights, IL: Waveland Press, 1990.

Dechesne, M.; Pyszczynski, T.; Arndt, J.; Ransom, S.; Sheldon, K.M. et al. "Literal and Symbolic Immortality: The Effect of Evidence of Literal Immortality on Self-Esteem Striving in Response to Mortality Salience." *Journal of Personality and Social Psychology*, 84, 722-737, 2003.

Dreger, Alice. *Galileo's Middle Finger*. New York: Penguin Press, 2015.

Fadiman, James. *The Psychedelic Explorer's Guide*. Rochester, VT: Park Street Press, 2011.

Ferriss, Tim. *Tools of Titans*. NY: Houghton Mifflin Harcourt, 2016.

Gangaji. *The Diamond in Your Pocket: Discovering Your True Radiance*. Boulder, CO: Sounds True, 2005.

—. *You Are That*. Boulder, CO: Sounds True, 2007.

Gardner, Howard. *Frames of Mind*. NY: Basic Books, 1983.

Gardner, Martin. *Are Universes Thicker Than Blackberries?* NY: W.W. Norton, 2003.

Gilligan, Carol. *In a Different Voice*. Cambridge: Harvard

University Press, 1982.

Goleman, Daniel and Davidson, Richard J. *Altered Traits: Science Reveals How Meditation Changes Your Mind, Brain, and Body*. NY: Penguin/Random House, 2017.

Greene, Joshua. *Moral Tribes*. NY: Penguin Press, 2013.

Griffiths, R.R.; Richards, W.A.; McCann, U., and Jesse, R. "Psilocybin Can Occasion Mystical-Type Experiences Having Substantial and Sustained Personal Meaning and Spiritual Significance." *Psychopharmacology*, Volume 187, no. 3, pp. 284-92, July 2006.

Griffiths, Roland R. and Grob, Charles. "Hallucinogens as Medicine." *Scientific American*, Volume 303, no. 6, pp. 76-9, December 2010.

Grob, Charles et al. "Pilot Study of Psilocybin Treatment for Anxiety in Advanced-Stage Cancer Patients." *Archives of General Psychiatry*, January 2011. Available at http://archpsyc. ama~assn.org.

Grossman, Neal. "Who's Afraid of Life After Death?" *Journal of Near-Death Studies*, 21(1), 5-24, 2002.

Hamilton, Allan. *The Scalpel and the Soul*. NY: Jeremy P. Tarcher/ Penguin, 2008.

Harris, Sam. *The Moral Landscape*. NY: The Free Press, 2010.

—. *Waking Up*. NY: Simon & Schuster, 2014.

Hart, Hornell. "ESP Projection: Spontaneous Cases and the Experimental Method." *Journal of the American Society for Psychical Research*, 48, 121, 1954.

Herrigel, Eugen. *Zen in the Art of Archery*. New York: Pantheon Books, 1953.

Hicks, Michael J. and Devaraj, Srikant. "The Myth and the Reality of Manufacturing in America." A report from Ball State University's Center for Business and Economic Research, 2015.

Holden, Janice; Greyson, Bruce, and James, Debbie (Eds.). *The Handbook of Near-Death Experiences*. Santa Barbara, CA:

Praeger Publishers, 2009.

James, William. "Address by the President." *Proceedings of the Society for Psychical Research* 12, pp. 2-10, 1896.

Kaag, John. *American Philosophy*. New York: Farrar, Straus and Giroux, 2016.

Kaplan, P. *Toward a Theology of Consciousness*, unpublished doctoral dissertation, Harvard University, 1976.

Kegan, Robert. *The Evolving Self*. Cambridge: Harvard University Press, 1982.

Kohlberg, Lawrence and Ryncarz, Robert A. "Beyond Justice Reasoning: Moral Development and Consideration of a Seventh Stage." In *Higher Stages of Human Development*. Charles N. Alexander and Ellen J. Langer (Eds.). New York: Oxford University Press, 1990.

Kolata, Gina. "Death Rates Rising for Middle-Aged White Americans." *The New York Times*, November 2, 2015.

Kuhn, Thomas. *The Structure of Scientific Revolutions*. Chicago, IL: University of Chicago Press, 1962.

Lazar, Sara W. et al. "Meditation Experience Is Associated with Increased Cortical Thickness." *NeuroReport* 16 (17), 2005, pp. 1893-7.

Leary, Mark. "Why Are (Some) Scientists So Opposed to Parapsychology?" *Explore*, Volume 7, no. 5, 2011.

Lewis-Williams, David. "Three-Dimensional Puzzles: Southern African and Upper Palaeolithic Rock Art." *Ethnos*, 67 (2): 245–264.

Lommel, Pim van. *Consciousness Beyond Life: The Science of the Near-Death Experience*. New York: HarperCollins, 2010.

Luhrmann, T.M. "Religion Without God." *The New York Times*, December 24, 2014. Available at https://www.nytimes.com/2014/12/25/opinion/religion-without-god.html.

Lukes, Steven and Hollis, Martin (Eds.). *Rationality and Relativism*. Cambridge, MA: The MIT Press, 1982.

Lutz, Antoine; Greischar, Lawrence L.; Rawlings, Nancy B.;

Ricard, Matthieu, and Davidson, Richard J. (Eds.). "Long-Term Meditators Self-Induce High-Amplitude Gamma Synchrony During Mental Practice." *Proceedings of the National Academy of Sciences* 101 (46), pp. 16369-16373, 2004.

Martin, Clancy. "Heaven Can Wait." *The New York Review of Books*, May 8, 2011.

Maslow, Abraham. *Religions, Values, and Peak Experiences*. NY: Penguin Books, 1964.

—. *The Farther Reaches of Human Nature*. NY: Viking Press, 1971.

McNamara, Patrick. *The Neuroscience of Religious Experience*. Cambridge, UK: Cambridge University Press, 2009.

Monastersky, Richard. "Religion on the Brain." *The Chronicle of Higher Education* 52 (38): A15-9, 2006.

Morin, Roc. "Prescribing Mushrooms for Anxiety." *The Atlantic*, April 22, 2014. Available at https://www.theatlantic.com/health/archive/2014/04/chemo-for-the-spirit-lsd-helps-cancer-patients-cope-with-death/360625/.

Newberg, Andrew. *Principles of Neurotheology*. New York: Routledge, 2010.

Newberg, Andrew and Waldman, Mark Robert. *How God Changes Your Brain: Breakthrough Findings from a Leading Neuroscientist*. New York: Ballantine Books, 2010.

Nietzsche, Friedrich. *The Gay Science*. Translated by Walter Kaufmann. New York: Vintage Books, 1974.

—. *The Portable Nietzsche*. Edited and translated by Walter Kaufmann. New York: Penguin, 1982.

—. *Basic Writings of Nietzsche*. Translated and edited by Walter Kaufmann. New York: The Modern Library, 1992.

—. *Daybreak: Thoughts on the Prejudices of Morality*. Cambridge, UK: Cambridge University Press, 1997.

Parijs, Philippe Van and Vanderborght, Yannick. *Basic Income: A Radical Proposal for a Free Society and a Sane Economy*. Cambridge, MA: Harvard University Press, 2017.

Philipps, Dave. "Ecstasy as a Remedy for PTSD? You Probably Have Some Questions." *The New York Times*, May 1, 2018, available at https://www.nytimes.com/2018/05/01/us/ecstasy-molly-ptsd-mdma.html.

Plato. *Complete Works*. John M. Cooper (Ed.). Indianapolis, IN: Hackett Publishing Co., 1997.

Pollan, Michael. "The Trip Treatment." *The New Yorker*, February 9, 2015. Available at http://www.newyorker.com/magazine/2015/02/09/trip-treatment.

—. *How to Change Your Mind*. New York: Penguin/Random House, 2018.

Popper, Karl. *The Logic of Scientific Discovery*. London: Routledge, 1992.

Powell, Diane Hennacy. *The ESP Enigma*. London: Walker Books, 2008.

Rivas, Titus. Book Review of *The Scalpel and the Soul: Encounters with Surgery, the Supernatural, and the Healing Power of Hope* by Allan J. Hamilton. In the *Journal of Near-Death Studies*, 2009, pp. 255-9.

Rivas, Titus; Dirven, Anny, and Smit, Rudolf H. *The Self Does Not Die*. Durham, NC: International Association for Near-Death Studies, 2016.

Roberts, Bernadette. *The Experience of No-Self*. Boston, MA: Shambhala, 1982.

Routledge, Clay. "Suicides Are Up. Is This an Existential Crisis?" *The New York Times*, Sunday Review section, June 24, 2018, p. 9.

Ruthven, Malise. *Fundamentalism*. NY: Oxford University Press, 2007.

Sabom, M. *Recollections of Death: A Medical Investigation*. New York: Harper and Row, 1982.

—. *Light and Death*. Nashville, TN: Zondervan/HarperCollins Christian Publishing, 1998.

Sage, Michael (Noralie Robertson, Trans.). *Mrs. Piper and the*

Society for Psychical Research. Charleston, SC: BiblioBazaar, 1904/2007.

Schuon, Frithjof. *The Transcendent Unity of Religions*. New York: Harper and Row, 1975.

Sharp, Kimberly Clark. *After the Light: What I Discovered on the Other Side of Life That Can Change Your World*. iUniverse, 2003.

Sheldrake, Rupert. *Dogs That Know When Their Owners Are Coming Home*. NY: Broadway Books, 2011.

—. *The Sense of Being Stared At*. Rochester, VT: Park Street Press/Inner Traditions, 2013.

Slater, Lauren. *Blue Dreams: The Science and the Story of the Drugs That Changed Our Minds*. New York: Little, Brown and Company, 2018.

Smit, Rudolf. "Corroboration of the Dentures Anecdote Involving Veridical Perception in a Near-Death Experience." *Journal of Near-Death Studies*, 27(1), pp. 47-61, 2008.

Smith, Huston. *Cleansing the Doors of Perception*. NY: Penguin Putnam, 2000.

Stace, W.T. *Mysticism and Philosophy*. Los Angeles, CA: Jeremy Tarcher, Inc., 1960.

Stevenson, Ian. *20 Cases Suggestive of Reincarnation*. Charlottesville, VA: University Press of Virginia, 1974.

Strassman, Rick. *DMT: The Spirit Molecule*. Rochester, VT: Park Street Press, 2001.

—. *DMT and the Soul of Prophecy*. Rochester, VT: Park Street Press, 2014.

Sunstein, Cass. *Designing Democracy*. NY: Oxford University Press, 2001.

Susskind, Richard and Susskind, Daniel. "Technology Will Replace Many Doctors, Lawyers, and Other Professionals." *Harvard Business Review*, October 11, 2016.

Taylor, Charles. "Responsibility for Self." In Rorty, Amelie Oksenberg (Ed.), *The Identities of Persons*. Berkeley, CA: The University of California Press, 1976.

—. *Philosophical Papers 1.* Cambridge, UK: Cambridge University Press, 1985.

Tierney, John. "Psychedelics Have Scientists Tuning in Again." *The New York Times*, April 11, 2010.

Tolle, Eckhart. *The Power of NOW.* Novato, CA: Namaste Press, 2004.

Tucker, Jim B. *Life Before Life.* NY: St. Martin's Press, 2005.

Tymn, Michael. *Resurrecting Leonora Piper: How Science Discovered the Afterlife.* Guildford, UK: White Crow Books, 2013.

Wilber, Ken. *Eye to Eye.* NY: Anchor Books, 1983.

—. *Sex, Ecology, Spirituality.* In *The Collected Works of Ken Wilber*, Volume 6. Boston, MA: Shambhala Publications, 2000.

—. *Integral Spirituality.* Boston, MA: Shambhala, 2006.

Yang, Andrew. *The War on Normal People: The Truth About America's Disappearing Jobs and Why Universal Basic Income Is Our Future.* New York: Hachette Books, 2018.

Zitter, Jessica Nutik. "First, Sex Ed. Then Death Ed." *The New York Times*, Sunday Review, February 19, 2017.

Author's Biography

Jack Crittenden, professor emeritus, taught political theory at Arizona State University for nearly 30 years. He has previously published four books, all related in some fashion to his specialty: democratic theory and practice. *Stalking White Crows*, as he and many of his readers will agree, is a welcomed departure. It is also a return to the work of his earlier years, when he and Ken Wilber started *ReVision*, a journal of knowledge and consciousness. Currently Jack serves on the Boards of Directors for Integral Life and for the Windbridge Research Center. He resides in Scottsdale, Arizona, which he and his wife escape as often as they can by heading to Santa Fe, New Mexico.

Previous Books

Beyond Individualism: Reconstituting the Liberal Self, Oxford
University Press, 1992.
ISBN: 978-0195073300

Democracy's Midwife: An Education in Deliberation, Rowman &
Littlefield/Lexington Books, 2002.
ISBN: 978-0739103289

*Wide As the World: Cosmopolitan Identity, Integral Politics, and
Democratic Dialogue*, Rowman & Littlefield/Lexington Books,
2011.
ISBN: 978-0739148549

Direct Deliberative Democracy: How Citizens Can Rule, Black Rose
Books, 2018.
ISBN: 978-1551646695

BOOKS

Iff Books

ACADEMIC AND SPECIALIST

Iff Books publishes non-fiction. It aims to work with authors and titles that augment our understanding of the human condition, society and civilisation, and the world or universe in which we live.
If you have enjoyed this book, why not tell other readers by posting a review on your preferred book site.

Recent bestsellers from Iff Books are:

Why Materialism Is Baloney
How true skeptics know there is no death and fathom answers to
life, the universe, and everything
Bernardo Kastrup
A hard-nosed, logical, and skeptic non-materialist metaphysics,
according to which the body is in mind, not mind in the body.
Paperback: 978-1-78279-362-5 ebook: 978-1-78279-361-8

The Fall
Steve Taylor
The Fall discusses human achievement versus the issues of war,
patriarchy and social inequality.
Paperback: 978-1-78535-804-3 ebook; 978-1-78535-805-0

Brief Peeks Beyond
Critical essays on metaphysics, neuroscience, free will, skepticism
and culture
Bernardo Kastrup
An incisive, original, compelling alternative to current mainstream
cultural views and assumptions.
Paperback: 978-1-78535-018-4 ebook: 978-1-78535-019-1

Framespotting
Changing how you look at things changes how you see them
Laurence & Alison Matthews
A punchy, upbeat guide to framespotting. Spot deceptions and
hidden assumptions; swap growth for growing up. See and be free.
Paperback: 978-1-78279-689-3 ebook: 978-1-78279-822-4

Is There an Afterlife?
David Fontana
Is there an Afterlife? If so what is it like? How do Western ideas of the afterlife compare with Eastern? David Fontana presents the historical and contemporary evidence for survival of physical death.
Paperback: 978-1-90381-690-5

Nothing Matters
a book about nothing
Ronald Green
Thinking about Nothing opens the world to everything by illuminating new angles to old problems and stimulating new ways of thinking.
Paperback: 978-1-84694-707-0 ebook: 978-1-78099-016-3

Panpsychism
The Philosophy of the Sensuous Cosmos
Peter Ells
Are free will and mind chimeras? This book, anti-materialistic but respecting science, answers: No! Mind is foundational to all existence.
Paperback: 978-1-84694-505-2 ebook: 978-1-78099-018-7

Punk Science
Inside the Mind of God
Manjir Samanta-Laughton
Many have experienced unexplainable phenomena; God, psychic abilities, extraordinary healing and angelic encounters. Can cutting-edge science actually explain phenomena previously thought of as 'paranormal'?
Paperback: 978-1-90504-793-2

The Vagabond Spirit of Poetry
Edward Clarke
Spend time with the wisest poets of the modern age and of the
past, and let Edward Clarke remind you of the importance of
poetry in our industrialized world.
Paperback: 978-1-78279-370-0 ebook: 978-1-78279-369-4

Readers of ebooks can buy or view any of these bestsellers by
clicking on the live link in the title. Most titles are published in
paperback and as an ebook. Paperbacks are available in traditional
bookshops. Both print and ebook formats are available online.

Find more titles and sign up to our readers' newsletter at
http://www.johnhuntpublishing.com/non-fiction

Follow us on Facebook at
https://www.facebook.com/JHPNonFiction
and Twitter at
https://twitter.com/JHPNonFiction